Teachers as collaborative learners

Challenging dominant forms of supervision

John Smyth

Open University Press
Milton Keynes · Philadelphia

Open University Press
Celtic Court
22 Ballmoor
Buckingham
MK18 1XW

and
1900 Frost Road, Suite 101
Bristol, PA 19007, US

First Published 1991

British Library Cataloguing-in-Publication Data

Smyth, John
    Teachers as collaborative learners: Challenging
    dominant forms of supervision. – (Developing
    teachers and teaching)
    I. Title   II. Series
    371.1

    ISBN 0-335-09588-7
    ISBN 0-335-09587-9 pbk

Library of Congress Cataloging-in-Publication Data

Smyth, W. John
    Teachers as collaborative learners: challenging dominant forms of
    supervision/John Smyth.
        p.   cm. – (Developing teachers and teaching)
    Includes bibliographical references and index.
    ISBN 0-335-09588-7. – ISBN 0-335-09587-9 (pbk.)
    1. School supervision – Great Britain.   2. Teacher participation in
    administration – Great Britain.   I. Title.   II. Series.
    LB2806.4.S69   1991   91-21337
    371.2′00941–dc20   CIP

Typeset by Rowland Phototypesetting Ltd, Bury St Edmunds, Suffolk
Printed in Great Britain by St Edmundsbury Press Ltd, Bury St Edmunds, Suffolk

Teachers as collaborative learners

Developing Teachers and Teaching

Series Editor: **Christopher Day**, Reader in Education Management and Director of Advanced Post-Graduate Courses in the School of Education, University of Nottingham.

Teachers and schools will wish not only to survive but also to flourish in a period which holds increased opportunities for self-management – albeit within centrally designed guidelines – combined with increased public and professional accountability. Each of the authors in the series provides perspectives which will both challenge and support practitioners at all levels who wish to extend their critical skills, qualities and knowledge of schools, pupils and teachers.

Current titles:

Contents

Series editor's introduction

John Smyth has produced an authoritative text, replete with references and consistent in its arguments for collegial approaches to teacher learning that gives more control to teachers themselves. The book provides a swingeing critique of prescriptive educational reforms and practices which, he argues, have produced alienation, demoralization and fragmentation among teachers and schools. He asserts that educational values must take precedence over bureaucratic and technically based judgements of teaching, that accountability is a two-way process, and that hierarchical forms of appraisal and curriculum development are fundamentally flawed. When one person is evaluating another, 'it is easy to forget that the moral and ethical imperative that we are really talking about is one that serves the interests of one party while silencing or denying the other!'

He proposes a liberal view of supervision in which so-called scientific knowledge is not regarded as superior to the artistic, intuitive knowledge of the teacher, in which teachers are viewed both as practitioners and intellectuals who should be enabled to examine and make judgements upon their own and one another's practice. Only in this way will the supervision of teachers be about reforming, transforming and changing practice rather than a means of maintaining the status quo.

The book represents a significant contribution to learning about teacher and school development, for it identifies the need for a 'major shift in perspective', from a view of supervision which essentially separates those who conceptualize from those who implement, from definitions of teaching which are expressed in terms of competencies and skills and schools which are viewed as tidy, rational organizations – to definitions of teaching and schools which are highly personalized, idiosyncratic and artistic.

The book presents supervision, *not* as a methodology for improving teaching, but as a means by which teachers may gain control over their own teaching and thus their development as professionals. The model of clinical supervision as a means of teacher learning which Smyth proposes, however, is not comfortable. It is both active and militant. It is active in the sense that reflection must be accompanied by theory-making and theory-testing. It is militant in that it asserts that action must be infused with a sense of power and politics. Teaching is a political process. Teachers, he writes, are only able to reclaim the power they have lost over their teaching if they place themselves in critical confrontation with their problems.

This is a powerful text for all those who are concerned with improving teaching and encouraging teacher professionalism. In addition to offering a much needed intellectual critique of dominant forms of curriculum, school and teacher development, it provides, through exemplars, a radical but realistic alternative.

Christopher Day

Acknowledgements

This book has been over a decade in the making and there are many colleagues and students who have had a hand in influencing my thinking. I want to thank them all, but at the same time acknowledge that responsibility for the ideas is mine and mine alone.

The latter stages of the writing of this book was made possible by a Senior Fulbright Research Award in 1990, and through the hospitality of Noreen Garman of Administrative and Policy Studies, and Mark Ginsburg of the Institute of International Studies in Education, both at the University of Pittsburgh. I am eternally grateful to Noreen for her guidance and support as a valued colleague over many years, and for her reading and the provision of insightful feedback on the original manuscript. Yvonne Jones and Pat Swanston provided cheerful secretarial assistance at the University of Pittsburgh, as did Leonie Taylor at Deakin University. The Faculty of Education at Monash University was also most generous in housing me during the final part of my sabbatical. My own institution, the School of Education, Deakin University, deserves considerable credit for providing a long-term environment in which ideas are able to be debated, contested and where they can ultimately flourish.

Throughout the entire project, my wife Solveiga did a magnificent job of maintaining interest (even when the issues were foreign to her), and was entirely responsible for the job of pulling together the large collection of references.

I am also most grateful to the various publishers who willingly provided permission for me to reproduce portions of my previously published papers, especially: *Curriculum Inquiry* and *Journal of Curriculum and Supervision*, Chapter 1; *Teachers College Record* and *Journal of Curriculum Studies*, Chapter 2; *Journal of Education Policy*, Chapter 3; *Journal of Curriculum and*

Supervision, Chapter 4; *Journal of Education for Teaching* and *Journal of Curriculum and Supervision*, Chapter 5; *Journal of Teacher Education*, Chapter 6; and *Journal of Curriculum Studies*, Chapter 7.

Introduction

The issue of teacher supervision and appraisal* of teaching is squarely back on the educational agenda, and it is not altogether hard to see why (see such disparate international sources as: Dockrell *et al.*, 1986; Evans and Tomlinson, 1989; Gitlin and Smyth, 1989; Lokan and McKenzie, 1989; McLaughlin and Pfeifer, 1988; Millman and Darling-Hammond, 1990; Preston, 1990; Simons and Elliott, 1989; Smyth, 1990; Suffolk Department of Education, 1985; Turner and Clift, 1988; Winter, 1989; Wise *et al.*, 1984). As Western governments of whatever political persuasion struggle with how to handle the crises of accumulation and legitimation afflicting them, education and schooling are firmly in their sights. What is most astounding is that extremely complex arguments about social, economic and cultural reconstruction are couched in terms that suggest that there are simplistic solutions – in short, whip the schools into shape and somehow all our economic woes will magically disappear. The major justifying rhetoric is that *more* control over what goes on in classrooms will arrest the decline in competitiveness of Western capitalist economies generally (see National Commission on Excellence in Education, 1983), and in the process ensure that schools (and teachers) do their economic work of skills formation. Accordingly, the range of so-called reform measures (Gibboney, in press) designed to check-up on teachers are justified as being needed as a way of ensuring that incompetent teachers are removed from schools, that wastage of educational resources is eliminated and that, in the process, schools produce 'outputs' that slot neatly into industry and improve national economic performance.

The major problem with this line of argument is that it is fundamentally flawed. Those who adhere to this line want simultaneously to believe that teachers can be blamed for poor economic performance, while at the same time portraying them as the major weapon by which we are to be extricated from this economic quagmire. It is difficult to see how they can have it both ways! Educational reform, of which teacher supervision/appraisal is a major component, has failed largely because the social and economic problems we face are not ones that can be sheeted home to schools. In reality, what we have is not a *crisis of competence* as alleged of our schools and teachers, but rather a deep-seated *crisis of confidence* going to the very heart of the system of Western capitalism. Trying to kick schools and teachers into shape is not going to come to grips with the fundamental structural inequalities and injustices that are at the root of our economic demise (Smyth, 1989c). By proposing educational reforms that focus on teacher appraisal, what our political masters have created is alienation, demoralization and fragmentation in schools. As Jonathan (1983) put it, moves towards such a 'manpower services model of education' with measures to introduce benchmark testing, national curricula, and national appraisal schemes, are all predicated on an impoverished and unsubstantiated view that somehow schools are failing to 'deliver the goods', and that teachers need to be held personally more accountable through more rigorous forms of appraisal for the 'right' sorts of learning. It is also clear that this economic labour market view of education regards 'the development of internationally competitive manufacturing and service industries . . . [as re-quiring] . . . a more highly skilled and better educated workforce' (Diamond, 1988: 4). Designing and implementing appropriate indicators of performance is viewed as being imperative to the overall agenda of quality control, and of ensuring that the products of schools fit easily into the national economic effort. Recent moves to mandate teacher appraisal in the UK (Walsh, 1987), for example, need to be considered for what they really are; namely, an interven-tionist desire on the part of the state to extend central control over education through proceduralizing the work of teachers in the guise of rational manage-ment procedures (D'Alcan *et al.*, 1986).

Against a background of this kind, this is a book about supervision and teacher appraisal that has a radically different perspective to the orthodox or dominant viewpoint (for a good example of this, see Trethowan, 1987). It starts out from the premise that there is something gravely wrong with construing supervision and appraisal of teaching merely as a *technical act* focusing exclusively on what *individual teachers do*. Instead, what this book seeks to do is to not only critique and show what is wrong with using supervision and appraisal as ways of 'working on teachers', but, at the same time, to replace those notions with an alternative that is less destructive of the educative process. The basic argument explored throughout the book is that technocratic and bureaucratic forms of supervision and appraisal are formulated on a set of false assumptions:

1 That teaching and learning are processes that can be broken down into discrete and unconnected skills.
2 That these skills have been verified and legitimated by people outside of classrooms who engage in scientific research.

3 That these skills can be observed and measured by another group, and some form of calibration conducted on them.
4 That having established these behaviours as being credible, that they are in fact enforceable in a moral and legal way with teachers.

The difficulty with such technicist approaches is that hierarchical values are accorded paramount status, and pursuing them amounts to undermining the social relationships that embody the lived educative experiences of people in schools. Herein lies the major contradiction: schools are organized and run as bureaucracies (concerned with taking orders and directives from above, and ultimately from the state), but in the nature of their work, they are inhabited by teachers who work as professionals relying largely on 'discretionary inter-pretation of specialist knowledge' (Winter, 1989: 50). As Winter (1989: 50) put it:

allegiance is therefore not upwards but downwards – to their clients – and inwards – to the specialism which they practice. Clients' cases are complex and unique: they cannot be decided upon by the application of general rules (given from above) but only by the discretionary interpretation of specialist knowledge in the individual instance.

Focusing forms of supervision and appraisal on the presumed deficits of individual teachers as if the problem were a lack of skills, also individualizes the problem in a way that misses the point completely – crises of this kind are *social* not *individual* constructions. Apple (1983: 4–5) makes this point eloquently when he argues that:

When government (the 'state') comes under attack for not being respon-sive enough to 'economic needs' and when fiscal crisis creates increasing pressures on the state to make the immediate needs of business and industry its primary goals, the crisis will be *exported downwards*. That is, rather than attention being directed toward the unequal results and benefits produced by the ways our economy is currently organized and controlled, schools and teachers will be focussed upon as major causes of social dislocation, unemployment, falling standards of work, declining productivity, and so on. Intense pressures will result in the form of at-tempts by government bureaucrats, ministry officials, and others to rationalize and tighten control of access to it and its outcomes. . . . Teacher grading systems, though initially less visibly connected to these more bureaucratic and technical models, need to be seen as part of the attempt by the larger government to solve its own economic and ideological problems by exporting them onto teachers.

Moore and Reid (1990) argue that the 'surveillance', and even the 'profes-sional' orientation that is often indistinguishable from it, rely on bureaucratic forms of evaluating teaching that are objectionable on three major counts. First, because it entrenches 'privatism' in teaching (when in reality teaching is much more of a relational, collective and collaborative enterprise), such methods promote competition among teachers that cut them off from dialogue that is crucial to the task of teaching. Secondly, by working from the 'quaint notion' that people in the administrative hierarchy know more about the work of teachers than teachers themselves, such viewpoints 'reinforce hierarchies' whereby those in positions of power in schools 'reaffirm the logic of their own assumptions' by ensuring that hierarchy becomes a taken-for-granted part of school life. Thirdly, by having appraisal schemes that treat teachers as if they were 'technicians' (in which the important work is left to outside experts), then the work of teaching is fractured into separate moments such that the phases of 'setting aims and objectives, curriculum policy development, implementation and evaluation' are undertaken by different people. The focus is upon technique, as the separation of 'conception' from 'execution' becomes complete. Moore and Reid (1990) see all of this as being quite contrary to a 'practice orientation' towards supervision and appraisal which regards: teaching and learning as a collective, corporate activity; ownership and control of the appraisal process as residing in the hands of school participants; participants as policy makers rather than technicians; and teaching as being rendered problematic through an analysis of the way in which issues of 'racism, sexism, elitism and ethnocentrism' are analysed in terms of how they inhibit the development of ethical and just relationships in schools.

Arguing for a 'critical' or counter view of supervisory practice and how it relates to teaching, therefore, amounts to endorsing a set of beliefs, assumptions and practices that are committed to a set of values quite different from those of a bureaucratic or technocratic mindset. Indeed, they are sufficiently important to be worth being explicit about right from the start.

First, within a critical perspective, *educational values* are given preference over administrative or hierarchical values. This means that judgements about what constitutes educational worth are based upon substantive academic and educational values internal to the educational work, rather than on the values, judgements and preferences of supervisors, superordinates or external researchers.

Secondly, the critical perspective is predicated on the view that *accountability is a two-way affair*. In most schemes of supervision, accountability is for performance. That is to say, the individual teacher is responsible for demonstrating how he or she is performing according to standardized criteria. This is a one-way system of accountability. What is missing, and which the critical perspective highlights, is the reciprocal form of accountability that *ought* to exist (between teachers and the system) to provide working conditions which permit teachers to fulfil designated responsibilities. That is to say, *accountability for provision* (Kemmis and Smyth, 1989). In other words, we should not consider 'performance effects' (how well staff perform in meeting targets) without attention to 'design effects' (how well the system is designed to permit the achievement of intended outcomes).

Thirdly, the critical perspective I adopt posits that many people within schools (as elsewhere) are unwittingly victims of causal processes that *exercise power* over them. This occurs because they are frequently unaware of how they have become implicated both individually and collectively in acquiescing to dominant views. Acting critically means working in ways that involve giving up illusions, or as Fay (1977) put it, abandoning practices we cling to and which give false meaning and false direction to our lives.

Fourthly, a critical view seeks to *locate and situate issues* within teaching and schooling so as to go beyond simple cause–effect connections. Increasingly, our society is coming to be characterized by 'technocratic' or 'instrumental' forms of rationality which are consciously structured to block, constrain and contain societal-wide reform (see Welton, in press). The emphasis in a critical view of supervision and appraisal is, therefore, on unmasking the systematic blocking process that stops schools from devising and implementing fair, just and equitable ways of living and working. Put another way, it is about uncovering the hidden message systems within teaching and the ways schools are organized that actually disfigure what education and learning ought to be like.

Fifthly, one of the major theoretical presuppositions of a critical perspective is that the *experience of school practitioners* (teachers as well as students) in solving day-to-day problems is considered to be on a par with that of theoreticians who try to explain practice (a process normally reserved for supervisors). The kind of relationship being fostered, then, is one of collaboration in which power relationships between the key players (supervisors, teachers, students, parents, administrators) are genuinely realigned in a much more symmetrical and equitable way. There is a commitment to the provision of much greater equality of access to information, by traditionally subordinated parties in schools.

Sixthly, the sense in which the term critical is used, is very special. As Little (1989) argues, theory and research about teaching is not something that ought to be generated exclusively through a process of detached observation by observers who act like neutral social scientists developing and verifying hypotheses. The conventional goals of science – explanation, prediction and control – are superseded in this approach by *improvements of practice* and the social relationships within which that practice is embedded. In other words, within a critical paradigm, theorist and practitioner collaborate with each other to achieve dialogically determined goals, interacting with one another in implementing and developing new theories.

Finally, because of the way it denies a dichotomous view of the relationship between theory and practice, a critical (or dialectical) view of supervision regards *knowledge as always being in an incomplete state*, in which theory is continually being modified by practice, constantly turning up new contradictions that serve as further sources of knowledge. There is a continual process of mutual modification underway. This applies as much to the relationship between theory and practice, as it does to the relationship between teachers and supervisors.

In Chapters 1–4, I articulate a range of arguments about what I see as being problematic with traditional or dominant approaches to the supervision and appraisal of teaching. I argue, for example, that an exclusive concern with matters to do with controlling the techniques of teaching are far too limiting and constraining. In our increasingly technologically driven societies, we need to pay far greater heed to emancipatory and educative agendas, based around notions of critical inquiry. The point–counterpoint approach I adopt is designed to show that there are a number of theoretical probes that have multiple agendas to them; for example, the view that it is possible to develop forms of evaluation of teaching (rather than of individual teachers) that are dialogical rather than monological; that it is possible to have problem-posing (and problem-raising) rather than problem-solving approaches; that contrary to conventional wisdom, teaching is a highly political rather than an apolitical activity; that evaluating what counts as teaching ought to be a reciprocal rather than an impositional process; and that communitarian rather than individual-istic values and norms should prevail. These and other points need to be made and vigorously argued for in a context in which viewpoints about what constitute supervision and appraisal are increasingly coming to be taken for granted.

Throughout I try to both critique mainstream views of supervision and appraisal, while at the same time offering cogent arguments and practical advice as to what an alternative conceptualization and practice might look like. In this I draw extensively on a reconstructed form of 'clinical supervision' as a collegial process (used *by* and *for* teachers) that has the potency and the capacity to hit the mark. From some fairly humble beginnings at Harvard University in the 1950s to provide another face for the professional develop-ment of teaching generally, clinical supervision has grown beyond the point of most educational fads to become widely regarded as having the theory of a 'consensual domain' (Garman, 1990) necessary to establish and sustain collab-orative learning relationships between teachers in schools. It is true that some people have taken the tenets of clinical supervision and co-opted it for their own narrow instrumental ends, but it is also true that there are many scholars and practitioners who see in the process the potentiality for genuine forms of teacher autonomy. As Garman (1990: 201) put it, one of the reasons clinical supervision continues to survive is because it has developed 'an intellectual tradition (albeit a modest one)' that has enabled issues in teaching to be canvassed and contested even in circumstances where there are strong pressures to reify particular versions of the way teaching should be. For Garman (1990: 202), the essence of this tradition lies in the way:

> Most educators accept establishing a relationship with the teacher, observ-ing classroom teaching, analyzing classroom scenarios, and holding a conference with the teacher as the basic events of clinical supervisory practice.

According to her, this collegial process has several crucial theoretic under-

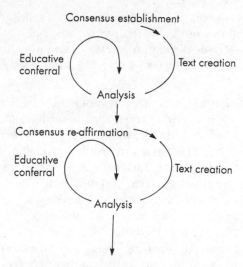

Figure 1   The spiral of clinical supervision

pinnings and 'immanent meanings' – a *consensual domain* in which teacher and supervisor (colleague) establish and maintain a collaborative relationship; an *observation phase* in which there is a joint commitment to creating a text about teaching; an *analytical aspect* in which teaching and its social/political contexts are rigorously and progressively unpicked for what they reveal; and an *educative act*, which has as its focus the conferral and exchange between colleagues committed to arriving not only at an understanding of what it means to be a teacher but what it might mean also to engage in strategic change. In many respects, this amounts to a spiral – one that starts out with conferral, and that involves problematizing, reflecting upon, and acting to create wider meanings and understandings of what constitutes teaching.

Without complicating the process excessively, nor oversimplifying it too much either, teacher and colleague (a term equated with 'supervisor' but without the hierarchical and sanction-ridden implications), are involved in a series of linked actions that might be summarized as follows:

- Teacher and colleague collaboratively plan (through *consensus establishment*) who is to enact which role (teaching or observation), what aspect of teaching or the context of teaching is to be looked at, where, when, and using what methods of data collection.
- The person who teaches carries out his or her part of the plan, while the observer collects information (i.e. engages in *text creation*) as agreed.
- Separately, teacher and observer *analyse* the collected information for what it means, what it reveals and what sense they can make of it.
- They meet to share their separate interpretations of the evidence and to

reflect (through an educative conferral process) on how the teacher might make changes to practise in the future.
- Once conversation turns to future strategies and modifications that might occur, they are in effect beginning to re-plan (or re-establish or *re-affirm consensus*).

Using clinical supervision in this way, teachers become active as distinct from passive agents, not only in changing the technicalities of their teaching but also in transforming the conditions, structures, practices and social relationships they come to see as frustrating their teaching. What is significant about clinical supervision used in this way is that it is not simply an instrumental way of solving problems. It is part of a much wider generative process of examining teaching, uncovering issues and working to reconstrue them in fundamentally different ways; it is part of a 'continuous cycle of critical analysis, education, and action' (Comstock, 1982: 387).

While the distinction between the theoretical and the practical is never sustainable in any real way in contexts such as this, Chapters 5–7 nevertheless try to rely less on argument and more on concrete illustrations of what different aspects of a critical practice of supervision and appraisal of teaching might look like. Starting out with teachers as collaborative learners of their own and one anothers' teaching contexts, and the fact that this may not rest easily with rational models of educational change, discussion canvasses what is known about adult learning, how this might provide a springboard for teachers to become 'critical inquirers', and the active role clinical supervision might play in all of this. In order for clinical supervision to become a critical practice in the sense of getting behind the habitual and taken-for-granted, teachers need assistance in highlighting a number of dimensions in the analysis of their teaching and its contexts; namely (1) in seeing how ideology comes to permeate and dominate so much of what they do, (2) in uncovering the interpretive understandings they have that often unwittingly shape their view of the world of teaching, (3) in coming to a realization of the importance of how historical conditions serve powerfully to shape and constrain present practices and understandings, (4) in making the linkages between historical conditions and the contemporary forces that sustain them, (5) in seizing upon the contradictions, paradoxes and dilemmas within current practices that plague them, and (6) in adopting educative ways of working that permit them to problematize the settings in which they work and to operate in ways that permit grassroots change. Consolidating the elements of a critical practice of teaching through supervision involves teachers in engaging with uncomfortable questions like:

- Why am I doing this?
- What are my reasons?
- What are the effects of my actions on my students?

One possible avenue through which to systematize the pursuit of questions like these is through teachers collaborating with one another in *describing*, *theorizing*, *confronting* and, where possible, *reconstructing* their teaching within the social, political and cultural contexts within which it is embedded.

Such a process is not 'clinical' in the sterile, objectivist or pathological medical sense of that term. Indeed, the term clinical as used here has its legacy in the Latin *clinicus*, or a person who rendered baptismal rites to a person on their deathbed. It was out of this ancient ecclesiastical process of tendering at the bedsides of patients, that this process came to take on its later metaphorical equivalent of teachers learning about teaching in the 'clinic of the classroom' – it has nothing to do with forms of pathology, or notions of neutral detachment, that have come to characterize modern-day usage of the term. The focus has more in common with medicos who came to learn about notions of their craft (science?) in close proximity to their patients/clients, as distinct from learning that occurred in laboratories, lecture halls and libraries. If there is a similarity between the usage here and the medical connection, then it has more to do with issues of immediacy as the *starting point* for learning about professional practice – I say starting point, because it is out of actual classroom contexts and the complexity that accompanies them that the real imponderables and intractable issues of education emerge.

The other major theme that keeps recurring, but which is most evident in Chapters 6 and 7, is how the political nature of reflection is embodied in the way in which the practice of clinical supervision is conceived of and discussed here. The kind of reflective stance argued as being central to a critical approach to clinical supervision, is one that endorses the propositions made about reflection as a form of political action made by Kemmis (1985: 140); namely, that:

1. Reflection is not a purely 'internal', psychological process; it is action-oriented and historically embedded.
2. Reflection is not a purely individual process; like language, it is a social process.
3. Reflection serves political interests; it is a political process.
4. Reflection is shaped by ideology; in turn, it shapes ideology.
5. Reflection is a practice which expresses our power to reconstitute social life by the way we participate in communication, decision-making and social action.

As Kemmis argues, reflection – and processes like clinical supervision which are manifestations of a reflective pose – are not solely internalized processes. While it is true that there is an internal or inward-looking deliberative dimension to it, it is the external objects, processes and purposes towards which those deliberative dimensions are directed that become the crucial aspect. In much the same vein, processes like teaching are never ahistorical either – they are always context-bound, and when we reflect on our teaching it is because we are confused or perplexed by some situation that is of some significance or consequence to us.

Critical reflection or critique is, therefore, concerned with 'how the forms and contexts of our thought shape and are shaped by the historical situations in which we find ourselves' (Kemmis, 1985: 142). There is a dialectical form to it, as thought is framed by lived experiences and as history is in turn shaped by and informs action. The point is that reflection has meaning and significance only in relation to historically embedded contexts and actions. The social and political nature of reflection becomes apparent enough once we begin to ask 'What interests are being served?' *Technical forms of reflection*, by being concerned only with problem solving, serve those who label the issue as 'a problem'. *Practical forms of reflection*, because of their concern with the moral rightness of actions in contexts, serve the interests of those who see themselves as the conscience of society. *Critical forms of reflection*, because they aim to assist people to discover the historical processes that led to their social formation as well as to discovering the ideological way in which thought and action become distorted, are directed towards emancipatory interests.

In addition to the social, political, historical and action-oriented nature of reflection, Kemmis (1985) maintains that it is ideological as well. He uses the term 'ideology' to refer to values, beliefs, attitudes and assumptions that sustain a society. Kemmis (1985: 147) says:

> Our ideas and the way we reflect betray our expectations about how our thinking will have its effect on society. Who our action is directed towards, who we believe our co-actors will be (and who we will act against), the specific modes and register of the language we use, and the issues we think about all locate us ideologically as people of a certain kind, striving towards certain things, and relating in definite ways to others around us.

All of this has profound implications for processes like supervision that are concerned with unexpressed (often disguised) power relationships. Indeed, no supervisory or appraisal practice can be morally or ethically sustainable unless it is itself opened up to the possibility of being turned back upon itself so as to establish through dialogical means the veracity of its own claims. As long as supervisory processes, unwittingly or not, are constituted as a bureaucratic means by which 'those deemed to know' are able to exercise surveillance and invoke sanctions over another group 'deemed to be deficient', questions will continue to exist about the moral and ethical defensibility of what is being attempted. This kind of unquestioning acceptance of 'regimes of power', as Foucault (1980) called it, is something we might expect to find in a totalitarian state, but not something we would expect to characterize educational institutions in a democracy.

Note

* I use the terms 'supervision' and 'appraisal' interchangeably throughout the Introduction. In the remainder of the book, however, I will use the term 'supervision' to mean 'appraisal' as well.

Critical consciousness: from supervision to critical inquiry

Introduction

The argument of this chapter is that in education we have been too reliant for too long on hierarchical and sanction-ridden modes of 'instructional supervision'. The counter-argument presented is that if teachers are to improve their pedagogy, then it will be as a consequence of *less* not *more* technical control of teaching. Rather than seeking to deliver 'effective' teaching based upon business management canons of accountability, inspection and quality control, the line pursued is that teachers will benefit from processes that enable them to gain insights, acquire understandings and a measure of empowerment over their own teaching. What this chapter attempts at the outset, from a largely historical perspective, is to question the values of business management as enshrined in the practices of instructional supervision as the dominant ones and to question whether these are necessarily the most desirable. Past practices in instructional supervision have taken the form of enveloping teachers in forms of bureaucratic and psychological control. Teachers as a result have been involved in a long, private cold war with supervisors (Blumberg, 1980), the effect of which has not been altogether productive for schools and learning.

The second part of the chapter considers an alternative form of professional interaction grounded in humility and geared towards liberating teachers from their taken-for-granted assumptions, rather than directed at domination and control of their work. It argues the need to move from close surveillance of teachers to teacher-initiated critical inquiry. Throughout the book and in this chapter in particular, the principles, practices and philosophy of 'clinical supervision' as espoused by Goldhammer (1969) and Cogan (1973) are explored as a responsive way in which teachers might use the collegial support of other teachers to acquire greater personal control over knowledge gained about their own teaching, ascribing meaning to that teaching, and learning what is involved in genuinely autonomous growth as a teacher. Clearly, much has happened educationally since Goldhammer (1969) and his associates at Harvard University made their first strident moves to free supervision from its 'watchdog origins' in the 1950s. At the time, they were looking for ways in which teachers could work collaboratively with one another that acknowledged the human worth and dignity of the people involved. It is interesting that despite the rapidity with which educational fads generally come and go, the notions of clinical supervision are still alive and thriving. The reasons for this are not hard to discern, at least from teachers' perspectives. In essence, clinical supervision stands for a view of teacher professionalism that moves considerably beyond leaving teachers alone in their classrooms and focuses instead on collectively investing them with control over pedagogical matters (Smyth, 1984a). *They* 'call the shots' in terms of what is looked at in teaching, what is considered feasible to change, how and under what circumstances. Clinical supervision, as a form of collaborative professional development is, therefore, posited as a more robust conceptualization of what it might mean for teachers to become actively involved in the collective and reflexive process of analysing and theorizing about *their own* teaching, its social antecedents and possible consequences. Through struggling to discover and reconstruct their own histories and the realities in which they are embedded, the proposal is that teachers acquire the capacity to understand, to challenge and, ultimately, to transform their own practices.

This represents a dramatic departure from other practices in supervision where certain categories of teachers are 'targeted' for treatment – the inexperienced, the weak or the incompetent. The effects of past unfortunate attempts at supervision were summed up well by Withall and Wood (1979: 55), when they said:

> [Supervision] connotes a situation that is unpleasant, possesses psychological threat, and typically culminates in unrewarding consequences. . . . [T]here are factors which encourage those undergoing supervision to see the activity with a worried, if not fearful eye. One is the manner in which supervisors have tended to project an image of superiority and omniscience in identifying the strengths and weaknesses of a teacher's performance and in offering advice concerning how to improve future performance.

The major problem with traditional forms of supervision (and clinical supervision is by no means completely immune from this criticism) is that they are conceptualized as a delivery of a service to those deemed to be in need of it. No matter how benevolently *it is done*, efforts of this kind are ultimately self-defeating because they are premised on managerial and undemocratic ways of working; such forms of supervision create *dependence* rather than *independence*. It is not the teachers' agendas, issues and concerns that are being addressed, but rather those of someone within the administrative or bureaucratic hierarchy. Put slightly differently, what is really at issue is the question of who exercises power. As Ryan (1971: 242–3) put it:

> What some are accustomed to thinking of as the enduring debilitating characteristics of the poor – such as apathy, fatalism, depression, and pessimism – are actually the straightforward manifestations of the dynamics arising from lack of power. Man powerless is not fully man. This concept can illuminate some vexing problems. Why didn't public housing fulfill the dreams of its planners, for example? Or why cannot slum schools educate? Why are so many of our young people robotized by, or alienated from, our major social institutions? The answers to these – and to an almost endless series of similar questions – is the same: we have failed to understand the nature of humanness and to provide for its nurturance; we have restricted people's ability to act effectively on their own behalf – that is, to exercise power.

Processes like clinical supervision, if they are implemented according to the spirit, ought to be primarily about 'empowerment', rather than the 'delivery of services' (Fried, 1980a) to colleagues who are perceived to have technical deficiencies or skill-related problems in need of correction. If we are to be serious about wanting to change and reform teaching and assisting colleagues to do likewise, then we need to view processes like clinical supervision as a way of posing problems about teaching (i.e. *problematizing* it) in a way that enables taken-for-granted assumptions to be challenged. In the process, we are likely to uncover the manifold contradictions, dilemmas and paradoxes that plague us in teaching and schooling.

None of this is to suggest that viewing teaching problematically will come easily, or that the process is comfortable. As Tom (1985: 37) argues, consciously suspending judgement about some aspect of teaching and considering alternatives is 'to raise doubts about what under ordinary circumstances appears to be effective or wise practice'. Carr (1982) and Kohl (1983) both claim that teachers who do this are in effect 'theorizing' about their practice in ways that enable them to transcend their teaching. But, as Carr (1984: 4) notes, they do this at some considerable personal and professional risk:

> It is one thing to acquire a stock of sophisticated teaching techniques and master the intricacies of modern technological aids; it is quite another to have the educational character of teaching as an ultimate professional concern. Within contemporary society, this kind of concern is often treated as a major weakness and to actually practice the educational philosophies that schools so often *say* are desirable, is to risk being thought a crank, a fool, or at best, somebody who has no interest in climbing up the ladder of his chosen profession.

The real and perplexing issue is whether it is the *ends* (i.e. broad goals of teaching) or the *means* (i.e. the technical skills) of teaching that ought to be regarded as problematic – this is an issue that remains the centre of some considerable contestation.

A problematic legacy

Much of the history of the 'improvement' of teaching has, therefore, taken the form of supervision or appraisal of some kind or other. Although there are an array of definitions and interpretations of what comprises instructional supervision, most emphasize interactive face-to-face classroom-based activity that purports to contribute directly to the improvement of teaching and learning. Sergiovanni (1982a: vi), for example, defines instructional supervision as comprising 'the task of helping teachers, working in classrooms with students, to be more effective'. Marks *et al.* (1978: 15) describe it as 'action and experimentation aimed at improving instruction'.

Arguably, one of the most distinctive feature of instructional supervision is its close connection with issues of immediacy and practicality. Indeed, its close association with the scientific management era of the 1920s, where the predominant concern was with inspection, control and efficiency, may not have left current practices in instructional supervision altogether untainted. Commentators upon that era, such as Karier (1982), argue that rather than *following* the lead of Frederick Taylor (1911) in industry and commerce, educationists may have been among the leading exponents and practitioners of the efficiency movement; industry may have learned much from schooling! While few people connected with schools today continue to espouse Taylorism openly, it is nevertheless important not to lose sight of the view of 'man' implicit in scientific management. As Taylor (1911: 59) put it:

> One of the first requirements for a man who is fit to handle pig iron is that he shall be so stupid and so phlegmatic that he more nearly resembles the ox than any other type. . . . (H)e must consequently be trained by a man more intelligent than himself.

The continued existence of the attitudes implicit in Taylorism is an interesting question. According to Baker (1977), little may have changed:

> Today we would shrink from voicing such a degrading point of view. Yet remnants of Taylor's ideology are deeply embedded in the way we organize our social systems. . . . The terms have changed but the ethos is the same. The language has the appearance of being objective, rational, scientific and value free. It is of course nothing of the kind. Each statement is intertwined with values related to efficiency, productivity and what *some* people regard as politically and administratively important. *It is easy to forget that what we are basically talking about is one group of people which uses technology and knowledge to do things at, and to another group of people, in a systematic and manipulative way* [my emphasis].

Despite half a century of cooperative supervision, human relations super-vision, supervision as curriculum development, and various other forms of enlightened supervision in schools, it is not altogether clear that we have severed the connection between instructional supervision and the industrial-managerial model with which it has been closely affiliated. According to With-all and Wood (1979), to talk of instructional supervision is to evoke feelings still among teachers of an impersonal hierarchical process of inspection, domina-tion and quality control.

Part of the image problem associated with instructional supervision stems from the kind of generative metaphor and analogy with its roots in scientific management often used to describe schooling. Schon (1979), for example, has argued that the way we frame social problems, closely affects the way we analyse them. According to Burlingame (1979), the continued prevalence of the school-as-a-factory metaphor has led to a hegemony of technical knowl-edge with primary importance being ascribed to a hierarchy of experts capable of standardizing procedures and ensuring smooth and efficient organizational functioning. Despite claims to the contrary that 'supervision in education is not the same as supervision in an industrial setting' (Wiles and Bondi, 1980: 4), it is often a case of action speaking more eloquently than words. Eisner (1982: 54) expressed his concern about the intent and practice in these words:

> It has connotations that seem at least somewhat incongruous with edu-cational practice. The relationship between supervisor and the teacher is hierarchical . . . (suggesting that the supervisor) . . . has the right to prescribe to the latter how the job is to be done. A sense of dialogue or interchange between two professionals trying to improve the educational experience of the young tends to get lost.

Unfortunately, it is not just a matter of changing the lexicon; the real issues go far deeper, frequently to the very basis of the intent and purpose of the supervisory process.

Instructional supervision has a long history as a method of social control in schools,[1] yet, for some reason, educationists have been reluctant to acknowl-edge the prominence of the control function in schools. Part of this stems from the view of schools as nurturant settings, to the desirability of individualism and self-expression, and to the oft-touted professionalism of teachers and administrators. Industry and commerce have been far less coy in extolling the alleged virtues of supervision through planning, organizing, leading, directing, commanding, co-ordinating, communicating and evaluating. In education, it is almost as if, by not talking about it, the control problem will go away.

An example from the Australian context with which I am familiar may serve to illustrate the point. Nineteenth-century Australian education represents a disturbing example of scientific management and bureaucratic control of schooling at its autocratic best. Because the bureaucratic form of organization lends itself so well to the breaking down of tasks into simple components and the supervision of the implementation of these sub-tasks, it seemed natural enough to apply this to schooling. Supervision of teaching and the careful prescription of the content of teaching were the two major requirements. Indeed, the nature of early Australian teachers made both of those imperative: 'with very rare exceptions [they were], vulgar, illiterate, sottish adventurers: the refuse and insolvent outcasts of some trade or mechanical occupation' (Smart, 1977: 7). It was the Church and the clergy who established schools in Australia and who exercised the supervisory control over teachers. Close supervision was deemed necessary because teachers were 'persons of the most worthless character who had formerly been convicts and who were notorious drunkards' (ibid., p. 7). The subsequent development of centralized government education systems in Australia merely meant that one form of bureaucratic control, through the Church, replaced another.

It was also not difficult either to control what passed as knowledge. It was simply a matter of rigorously prescribing the textbooks and specifying the time teachers should allocate to the teaching of various topics – both were done assiduously. And, as if these controls were insufficient, the Australian colonies enjoyed the dubious privilege of being among the leading practitioners of the 'payment by results system'. Teachers were paid a low salary, plus an additional supplement for each child who passed a basic examination in literacy and numeracy. The elaborate system of standardization and task-specification of what was deemed desirable in teaching and learning, were guaranteed through an efficient system of inspection. Giving evidence before the Royal Commission of 1882, one inspector lamented that in the teaching of hand-writing (Austin, 1961: 240):

> that in the M's and N's the second stroke has to come from the bottom of the previous one and not from the top . . . I am constantly pointing out some of these minute things to the teachers . . . I say the down strokes must be complete. . . . Individuality should be suppressed beforehand, not only in the way of moral training, but in order to improve the writing itself. . . . All inspectors are agreed that there should not be latitude in this respect, as it will be productive of evil.

With the pursuit of standardization and efficiency in the first two decades of this century, control became an even more 'respectable' form of legitimation. On the other side of the Pacific, in the USA, proponents like Cubberley (1922) made it clear through their writing that schools, rather than being victims of the movement and following the lead of business and commerce in the quest for order, control and efficiency, were instead at the leading edge in terms of the application of these ideas. The development of a self-styled scientific approach to the supervision of instruction was, therefore, a response to the absence of any clearly defined standards in schooling, and were a way of circumscribing which methods *worked*, *when* and with *which* children. Needless to say, it also enabled the sorting of effective from ineffective teachers. According to McNeil (1982: 19), those involved in instructional supervision were expected 'to discover best procedures for performing teaching tasks and to help teachers acquire those methods in order to ensure maximum pupil achievement'.

During the 1930s, there were the beginnings of what appeared to be a shift in emphasis. Supervisors of instruction were still expected to attain the given ends of efficiency, but the method was to be through assisting teachers to understand the mission of their respective schools, with supervisors assisting in the selection of appropriate strategies through which to generate the desired achievement-related results. This was really an attempt to generate freedom within a tightly controlled structure. As Sergiovanni and Starratt (1979) argue, nothing in the way of change occurred during this supposedly humane and democratic 'human relations' epoch. Even though there were outward appearances of a heightened concern with the individual as a person, the human relations approach was little more than a carefully contrived attempt to gloss over existing social relationships. Applied to teaching, there was little that could be construed as liberating or emancipatory. Obvious by its absence was a lack of concern about the classroom practitioner as a teacher, and of the need to attend to personal and professional concerns relating to pedagogy and curriculum. While there were outward signs of change in the direction of participation and away from a bureaucratic stance, underneath there was still a dominant and manipulative agenda. Sergiovanni and Starratt (1979: 4) expressed it in these words:

> Supervisors worked to create a feeling of satisfaction among teachers by showing interest in them as people. . . . Participation was to be an important method, and its objective was to make teachers *feel* that they were useful and important to the school. . . . [But] the focus of human relations supervision was and still is an emphasis on 'winning friends' in an attempt to influence people. To many, 'winning friends' was a slick tactic which made the movement seem manipulative and inauthentic, even dishonest.

In summary, the point being made is simple enough. Until fairly recently, there was an exclusive pre-occupation with the bureaucratic use of instructional supervision as a form of social control over teachers and teaching, albeit in the guise of enhancing efficiency. There was a quite deliberate attempt to control and regulate from the centre the pedagogy, knowledge and behaviour of teachers through elaborate systems of prescription, inspection and evaluation.

It is also important to note that as early as the 1930s, and following through into the 1960s, that there was evidence of a more indirect form of control over teaching and teachers. In the wake of the innovative practices of the Dalton Plan and the Winnetka Scheme in the USA, there was promise of a respite from the heavy-hand of bureaucratic control. There was a problem, however, between the rhetoric and the reality. Modes of instructional supervision were beginning to be influenced by the paradigm shift to a behavioural science view of research. Behavioural scientists believed, for example: that it was possible to

use a natural sciences perspective (with its ethos and values) in the study of
social phenomena; that social phenomena can be meaningfully analysed using
natural science methods; and that the underlying investigative purposes are the
same, namely, to generate empirically grounded theory and predictive statements. The behavioural sciences approach assumed particular significance
through the development of psychological theories of learning, as well as
through the 'research', 'development' and 'diffusion' model (RD&D) of educational change. As a wave of educational innovations occurred through the
1960s, including teaching machines, programmed instruction, mastery learning and individually guided instruction, there was an accompanying shift in the
emphasis on instructional supervision. Those changes, although they involved
a relaxation of the inspection of teachers and heralded the move towards
'teacher-proof' educational materials requiring minimum surveillance, they
also signalled that the route to educational improvement was to lie in
programmes rather than people.

In practical terms, this meant that the reduction in overt bureaucratic control
was accompanied by an intensification of covert control over curricula and
pedagogy by agencies outside of schools such as research and development
laboratories, educational publishers, test designers and curriculum developers. Indeed, with the boom conditions of the 1960s, it was hard for
schools not to get caught up in the pedagogical consumerism generated
outside of schools. It was equally hard for them to avoid the psychological
pressures upon them from educational 'peddlers', as well as pressures from
their local communities, not to be seen to 'keep up with the times'. As Bates
(1980: 55) has noted, these new developments influenced teachers' practices
in subtle and pervasive ways:

> Rather than direction and supervision, a subtler 'band wagon' effect is
> created, which defines publicly and privately what 'good teaching' is
> about, and creates divisions within the teaching population, between
> those who know about and employ the new curricular technique, and
> those who do not. Status is therefore re-defined in terms which are
> ideologically produced and manipulated. . . . Once again, while greater
> autonomy is promised, the effect is to shift the basis of control, rather than
> to reduce its extent.

The problem with control of this kind is its insidious nature. While it is no
less real than its bureaucratic counterpart, it in fact belies its outward appearances of freedom and autonomy. The pressure to conform, while partly
inherent in the curriculum and material packages themselves, was all the more
effective because of consumer desire to partake of the goodies. Any real
reduction in control over knowledge and classroom practice was therefore
quite spurious.

What discussion so far in this chapter highlights is not that there should be
no external control of public education, nor that teachers should not be
accountable for what transpires in their classrooms. The issue is really one

of the balance between social control, and the personal freedom from persecution, coercion, domination, ignorance and oppression. The question is how to provide the certainty and stability possible through an infrastructure, while preserving and nurturing individual rights.

While not pretending to have a simple answer to the problematic issue, the next section attempts to provide an alternative ideological framework within which teachers can begin to assume greater control over the improvement of teaching for their own professional development. It is argued that this might occur by assisting teachers to penetrate their everyday experiences in more practical and insightful ways. The proposal is that this involves obtaining meaning out of confusion, extracting understanding from repetition, uncovering intentions behind actions, replacing prejudice with sensitivity; in short, it involves articulating an ideology for making sense of one's world. In Hunt's (1978) terms, there are messages embedded in the personal experiences of teachers, and teachers are probably their own best theorists. What is required, therefore, is that 'outsiders' view their role as working with teachers to assist *them* to develop common frameworks of meaning about teaching.

One way for teachers to engage in critical inquiry is for them to become active 'clinicians' of their own and each other's teaching. What we need to do is to fundamentally transform the basis upon which changes purportedly occur in teaching and supervision – from one that endorses (however subtly) an authoritarian and manipulative approach, to one that actively empowers teachers, providing them with an ideological framework for uncovering the myths, metaphors and constraints of that teaching. Accordingly, teachers would cease to be the passive recipients of other people's theories and become participants in codifying meaning and understanding in what they do.

'Best existing practice'?

The type of process most likely to generate benefit for teachers is that which recognizes teachers' pragmatic on-the-job style of learning, and which enables them to experience the benefit of autonomous professional development possible through the systematic study of their own teaching. Elliott (1976b) has described as 'practical reflection' the process of engaging teachers in an analysis of their own practice so that emerging problems can be resolved through the generation and testing of hypotheses in teachers' own classrooms. He proposes that this be done by assisting teachers to identify and diagnose practical problems of importance to them, and over which they exercise discretionary control. Under these conditions, the teacher becomes 'an autonomous person who is capable of improving his [sic] own performance' (p. 55). Bodine (1973: 171) has also spoken of the potential gains in analysing one's own practice:

Self-assessment is probably the most powerful means yet developed for a teacher to be the master of his [sic] own professional growth. . . . Self-assessment, like opening a door, allows a person to look and see what he [*sic*] is actually doing in the classroom. It is the mirror of his [*sic*] present teaching behavior. It gives the teacher objective information about this role in the classroom and enables the teacher to learn as much as he [*sic*] can about his [*sic*] own methods of working with and influencing children and other people.

Yet, even where there are demonstrable benefits associated with the critical analysis of practice, there are problems of a very real kind too, as House (1972: 406) has indicated: 'since there are no punishments for not exposing one's behavior and many dangers in doing so, the prudent teacher gives lip-service to the idea and drags both feet'. As MacKay and Marland (1978) put it, asking teachers to distance themselves from the kaleidoscope of classroom events is an extraordinarily difficult process for most of them. The variety, complexity and simultaneity of classroom events do not provide good reflecting surfaces for teachers to see themselves at work. Teachers *can* and *do* seek opportunities to be reflective and to scrutinize their teaching, when introduced to acceptable methods. However, as Cogan (1973: 262) noted, 'the teacher needs help in disengaging himself from familiar patterns and he needs professional-technical support during the novel behavior'.

Actually divesting instructional supervision of its lingering bureaucratic and sanction-ridden connotations and the accompanying 'expert' and 'inexpert' syndrome is clearly a substantial challenge. Teachers need processes with which in collaboration to analyse and appraise *their own* teaching, but they need at the same time to be introduced to paradigms and methodologies that enable them to engage in the process of discovering what they do, appropriating that knowledge and legitimating their pedagogy.

In the final analysis, being clear about the type of practice which is robust enough to be revealing, may carry us considerably beyond best existing practices in instructional supervision. The type of process most likely to succeed, in my opinion, is not that which relies on the classification, objectification and modification of behaviour through the generation of 'brute data' (Taylor, 1971) about teaching, but rather that which comes closer to Geertz's (1973) 'thick descriptions' of teaching where the values, cultural significance and meaning of teaching experiences are paramount. Hymes (1979), for example, describes as 'ethnographic monitoring', the process of going beyond merely focusing upon problem areas within teaching and providing technical solutions, to discovering instead what is working already, and then to provide support, explanation and legitimacy for these practices.

The philosophy, rationale and constructs of clinical supervision (Goldhammer, 1969; Cogan, 1973) move us substantially in that direction. The major difficulty with it is that it has often been imposed upon teachers by outside supervisors as a process that is supposedly 'good' for them. Commenting on the burgeoning interest in clinical supervision, Snyder (1981) noted that clinical supervision *can* provide a philosophical as well as a methodological framework for teachers and supervisors as they work together. The reality for Sergiovanni (1982b), however, is that while clinical supervision should be construed as a way of thinking about improving teaching, for many adherents it is simply a neat set of mechanical steps to be followed. As Garman (1982: 36) notes, this technocratic orientation manifests itself in a surfeit of itinerant clinical supervisors: 'Itinerant supervisors often report. "We are *doing* clinical supervision in our school" (meaning we are following the plan of the method) or more direct "I am using the cycle on a group of teachers".'

The tragedy for these practitioners is that they are unable to distinguish between the cultural habitus (the beliefs, traditions, myths, language and implicit conventions) of clinical supervision, and the process of 'going through the motions' of using clinical supervision (Smyth *et al.*, 1982b).

The challenge for Garman (1982) and others concerned about supervision lies in converting ritualistic encounters between would-be collaborators into meaningful educational alliances through the development of a culture-like approach to clinical supervision, where participants are working towards the articulation of a similar definition of reality. This will in all likelihood come through a careful and deliberate analysis of the negotiation process that occurs both during the pre- and post-observation conference sessions, as teachers question their own motives for adopting particular negotiating positions. What is at risk is the need to recognize the existence of multiple realities and the legitimacy and power of others' values and expectations. This implies that there are serious moral and ethical questions in denying teachers an equal and authentic partnership in deliberating upon choices that affect them and their teaching.

In all of this there is clearly a need to move beyond a concern with the process and the method of clinical supervision, and work at developing the kind of ideology that goes with those practical constructs. Success at doing that task could ultimately affect the way teachers are prepared to develop a thorough-going sense of ownership of the strategy and what it stands for. Success shall also be dependent, in part, on teachers developing a personal and institutional commitment towards being reflective about teaching, pursuing questions like:

1 To what extent are the practices of clinical supervision *just* in treating teachers as rational and capable of participating fully in the determination of their own destiny?
2 To what extent is the process of clinical supervision *practical* in allowing teachers to discover aspects about their own teaching through actions?
3 To what extent is clinical supervision *realistic* in acknowledging the facts of school and classroom life.

If we are to be honest in the answers to these questions, then those of us who work with teachers in introducing clinical supervision into schools will have to accept some of the responsibility for the *nominal* acceptance of clinical supervision. In this we need to be much better at heading off what Romberg

(1979) described as the *illusory* (or mechanical) adoption of clinical supervision by those who carefully adopt the language, rituals and the routines, but
who fail to engage in the development of shared frameworks of meaning about
what they are doing. For example, where teachers and schools adopt the labels
of clinical supervision and claim that what they are currently doing is clinical
supervision, '. . . and we've been doing it for some time, too'. We need to begin
to see that within this kind of mindset the 'how' of teaching is often emphasized
to the exclusion of the 'why', and that what is missing is reflection and
understanding about purpose. Occasionally, we can take some of the credit for
those instances where there is *constructive* adoption of clinical supervision –
where the larger educative purpose is understood and the language, rituals
and procedures are used in the light of that purpose. While teachers are not
entirely blameless when clinical supervision does not work out, if we expect
them to adopt it as 'a way of life' in schools, then we shall need to pay close and
continuing attention to ensuring that clinical supervision is 'realistic, practical
and just'.

In a real sense, we are all the products of our history, notwithstanding the
fact that we are also able to shape in some small measure the course of that
history through some of our actions. All teachers have vivid memories of
having had their teaching observed in one way or another, usually for purposes
of inspection or evaluation. An example may serve to clarify the way professional histories continue to live on into the present. A colleague of mine,
now a Professor of Education in the UK, reflected on his own memories as a
teacher and what it meant to him, to have been 'evaluated' by an outside
observer (Eggleston, 1979: 41):

> I can still vividly recall after 25 years my first General Inspection. Form 5b
> were wrestling with the structure and physiology of the vertebrate eye.
> Vitreous humor flowed freely over the laboratory benches. At one point
> the class lapsed into a metaphysical exposition concerning the existence
> of the 'phantom' made visible by gently poking the inner corner of a
> closed eye. What my Inspector made of this activity was and remained
> beyond my ken. He uttered four words during 45 minutes, 'good morn-
> ing' and 'thank you'. There may be, lodged in the archives of the
> [Department] a more articulate report of the Inspector's observations,
> perceptions and judgements of the events of that possibly unique occa-
> sion. But any expectation I might have had that I would be the recipient of
> feedback rich in pedagogical insight was not realized.

Speculating on what the evaluator as an observer may have focused upon, and
indeed gleaned from the experience, Eggleston (1979: 41) continued:

> The focus must have been on my ability to engage the class in tactical
> manoeuvres. My intentions might have been inferred, my strategies to a
> limited degree have been discernible, the effect of the lesson on my pupils
> visible only from their performance as participants. Any cognitive gains

which may have occurred, any developments of attitudes to the business of learning biology were not manifest in any way observable by the Inspector. At no point during this inspection was I asked to give an account of my intentions.

Was I teaching the vertebrate eye to give my pupils experience of scientific ways of thinking? Was I merely presenting facts about the eye and of its functions? Was I mainly concerned to develop my pupils' abilities to develop mathematical algorithms from physiological data? Did I intend to advance my pupils' development in the use of descriptive language to describe accurately biological processes? Was my purpose to give my pupils a sense of awe when brought face to face with the fitness for function of the mammalian eye? No such issue was raised. The equally significant question of the effects of the lesson on my pupils was also not called into question. Had they learnt what I was trying to teach them? No evidence was available, none called for.

The term 'evaluation' (or appraisal) is, therefore, one of the most loaded and disliked words in the language of teachers. There is extensive occupational myth, much of it well-founded, surrounding the personage of the inspector, supervisor or the evaluator (Tronc and Harris, 1985). There is little doubt that the unfortunate occupant of this role is treated with the universal scorn afforded any unwanted, unfriendly invader of the teacher's classroom space. Yet, when we consider the legacy of the very considerable preoccupation of education systems with order, efficiency and control in education, spawned largely in the USA through the work of people like Bobbitt (1924), Cubberley (1922) and Bagley (1907), it is not hard to understand teachers' longstanding resentment to evaluation. Let us take an illustration that is broadly similar to what has happened in a variety of other contexts. In Australia, the role of inspector became an official government appointment when schooling was systematized in the middle of the nineteenth century. The emphasis at the time was upon control and efficiency, and the role of inspectors was that of acting as a 'watchdog' to ensure that public monies were spent effectively. Added to this was the 'ruthless, capricious and arbitrary way in which the duties of inspection were sometimes performed', with the result that they were often ascribed a 'head-hunting' image of 'fact-finding examiner, conservative keeper of standards and preserver of the status quo' (Tronc and Harris, 1985: 45). As Tronc and Harris (1985: 45) put it, 'Inspection became an almost un-bearable authoritarian inquisition, with teachers sacrificed on the altar of efficiency.'

Even though the language may have mellowed a little, much of what passes as the appraisal of teachers today is little different in intent from the scientific management notions from which it derives. While done with the best of intentions, the oppressive ideology is still intact (see Hunter, 1984, for a good illustration of what I mean). When one person is 'evaluating' the teaching of another it is easy to forget that the moral and ethical imperative that we are really talking about is one that serves the interests of one party while silencing or denying the other.

Because of the unwritten but powerful mythology of teaching, the inspectorial, evaluation and appraisal legacy has left teachers understandably reluctant to open their classrooms voluntarily to outside visitations no matter how benevolent the apparent intent. Outsiders, and this can include colleagues from down the corridor, still experience difficulty in living down the reputation of their inspectorial predecessors when it comes to observing teaching. Even though the rhetoric of clinical supervision is couched clearly enough in terms that disavow any connection with matters 'evaluative' or 'judgemental', it is difficult for teachers to grasp readily how observation can be anything other than inquisitorial. It is only when they experience the data-based nature of observations and become actively involved in determining the focus of observation in their teaching, that teachers learn how this can be possible.

Living down our unfortunate educational history alluded to earlier in this chapter may, however, only be *one* aspect of the problem of getting clinical supervision working in schools.

The context for clinical supervision

There is no shortage of sceptics prepared to scornfully accuse collegial and collaborative processes like clinical supervision as being doomed. They advance the argument that the democratic conditions necessary for clinical supervision to flourish and take hold do not exist in schools, and that, as a consequence, it is not surprising that it cannot or does not work. McFaul and Cooper (1984), for example, claim that teacher isolation within the school, fragmentation among teaching staff in terms of experience, and frustration among teachers because of a lack of time, are all contributing reasons preventing clinical supervision from catching on. And, they may be right!

My concern is somewhat different; I am concerned about McFaul and Cooper's (1984) logic. Their case rests on the unfounded, or at least unquestioned assumption, that in order to introduce processes like clinical supervision into schools you first need a healthy organizational climate. What viewpoints like this fail to grasp fully is that processes like clinical supervision, rather than *requiring* utopian pre-conditions, in fact, have the *capacity* within them to enable school people to generate the kind of circumstances that *can* lead a school towards becoming a more reflective, enlivening and vibrant kind of place. To argue as McFaul and Cooper (1984) do that clinical supervision is *impossible*, and therefore is not worth attempting, because of the absence of certain idealistic conditions, is like saying that children of the poor are so because they lack an education and cannot read or write! The analogy is interesting, because in both cases the victim is blamed.

Rather than arguing that clinical supervision is unlikely to work in schools because of the absence of an environment congruent with sustained professional development, it would be more productive to move beyond the victim-blaming rhetoric to ask more penetrating questions like why it is that schools are effectively precluded from engaging in uplifting processes like clinical supervision? On a broader front, I suspect the issue is similar in nature to the reform of wider social issues like inequality, injustice and discrimination. On these fronts, we are constrained in ways we do not even know about – we are victims of our own limited consciousness.

Because of our inability to transcend and question the efficacy of our taken-for-granted practices and the ideology and axiology that sustain them, we resort to examining issues in tired old ways. Discussion about the alleged unworkability of clinical supervision, for example, tends to be in *individualistic* terms, which portrays teachers as being unprepared to challenge one another, or as implicitly endorsing mediocrity in teaching through an unwillingness to act reflectively. Lortie (1975) had some harsh words to say about teachers' 'reflexive conservatism' when he described them as not having a tradition of thinking carefully about their professional beliefs and practices, and not having a history of regularly testing the validity of their actions. Wehlage (1981) also found that even when teachers were provided with 'enabling time' to reflect on their practices, they tended not to conceive their work in problematic terms, but rather as procedural tasks to be enhanced. According to McFaul and Cooper (1984), even when provided with the clinical supervision framework and the opportunity to work with peers, teachers were still reluctant to collect classroom data and to engage in the task of transcending it for meaning.

I find such portrayals that rely on the presumed personal inadequacies of teachers to be unhelpful, not to mention a trifle arrogant. In a more positive vein, I am inclined towards Yonemura's (1982) view that teachers have a long history of oppression to be overcome before they are able to accept fully that valid knowledge about teaching does not reside *only* in outside experts. Once teachers begin to re-learn the sobering fact that they *can* have theories of action that amount to valid and plausible knowledge about teaching, then they will have begun to overcome the institutional barriers that have hitherto inhibited them from developing and publicly articulating repertoires about 'what works in teaching'.

Implicit in what I am saying is that to argue that clinical supervision (or processes like it) does not work in schools because of disaffected or incapable teachers is to ignore the overwhelming and systematically distorting effect of educational structures themselves. Where clinical supervision does not work out, we need to move beyond blaming the teacher (as victim) to a wider examination of what is at work in schools generally, that prevents self-reflective processes like clinical supervision from gaining a hold. We need not only to consider the *structural character of schooling* that prevents reflection from occurring, but look also at how those conditions have historically come about and how they continue to sustain and maintain conditions that effectively thwart reflective processes.

In this regard, Bullough *et al.* (1984) argue that there are two inherited aspects of our culture that have powerfully shaped teachers' roles and that serve to inform the way teachers interpret and understand the nature of their work. They label these 'the tradition of public service' (or the unquestioning submission to bureaucratic authority) and the ideology of 'technocratic mindedness' (or the supremacy of technical rational values). We hardly need reminding of the extensive body of literature (Karier, 1982) that portrays the teacher as historically conforming to the image of the public servant. This literature says that for reasons of efficiency and control there are dangers in allowing teachers the power to establish the ends towards which they work; even their freedom to work out instructional methods is limited only by the inability of science and research to define and prescribe precisely the most effective strategies. Put bluntly: 'the teacher is free only because control is not yet fully [and technically] possible' (Bullough *et al.*, 1984: 345). Even though the humanistic and democratic language used generally tends to mask it, teachers are still often construed as being submissive and unquestioning, having no political interests beyond the classroom, and as concerned only with the implementation of somebody else's agendas. This is part of the technocratic ideology that regards schooling as essentially value-free and construes protracted social questions relating to morals, ethics and politics as nothing more than another species of technical decisions to be implemented by instrumentally thinking bureaucrats (Bullough *et al.*, 1984: 343). This unbounded faith in the ability of educational experts to solve the problems of schooling means that there is a deliberate division of labour between those who *know about teaching* and those *who do it.* Wherever the 'expert' tenders to the 'inexpert', it is not surprising to find a wide discrepancy between the opportunities afforded teachers to question the efficacy of what they do, and the disproportionate influence outside experts are able to wield psychologically and bureaucratically over the work of teachers.

It is not hard to see, therefore, how a process like clinical supervision, which involves personal disclosure of teaching aspirations and the collection and analysis of evidence about that teaching, could be used by 'outsiders' to the disadvantage of teachers. Rather than investing teachers with the capacity to gain more control over their own professional lives and destinies, clinical supervision can become a quite sinister form of teacher surveillance. To rephrase some remarks made by Hargreaves (1982), we have become so accustomed to the unsubtle attempts by school systems 'to storm the front gates of the citadel of teacher autonomy, that its quiet entry through the backdoor [via processes like clinical supervision] has been virtually undetected' (p. 258). None of this is to suggest there is anything wrong with the *form* of clinical supervision; rather, it is an indictment on how it has been misused. Amid this gloom and doom, there are, however, possibilities as well.

An emancipatory possibility

If clinical supervision is to be a way of 'empowering' teachers, which is to say, 'helping [them] to take charge of their lives . . . [in the light of having] been restrained by social or political forces, from assuming such control' (Fried, 1980a: 8) and not construed as a 'delivery of a service' to targeted audiences of teachers deemed to be inexperienced, inefficient, incompetent or in need of re-skilling, then it is imperative that we adopt a 'critical' view of what is involved. Being critical does not mean being negative, but refers rather to the stance of enabling teachers to see their classroom actions in relation to the historical, social and cultural context in which their teaching is actually embedded. This means creating conditions under which teachers, both indi-vidually and collectively, can develop for themselves the capacity to view teaching historically; to treat the contemporary events, practices and structures of teaching problematically (and not take them for granted); and to examine the surface realities of institutionalized schooling in a search for explanations of its form, and thereby to clarify for themselves alternative courses of educational action that are open to them. Acting critically, therefore, refers to collaboration in marshalling intellectual capacity so as to focus upon analysing, reflecting on and engaging in discourse about the nature and effects of practical aspects of teaching and how they might be altered (Smyth, 1985a).

Becoming critical and acting reflectively involves acknowledging Berlak and Berlak's (1981) point that teachers are both the products and the creators of their own history. In practical terms, this means teachers engaging themselves in systematic individual and social forms of investigation that examine the origins and consequences of everyday teaching behaviour so they come to see those factors that represent impediments to change. The intent is through collective action to overcome the fatalistic view that change in teaching is 'impossible for me', and seeing that circumstances *can be* different from what they are. It means teachers moving from a passive, dependent and adaptive (Fay, 1977) view of themselves and their potentialities, to one in which teachers are able to 'analyze and expose the hiatus between the actual and the possible, between the existing order of contradictions and a potential future state' (Held, 1980: 22). In short, it involves teachers becoming oriented to the development of an enhanced 'consciousness' of their own circumstances and political involvement in working towards actively changing the frustrating and debilitating conditions that characterize their work lives (Smyth, 1986a).

The major problem with extant views of clinical supervision is that they lack this kind of a critical dimension; they are inherently conservative. While their espoused concern is for teacher autonomy, dignity and worth, and with seeking to release teachers from the passive consumerism and domination by outside experts, clinical supervision operates largely on the basis of an individualistic view of what it means to engage in self-evaluation. Certainly, there is opportunity for dialogue, but it is severely constrained by the working requirement of teachers to form dyad arrangements as the basis for the collaborative alliances to examine their own and each other's teaching. There is no provision for *extended* discourse about the ends of teaching, nor about the social purposes of schooling, or the nature of this form of inquiry. In short, clinical supervision as normally construed celebrates a view of change that is limited to working *within* existing institutional structures and frameworks. While the means of teaching may be subjected to questioning, the ends are not. Herein lies its major drawback. Arguably, the most serious issues confronting teachers are not matters of teaching techniques, but impediments that exist because of power relationships and organizational inertia. As a community of scholars and practitioners, we have not yet begun to embrace, let alone practise, how to move clinical supervision outside of itself. As Sergiovanni (1976: 21–2) expressed it:

> clinical supervision at present is too closely associated with a workflow – a pattern of action, and not associated enough with a set of concepts from which a variety of patterns could be generated. The intellectual capital inherent in clinical supervision is . . . more important than its workflow as articulated into steps, strategies and procedures.

We need to reduce our concern with the process and procedural aspects and deepen our commitment to tackling the broader issues of how clinical supervision might assist teachers to achieve forms of teaching that contribute to ways of learning that are more realistic, practical and just for students (Smyth, 1984b).

None of this is to suggest that the technical aspects of teaching are unimportant or should be ignored; rather, I am entering a plea to restore them to their rightful status, not as ends in themselves, but as important means to valued social purposes. As long as we have an excessive concern in clinical supervision with the instrumental and technical aspects of teaching, then these get in the way of asking questions about how schooling perpetuates injustices and inequalities in our society, and actually 'prevents the more consequential questions from being asked' (van Manen, 1977: 209).

Conclusion

The argument presented in this chapter has been that instructional supervision as generally conceptualized and practised in schools suffers because of its heritage and historical affiliation with matters relating to scientific management. Overt bureaucratic forms of control through inspection of teaching were shown to have been replaced by less obvious psychological forms of controlling teachers by agencies outside of schools and school systems. Even in those circumstances where schools and authorities were seen to espouse a more humanistic view of what it means to be a professional in a school setting, there are still important, largely undiscussed ideological issues associated with the job-related growth of teachers. Argument in the chapter has suggested that it is possible to treat teachers in non-coercive ways, while ensuring that they be sensitive, responsive and responsible to their various constituencies. This enhanced ownership and control by teachers over their own teaching was argued to occur through a more historically reflexive view of teaching that culminates in a commitment to action.

What was proposed were practices that focus upon developing forms of consciousness among teachers that emphasize critical inquiry as a way of generating theories about their own practice. Clinical supervision was portrayed as an existing practice that moves us towards a more just, practical and realistic theory of social action. If clinical supervision is, *in fact*, to provide a paradigm for assisting teachers to develop and articulate ideological frameworks about their own teaching, then there is a need for greater attention to the philosophy and rationale of clinical supervision, rather than a concern only with the methodology itself. In this regard, the future direction is reasonably clear. We need to move away from sole reliance upon the idea of clinical supervision as a methodology for improving teaching, and to think of it in terms by which teachers are able to gain control over their own teaching and, as a consequence, their development as professionals.

Note

1 The argument here follows Bates, 1980.

2

Supervision: a field of study?

Introduction

The major claim I make in this chapter is that what passes as the theory, research and practice of supervision in schools generally, is desperately in need of overhaul. There has been a plethora of research and much hortative literature on the practicalities of doing supervision, but virtually no attempt has been made to stand back and look at the area of study itself (Smyth, 1985b), what it purports to be, where it has come from, what it aspires to, where it is headed, and how it relates to discussion and debate in the broader area of the philosophy of science. As Toulmin (1972) argued, any field that hopes to make any conceptual advances must remain continually open to criticism and change if it is to move beyond being a mere pretender. It is, above all, this ability to develop an inquiring inner eye on itself, that represents the hallmark of a genuine field of study.

In this chapter, I argue that supervision like the field of professional development generally is suffering from a legacy of being affiliated with an outmoded interpretation of science and technology. Value-free objectivist views of science and the notions of technical rationality that accompany them have broken down in the face of protracted social problems – social engineering in the guise of neutral science no longer suffices. I discuss the crisis of confidence in the professions generally, and in supervision and research on teaching in particular. As a way out of this quagmire, I propose a dialectical possibility that opens up for contestation and debate implicit power relationships and the question of who has 'the right to know' about teaching. I see supervision, enacted in the ways I envisage in the latter part of the chapter, as a potent means by which teachers can reclaim their professional lives.

For starters, I want to locate supervision in some kind of historical context and to acknowledge Giroux's (1983) point about the need to recover our sedimented histories if we are to have any hope of resolving current issues. Acknowledging Giroux's critical perspective requires that, in order to decide what to do next, we have to ascertain why things are currently the way they are, how they got that way, and what conditions sustain and support them.

The roots of supervision

The pedigree of supervision is not an entirely irrelevant one in the context of current discussions. From the educational literature, it is clear that the intention of the common schools, at least in the USA in the nineteenth century (and I suspect elsewhere as well), was unashamedly that of changing the nature of society; those who assumed the title of 'supervisor' were to be the front-line evangelists in changing the social order. Using evidence from the *Annual Reports of the Superintendent of Common Schools in the State of New York* (1845), Blumberg (1984) leaves little doubt as to the social reconstructionist nature of the supervisory role:

> The future of this country and its republican form of government, as they [the supervisors] saw it, was intimately connected with the schools. It would only be through [the] success and popularization [of schools] that the country would have an educated populace capable of making informed decisions and learning the skills necessary for productive adult life. . . . Failing to develop a viable widespread school system would result . . . in the replication in this country of the condition of the South American republics which 'have fallen into revolutionary decrepitude and degenerated into military despotisms . . .' (p. 3).

> Without a good system of public schools, the thinking went, the great experiment in republican government that was America, where each person had the opportunity to be what he or she could be, would degenerate. Wealth would be concentrated in the hands of a few and such concentration of wealth 'enables its possessor to monopolize intellectual attainment, and robs the mass of motive power to effort'. Public schools were the antidote to this possibility (p. 5).

What was at issue was the right of these supervisory superintendents to grant and withdraw teacher certification. Doyle (1978) has argued that it was the push by superintendents to professionalize US education in the nineteenth century and thereby gain autonomy for themselves that led directly to the search for scientific justifications (and hence the quest for indicators of 'teacher effectiveness') to support the exercise of power and control. According to Doyle (1978: 144):

> A profession is an occupation that gains control over the substance of its work because its assertions about importance and efficacy are ultimately

believed by society. Such a view of professionalization places special emphasis . . . on the elements of power and control that influence the location of an occupation within the structure of a particular domain of work.

In schools that occurred at the supervisory level, where the battle for the right to control teaching was fought.

The struggle was about wresting control over the recruitment of teachers away from the influence of local political patronage and investing it in the hands of a civil servant class proclaimed to be above and beyond reproach (Smyth, 1984b); hence the recourse to scientism as a way of legitimating supervisory actions. Cubberley (1922), for example, saw in testing the opportunity for supervisors to establish standards against which to be able to defend what they were doing. It was argued, that by this means, control over education could be shifted out of the emotionally charged world of whim and local political influence, and placed within the jurisdiction of civil servants able to legitimate their actions by reference to scientifically established standards.

It thus became possible to link the actions of supervisors to the outcomes of schooling through various indicators of efficiency and effectiveness. As Doyle (1978: 145) argued:

Effectiveness indicators would thus have substantial symbolic value in establishing the technical qualifications of administrators to manage the affairs of education. Of equal importance were the immediate practical consequences of control over entry into the classroom. Possession of a scientifically-derived set of teacher qualities related systematically to effectiveness would enable superintendents to decide on disinterested, rational grounds who would be appointed to teaching positions. In this manner, the profession would gain a powerful weapon in the fight against the political patronage system. Who could reasonably question a decision not to hire the ward boss' niece when she did not meet 'scientific' criteria of effectiveness?

For Karier (1982), the blueprint for supervision established for schools at this time had quite sinister and long-ranging implications:

The same year Karl Marx wrote *The Communist Manifesto* (1848) Horace Mann penned his last Annual Report to the Massachusetts Board of Education. In that report was embedded a theory of human capital that conceptually linked schooling to economic and social growth within a meritocratically-organized social and economic class system. Here, then, was the rationale for public schooling that would sustain the American nation for the next century. Implicit in that rationale was an ideology of competitive and possessive individualism packaged in the context of equal opportunity for all within a system of schools locally managed under state authorization (p. 6).

. . . As the system became more bureaucratic, the primary values became standardization and efficiency. As means became evaluated more on efficiency grounds, the role of the professional teacher and supervisor entered the highly charged problematic world of social engineering (p. 4).

The problem appears to be that the metaphors we choose to frame our thinking, actually drive our descriptive language about schooling, which in turn has a bearing on the way we work with school people – if you like, the way we 'supervise'. Sawada and Calley (1985: 14–15) put it as follows:

The dominant metaphor for today's education is the Newtonian Machine: the school is a more or less well oiled machine that processes (educates?) children. In this sense, the education system (school) comes complete with production goals (desired end states); objectives (precise intermediate end states); raw material (children); a physical plant (school building); a 13-stage assembly line (grades K-12); directives for each stage (curriculum guides); processes for each stage (instruction); managers for each stage (teachers); plant supervisors (principals); trouble shooters (consultants, diagnosticians); quality control mechanisms (discipline, rules, lockstep progress through stages, conformity); interchangeability of parts (teacher-proof curriculum, 25 students per processing unit, equality of treatment); uniform criteria for all (standardized testing interpreted on the normal curve); and basic product available in several lines of trim (academic, vocational, business, general). Is this reminiscent of Fords, Apples, and Big Macs?

Sergiovanni (1984a: 8) has also argued that the way we choose to view teaching has a profound influence on our notion of supervision:

The pipeline or conduit metaphor is often used to depict teaching. 'Instructional delivery systems' are conceived as pipelines through which knowledge and information must travel. Student outcomes are at one end of this line and teaching inputs are at the other end. Care must be taken to keep this instructional pipeline flowing smoothly; obstructions in the line must be eliminated; and the line itself must be shaped to avoid blockage kinks. Inputs must be properly sized to fit the pipeline and a system of monitoring must be established to ensure easy movement of this input through the line. Student outcomes need to be carefully checked to assure that they fit input intents. Improvements need to be made in the composition and arrangement of the pipeline itself in an effort to maximize, even further, student outcomes at lowest cost and so on.

The purpose of this discussion of metaphors is to underscore the point that if the prevailing metaphor that drives educational thought, discussion and action derives from Newtonian physics, and given what we know about the boundedness and limitations of that view of physics, then we need ways of challenging these awesome stabilizing forces.

Crisis of confidence in professional knowledge[1]

The most pressing issue in supervision is whether to focus on the 'figure' or the 'ground'; that is to say, whether to focus on the technicalities of supervision, or the values and ideals purportedly implicit in the notion of supervision. To date there has been an excessive preoccupation with the former, to the exclusion of the latter. Sergiovanni (1984b: 54–5) captured it neatly when he said, we err:

> by looking in the same places, relying on the same intellectual frames of reference, . . . travelling the same roads in seeking improved practices. Supervision will not improve much by doing *better* that which we are now doing. The models upon which our practices rest and the theoretical bases for generating these models . . . are the problem. Basic knowledge perspectives will need to be changed before practices will change.

Continuing to focus exclusively on *better* ways of doing *more of the same* will prevent the crucial 'educative' issues within supervision from ever emerging. As long as the preoccupation is with the technical and the instrumental, then the important moral, ethical, political and philosophical questions will continue to be ignored.

One way of characterizing the current scene in supervision is to say that it is suffering from a 'crisis of confidence'. The claims to professional knowledge about supervision are out of step with the changing situations of practice. The point can best be made by drawing on the work of Schön (1983) in his *Reflective Practitioner*, in which he argues that in the professions generally, 'the complexity, uncertainty, instability, uniqueness, and value conflicts which are increasingly perceived as central to the world of (current) professional practice' (p. 14), are not able to be handled by recourse to existing bodies of knowledge, or accepted ways of acquiring such knowledge. What Schön (1983) is saying is that the rules of the game have changed radically. Accepted and taken-for-granted ways of applying specialized knowledge to resolve particular recurring problems no longer seem to work. The foundations of professional practice seem to have shifted dramatically from that of 'problem solving' to one of 'problem setting' (or problem posing); that is to say, from a rational process of choosing from among possibilities that best suit agreed-upon ends, to a situation that opens up for contestation and debate the nature of those decisions, the ends to which they are to be directed, and the means by which they are achievable. Rather than relying upon tried-and-tested knowledge to be applied in all circumstances of a similar kind, the scene is increasingly characterized by the application of knowledge acquired from previous particular cases. What this has meant for professionals is a transformation:

from a position where scientifically derived knowledge is deemed superior, to a circumstance in which artistic and intuitive knowledge may be equally as appropriate; from an *a priori* instrumental view of knowledge, to one that reflects knowledge as being tentative and problematic; from a view which presupposes answers to complex social questions, to one that endorses the importance of problem posing and negotiated resolution (Smyth, 1986b: 7).

There are a number of interrelated explanations for this shifting position, not the least of which has to do with the inability of the professions to maintain public credibility in the face of changing social conditions. In particular, the issues confronting the professions are far more complex, problematic and protracted, and the nature of knowledge far too tentative and incomplete, to enable issues to be resolved through the mere application of 'technical' knowledge. In the US scene, Schön (1983) summarized it thus:

A series of announced national crises – the deteriorating cities, the pollution of the environment, the shortage of energy – seemed to have roots in the very practice of science, technology, and public policy that were being called upon to alleviate them.

Government sponsored 'wars' against such crises seemed not to produce the expected results; indeed, they often seemed to exacerbate the crises (p. 9).

. . . the public predicaments of society began to seem less like problems to be solved through expertise than like dilemmas whose resolution could come about through moral and political choice (p. 10).

These problems have been further compounded by the professions' growing disregard for their own espoused tenets; namely, a contribution to the social good, placing clients' needs above personal self-interest, and self-regulation of standards of competence and morals. Added to this is Schön's (1983) observation that as professionals become increasingly unionized and industrialized, they move towards a state of bureaucratization with an accompanying decline in the perceived importance of autonomy and independence of action which had hitherto characterized them.

The crisis in the professions is, therefore, related to an increased questioning by the community of the concept of professional standing, but also to a growing feeling of the inability of the professions to 'deliver' solutions on important social issues. This crisis of confidence manifests itself in the realignment of interests away from client needs, towards those of business and government. These may, however, be only a partial explanation of the growing disillusionment with the professions; the more significant explanation may have to do with whether existing forms of professional knowledge are indeed capable of meeting the problems and needs of society.

It is not surprising, therefore, to find a babble of voices within the professions as they seek to unravel the tangled web of competing and conflicting values, goals, purposes and interests that comprise professional practice. Neither does it come as any surprise to hear of the multiple and shifting images that constitute the practices within these professions. What *is* surprising is that so many practitioners have begun to develop the capacity for reducing what Schön (1983: 18) describes as 'messes to manageable plans', and to make as much sense as they have of the conflicting demands made on them by so many different groups.

What is really at issue here is the epistemology or ways of knowing and acquiring professional knowledge. The tension is between the dominant epistemology of technical rationality where theory is separate from practice, and the emergent paradigm of reflection-in-action which emphasizes forms of knowing that disavow the separation of theory from practice, one in which theory emerges out of practice and practice informs theory; in a word, 'praxis', a notion I shall return to later in the final section of this chapter.

Technical rationality (embedded in the positivist epistemology) has powerfully shaped our Western institutions, ideas and ways of thinking and acting. It had its origins in the Reformation as a way of bringing science and technology to bear in purging thought and action of mysticism, superstition and metaphysics. Originally intended as a way of extending technical control over the physical environment, it came to be applied to social, moral and political issues as well. Its major hallmark was a disciplined and rigorous approach to problem solving based upon the application of empirically verified, cumulative, scientific knowledge.

This knowledge was, and still is, applied to the solving of problems in stable institutional settings where the ends have been unambiguously determined and where technical procedures can be vigorously applied. According to the technical rational view, *basic research* is undertaken in order to yield practical results to be utilized in *applied research* which will eventually generate problem-solving techniques that will increase the efficiency and effectiveness of services provided. Positive science regards these forms of knowing and doing as being related, one to the other, in hierarchical ways; basic research is more important than applied research, which in turn is superior and separate from practice.

Leaving aside the questionable nature of the distinction between applied and basic research, a major difficulty with technical rationality is that it presumes that problems are able to be solved by selecting from among available means and that the ends to which activities are directed are established and unquestionable. In the real world, ends are much more complex, ill-defined and problematic. It is becoming clear that the technical-rational model has become inadequate, incomplete and discredited as a way of dealing with complex and ill-defined issues in times of uncertainty, instability and unpredictability.

Closer attention, therefore, needs to be paid to the intuitive ways in which skilful and artistic practitioners are able to make sense of confusing and contradictory circumstances. However, as Schön (1983) reminds us, this involves a choice; whether to occupy the high moral ground of certainty and predictability of research-based theory for the resolution of our problems, or descend into the swampy lowlands where situations are murky and characterized by confusing 'messes' with no easy solution (Schön, 1983: 42). Opting for the latter means adopting a stance in which knowledge is treated in a tentative fashion. Greater attention is therefore given to the 'playfulness' of knowledge and to the job-embedded ways of learning that acknowledge the fundamental importance of questioning, criticizing and reformulating taken-for-granted assumptions about the nature of work. It means engaging in what Schön (1984: 42) describes as reflection-in-action, or 'a reflective conversation with the situation'. Schön (1983) claims that individuals and communities acquire knowledge, skills and concepts that empower them to re-make, and if necessary re-order, the world in which they live. It takes the form of 'on-the-spot surfacing, criticizing, restructuring and testing of intuitive understandings of experienced phenomena' (Schön, 1984: 42). Indeed, in struggling to describe what it is that is occurring, we often cannot locate conventional rules and procedures to account for what we know: 'We find ourselves at a loss, or produce descriptions that are obviously inappropriate. . . . [O]ur knowing is in our action' (Schön, 1983: 49).

Even though we may be unconscious of doing it, we often engage in a dialectical process of conversing with the unique aspects of the settings in which we work so as to generate forms of knowledge of a kind characterized as 'what works for us'. This is a legitimate way of knowing that amounts to engaging in a form of experimentation that enables us not only to check out hunches and resolve issues of immediacy, but also to develop a repertoire of knowledge that helps us to make sense out of confusion, ambiguity and contradiction. In what amounts to a recant of his earlier writing, Tyler (in Hosford, 1984) claims that researchers and academics develop a misguided view of the importance of technical-rational knowledge. As he put it:

> The practice of every profession evolves informally, and professional procedures are not generally derived from a systematic design based on research findings. Professional practice has largely developed through trial and error and intuitive efforts. Practitioners, over the years, discover procedures that appear to work and others that fail. The professional practice of teaching, as well as that of law, medicine and theology, is largely a product of the experience of practitioners, particularly those who are more creative, inventive, and observant than the average (p. 9).

Knowledge gained in this way – through exposing practice to critical scrutiny – is different in form and substance to knowledge acquired through technical-rational means. For one thing, it does not have to be applied to a problem situation; it is already being used to transform the nature of practice. There is no separation between the developer and the user of knowledge – they are one and the same person. Professional knowledge acquired in this way is not, therefore, static and dependent on legitimation by outside 'experts'.

There is a quality to it that acknowledges a certain willingness to take risks and to confront circumstances of uncertainty in an enterprising way. For those who rely on the certainty and predictability guaranteed by technical knowledge, 'uncertainty is a threat; its admission is a sign of weakness' (Schön, 1983: 69).

Reflection-in-action can occur in deliberate and calculated ways after the event, but it is just as likely to be an inseparable part of on-going practice. Where it occurs in the latter way, practitioners are in fact modifying their action in the light of feelings and information about their own effects. They are not circumscribed by having to rely on knowledge generated by outside authorities; through monitoring what they do themselves, they have a way of knowing that is inherent in intelligent action. What is interesting is that although we can, and do, reflect-in-action, we seldom reflect on our reflection-in-action. This may seem to imply an infinite regression, but it can be overcome by keeping in mind that all actions are ultimately practical. According to Schön (1984: 43), 'a crucially important dimension . . . tends to remain private and inaccessible to others'. Because awareness of our own thinking usually grows out of the process of articulating it to others, as practitioners we often have little access to our own reflection-in-action. In other words, we do not have the disposition or the grammar for talking about the way in which we reflect on what we do; we are unable to communicate to others about it; if others learn, it is by some fortuitous process like contagion.

Reconstructing the teaching–supervision interface

These notions become especially poignant when considering an area of study like supervision in which there is an entrenched presumption that a definitive body of knowledge exists about teaching, that this knowledge is possessed by one group (described as 'supervisors'), while deemed to be absent in varying degrees among teachers. There is the added presumption that this knowledge is indeed capable of transference from one to the other. Hawkins (1973: 8) captured the implicit power relationship in this when he said, 'We . . . are sometimes inclined to the view that nothing is known which is not known to a group of people campaigning to have it decided that they are the official knowers.'

When we talk about supervision we are really talking about a social relationship in which one person is presumed to be an expert, and as such 'knows, or is believed by others to know, everything about a particular activity. He wants to, and is expected to offer "solutions" to problems' (Parekh, 1970: 461). The difficulty with expertise of this kind is that it is of a technical kind that is severely constrained and does not permit the analysis of issues from alternative viewpoints. As Apple (1981: 89) expressed it:

　　the bureaucratic institution . . . furnishes the problems to be investigated
　　. . . the type of knowledge that the expert has to supply is determined in

advance . . . [and] . . . the expert is expected to work on the practical problems as defined by the institution, and not offer advice outside these boundaries.

Because experts are ideologically bound by concepts, beliefs and values that are largely taken-for-granted, Apple (1981: 92), paraphrasing Mannheim, argues that there is a likely insistence on predictability and control with the real risk of 'substituting the search for a smoothly running factory for the critically important debate over the purposes and means of the institution'. Hartnett and Naish (1980) claim that questions about the educational ends to which teachers work are taken as settled or largely irrelevant. Where teachers are treated as technicians unquestioningly following agendas determined by others, such emphasis on means to the exclusion of ends 'is at best, amoral' (Hartnett and Naish, 1980: 265). There is little solace to be found either in the research on teaching. Given what we know about the tentative, inconclusive and problematic nature of research on teaching (Berliner, 1984; Buchmann, 1984; Smyth, 1984c; Garrison and MacMillan, 1984), we must be circumspect about the utility of such research. To argue as Hunter (1984: 174) does that 'translation of research-based theory into practice has now been accomplished, so we can describe and substantiate much of what is effective in teaching', is to put a form of legitimation on this kind of work, that even the researchers themselves hesitate to do. It is to claim a degree of conclusiveness that does not exist. Stenhouse (1983: 212) put it neatly:

> The provisional knowledge created in the educational academy may be seen as second-order . . . knowledge about educational practice offered to teachers. . . . [K]nowledge expressed as generalizations, more or less reliable, contributes to the teachers . . . understanding of the world in which they have to act. However, few such generalizations offer guidance as to how to act since they cannot by definition . . . take account either of the professional biographical development of the teacher . . . or of the crucial contextual and temporal variables. Hence, at this level of action, research can offer only relatively insecure hypotheses, principles, and theories.

Therefore, before we accept the products of other people's research about teaching and 'apply' them through the supervisory process, we need to be clear about the power relationships that are at work. As Fenstermacher (1983: 498) put it:

> Instead of asking how the implications shall be used, we might ask who is to decide what the implications of research for practice are. In one sense, every knowledgeable, competent person may help derive implications. But in the end the critical question is whether these pre-formulated implications are truly implications for you or me, given our contexts and situations. The ultimate arbitrator of whether some finding has implications for practice is the person engaged in the practice.

Embedded in the 'applied' view of research on teaching is the notion of supervision as a bureaucratic relationship in which a corrective service is delivered by those of superior wisdom to those who are less experienced, less capable and less competent. Sergiovanni (1984c: 358) argues that such views of supervision 'typically emphasize goal setting, rational planning, accepting events at face value, objective truth-seeking verified by public knowledge, and rational responses to the process from teachers'. These are real-world conditions that are, at best, highly suspect. They are predicated on a view that school people operate according to notions of rationality that embrace a determination of unambiguous goals, clear statements of objectives, a search for valid alternatives and objectivist forms of knowledge. Teaching is far more indeterminate, ambiguous and value-laden than that. As Hawkins (1973: 8–9) argues, teaching involves a relationship that:

> lies inescapably in the moral domain and is subject to moral scrutiny and judgement. If teaching is good or bad, it is morally good or bad. This claim . . . is not a recommendation or a hoped-for view of the case, but it is a claim of fact.
>
> The relationship [implicit in teaching and learning], by its very nature, involves an offer of control by one individual over the functioning of another, who in accepting this offer, is tacitly assured that control will not be exploitative but will be used to enhance the competence and extend the independence of the one controlled, and in due course will be seen to do so.

Addressing the interface between supervision and teaching requires a serious consideration of the ethical, moral and political questions about the nature of the social relationship between supervisors, teachers and children. Above all, it involves asking why we are engaging in supervision. From my reading of the supervision literature, once we remove the rhetoric of 'improvement', 'teacher development' and 'enhanced professional enactment' that tends to surround supervision, we are left with the threadbare notions of efficiency and effectiveness that sound suspiciously like the business management canons of accountability, inspection and quality control.

A dialectical view

The issues to do with supervision become somewhat clearer when we focus on the medieval Latin origins of supervision as a process of perusing or scanning a text for errors or deviations from the original text. Like its more recent educational counterpart, the original notion of supervision was problematic. While there were obvious instrumental aspects to the process of inspecting liturgical text, there were also unanswered questions. In Grumet's (1979: 19) words:

What does the supervisor look for? Smudges? Omissions? Does he [*sic*] bend to the work eyeing each word and disregarding the meaning of the aggregate as the skilled copy reader who trains himself [*sic*] to examine the surface content only? Are his [*sic*] standards for the work shared by the one who executed it, both participating in a practice so saturated with their common faith that the criteria for scrutiny need scarcely be uttered?

Grumet's (1979) idealized backwards glance at supervision highlights a range of contentious issues including 'ambiguity', 'role conflict' and 'the problem of interpretation' – issues that continue to plague us in modern-day supervision of teaching. While I am unclear how we came to make the transition from the medieval Latin to present-day connotations, the parallels are nevertheless quite striking. Where the medieval monks were confronted with difficult issues of 'style, design, interpretation and intent to be negotiated' in their liturgical work (Grumet, 1979: 191), the supervision of teaching has to contend with the same issues of contestation and legitimation, albeit in somewhat different forms. Indeed, Grumet (1979: 191) sees the supervisor of teaching as facing 'his [*sic*] situations with less faith in his [*sic*] theory and less authority among his [*sic*] peers than did his [*sic*] medieval namesake'.

A somewhat more oppositional view to hierarchical forms of supervision lies in what I shall term a dialectical view of supervision (Smyth, 1985c). What I mean by this may become more clear by reference to its anthesis. Gitlin and Goldstein (n.d.: 3–4) portray standard forms of supervision (and evaluation) thus:

Typically, teachers are not involved. . . . Instead, an administrator, under the constraint of district guidelines, visits a teacher's class two or three times during the school year to make judgements about retention, promotion and tenure. These abrupt observation visits are initiated with little sense of the classroom's history and upon completion are not integrated into its ongoing history. In making these judgements the administrator is usually armed with a summative rating scale which lists any number of desirable teaching outcomes. . . . The [supervisor] acts as the expert who knows the script and score and has in mind how it can best be realized. The teachers satisfy or do not satisfy the expert in varying degrees. If the teacher is fortunate, she will learn the reasons for her . . . assessment and ways to modify what needs improvement. The activity is essentially monologic, essentially a process of communiques, of one-way declarations about the state of things: the goal is to change practice to be more congruent with the expert's standards of how classrooms should be controlled or ventilated or how to introduce the Pythagorean theorem.

What stands out as characteristic of this procedure is that it is unilateral. Those who are thought to be experts impose standards concerning desirable teaching outcomes on those who supposedly need the feed-back. The problem is that even if feedback changes teacher behavior in accceptable ways, the hierarchical relation between the expert and the teacher is reproduced. And, if change occurs it will not be based on a joint inquiry into the rightness of particular teaching outcomes, but rather based on standards that are imposed solely by a group's position in the hierarchy. This type of strategic action, which characterizes most [supervisory] processes, therefore, guarantees that the expert/teacher relation will be one of domination.

Given the hegemonic and exploitative relationship inherent in traditional forms of supervision, I propose in their place a dialectical notion that not only regards teaching problematically, but which mobilizes teachers into dialogue among themselves towards pedagogical consciousness about their teaching and the broader social context of their work.

The notion of dialectical takes its fullest expression in 'praxis' (Small, 1978), where the unity of theory and practice is bound up with the inescapable moral and political nature of human activity. In deliberate and conscious social practices, the individual acts upon and changes others, but in the process is transformed him or herself. It is the 'critical' nature of praxis and its concern with consciousness, evaluation, choice and decision that distinguishes it from other habitual routines and unreflective ways of life. Actors cannot, therefore, be spectators or onlookers. It is in uncovering the taken-for-grantedness of existing communicative and social relationships that participants are liberated from power relationships that have become frozen and unquestioned over time. Praxis is, therefore, about the removal of impediments and the transformation of people that enables the 'emergence of new faculties or the development of existing ones' (Small, 1978: 218). It is also concerned with the creation of genuinely harmonious relationships. By way of contrast, Small (1978: 219) states:

> the one-sidedness of purely self-directed activity accounts for the one-sidedness of theory isolated from real activity, while the one-sidedness of purely other-directed activity is the one-sidedness of an unthinking activism. . . . If the opposite to . . . one-sidedness . . . is taken to be balance and harmony . . . then the threat of a narrowly constricting definition of the fully human life may be seen as unfounded.

To talk of supervision in 'praxis-like' terms and to construe it dialectically is to jettison the dominant hierarchical and instrumentalist approach and to posit a view of supervision that is more inclusive of oppositional viewpoints of teaching and learning. Dialectical, as used in this context, 'is a convenient term for the kind of thinking which takes place when human beings enter into a friendly (meaning: well intentioned, cooperative, genial, and genuine) dialogue in order to find a synthesis, or when they engage in reflection and self-reflection' (Proppe, 1982: 18). Such a dialectical perspective would involve participants in self-formative processes, whereby they are able to reconstruct analytically accounts of their own histories, and while locating themselves therein, being able to see how elements of their past live-on into the present. Such a view would begin to acknowledge that:

both personal beliefs and values are relative in the sense that they can never be final, can always be superseded. They are absolute in that, even as errors – as approximations – they contribute to further possibilities of understanding. . . . As we become aware, our perceptions are recognized as simplifications of reality. We realize we systematically ignore details, discrepancies, and distortions. Every act of perception simplifies the object. We come to know through successions of these erroneous simplifications (Proppe, 1982: 17).

Teachers and supervisors within such a conceptualization would focus not only on the specifics of teaching, but do so in an inquiring way so as to articulate a relationship between teaching and the social and political ends towards which it is directed. They would come to see their teaching, as well as the process of supervision itself, as a part of a broader social purpose, the hallmark of which would be a willing sharing and acceptance of each other's beliefs, values, preferences and opinions through symmetrical and undistorted forms of communication.

There is an impressive and growing body of practitioners and scholars who, through their actions, have endorsed many of the notions implicit in such a dialectical viewpoint (Bullough *et al.*, 1984; Gitlin and Goldstein, n.d.; Bullough and Gitlin, 1985; Tripp, 1984; Day, 1985; Apple, 1981; Garman, 1982; Sergiovanni, 1984b; Berlak and Berlak, 1981; Tom, 1985; Rudduck, 1985), even though there are unresolved questions as to what should be regarded as the 'arena of the problematic' in teaching – teaching strategies, the moral bases of teaching or the social ends towards which teaching is directed. As Tom (1985: 37) expressed it:

To make teaching problematic is to raise doubts about what, under ordinary circumstances, appears to be effective or wise practice. The objects of our doubts might be accepted principles of good pedagogy, typical ways teachers respond to classroom management issues, customary beliefs about the relationship of schooling and society, or ordinary definitions of teacher authority – both in the classroom and in the broader school context.

Supervision that starts with teachers' and supervisors' understanding and awareness of themselves as social actors and helps them to develop through autonomy and responsibility, provides a way of working within teaching that is more practical, realistic and just. It acknowledges participants as conscious and reflective beings, existing in a world they are constantly questioning, re-creating and transforming. As Grumet (1979: 255) put it, the experiential and reflective aspects 'serve to help the teacher to become a student of her own work and to assume a dialectical relationship to that work', such that 'the questioner and the questioned constantly appear to each other in a different light' (Streeter, 1967: 508).

Throughout, the presumption is that when construed in dialectical terms the supervisor will 'monitor her own investment in the relationship she develops with the teachers with whom she works . . . examining with rigor, whose interests are being served' (Grumet, 1979: 254). It involves helping teachers to place themselves 'in consciously critical confrontation with their problems [and in the process] to make them agents for their own recuperation' (Fried, 1980a: 8). Dialectical encounters of the kind envisaged are concerned above all with 'reflexivity'. To act reflexively (Bolster, 1983: 303):

> People must be considered both the creators and the products of the social situations in which they live. . . . In all our activities we act on the basis of intent, observe the reactions of others to our behavior, and act purposefully again. The most important elements of any social situation are the shared meanings which participants take from the process of interaction and which ultimately shape their behavior. Significant knowledge of any social situation, therefore, consists of an awareness of the emerging meanings that participants are developing and the specific ways that these meanings are functioning to shape their endeavors and thus the characteristics of the situation itself.

What is being proposed is really a 'liberating' view of supervision (Sergiovanni, 1984b), one that frees teachers from dependence upon conventional axioms about teaching and the habitual and taken-for-grantedness that unconsciously characterizes their teaching. Berlak (1985: 2) encapsulated the meaning of liberation when she said:

> People are liberated to the extent that they are, at the same time, increasingly free to choose from a range of alternative perspectives on themselves and their social worlds. This freedom of choice requires the ability to see one's own views of what is good or right, possible or impossible, true or false, as problematic, socially constructed, subject to social and political influence.

Viewed in this way, teachers take on the characteristics of 'intellectuals' rather than those of 'technicians'. As Kohl put it, teachers should be intellectuals as well as practitioners. For Kohl (1983: 30), an intellectual is:

> someone who knows about his or her field, has a wide breadth of knowledge about other aspects of the world, who uses experience to develop theory and question practice. An intellectual is also someone who has the courage to question authority and who refuses to act counter to his own or her own experience and judgement.

When teachers are encouraged to take the kind of critical stance where moral issues are inseparable from educational ones, they are considered capable because of their engagement with practice to be able to offer 'an informed commentary on, and critique of, current policies and practices' (Hartnett and Naish, 1980: 269). They are, for example, able to offer insightful accounts on the nature of the school system, what it aspires to achieve, how power is used and how it might be redistributed.

Within a dialectical approach to supervision, the purpose and intent of research is no longer the development of universal prescriptions to be applied in the remediation of teaching. Indeed, the reflexive relationship between research and teaching requires, according to Bolster (1983: 303–4):

> envisioning each classroom as a small culture created by teacher and student as they work together over a period of time. The basic elements of the process of teaching in such a conceptualization are not defined as specific teacher initiatives which cause students to master skills or process information in predictable ways, but rather as constant demands that a specific classroom environment places on those who work in it. The ultimate purpose of research based on this view of teaching is not to generate universal propositions that predict teacher effectiveness, but rather to build and verify a coherent explanation of how a particular classroom works. The resultant knowledge will not be expressed as nostrums to improve teacher competence, but as systematic and reliable information which teachers can use to shed light on their own pedagogical situations.

Developing within teachers and supervisors these questioning ways of working in which universal propositions are replaced by more problematic views, will hopefully follow through in the way teachers work with students. As Berlak (1985: 8–9) put it:

> In order for students to become freed from dependence upon ideological elements of their common wisdom . . . , they must see [that] what they have come to believe is truth is socially constructed . . . ; they must develop a critical stance towards knowledge itself.

Above all, it involves a willingness to regard both students' and teachers' knowledge as purposeful and relevant. The kind of questions that become relevant in a collaborative alliance in the analysis of teaching are ones like the following (Kohl, 1983: 28):

> How do you think children learn?
> How does your practice in the classroom relate to how you think children learn?
> How does the organization of the school program reflect ideas of learning?
> What books, theories, ideas or other sources do you use to guide you in your teaching?

If we start out in this less constrained way with teachers collaborating to examine what they are doing, why and with what effects, then maybe we can turn schools around so they become the inquiring vibrant kinds of places we want them to be. The effect is to develop a more collegial atmosphere in which becoming informed about personal strengths, weaknesses and alternative possibilities in teaching supplant the relentless sanction-ridden supervisory quest for accountability. As Gitlin and Goldstein (n.d.: 4) put it:

> By such means, teachers begin to establish relations where change is based on mutual consideration of what makes a good teacher. This type of relation in turn challenges the legitimacy of hierarchies which enable particular groups to impose standards and dominate others.

Elements of a critical practice of supervision

One of the recurring themes so far in this chapter and the book generally, has been that if we want schools to be vibrant and inquiring places, then teachers must be engaged in a continual search for meaning in their work, dialoguing and sharing with colleagues, and constantly asking engaging questions like:

- What am I doing?
- What are my reasons?
- What effects do my actions have on my students?

Sadly, this inquiring mode is not part of the usual apparatus of most schools; indeed, there is a substantial body of literature advancing what appear to be plausible reasons why teachers are not avid inquirers into their own professional practice. At root is the alleged cellular nature of the way schools are organized. Anderson and Snyder (1982: 3) put it in these terms:

> To us it seems that education is among the last vocations within which it is still legitimate to work by yourself, in a space that is secure against invaders . . . . 'Teachers helping teachers' is in many respects an ideal form . . . and schools within which all professionals are spending significant chunks of time analyzing live samples of pedagogical activity are destined to be far more productive, as well as far more stimulating environments within which to work, than schools in which the word 'colleague' refers to a relative stranger on the other side of a wall.

What we tend to find in education, therefore, is a history of various forms of supervision designed to 'keep teachers on their toes'. As van Manen (1977: 209) put it:

> In a culture where the knowledge industry is dominated strongly by an attitude of accountability and human engineering, it is not surprising that the predominant concern of educational practice has become an instrumental preoccupation with *techniques*, *control*, and with means–end criteria of *efficiency* and *effectiveness*.

Indeed, even in those instances where enlightened practices have been developed that aim to invest teachers with a modicum of control over their working lives, they have either been regarded by teachers with suspicion, or bureaucratically sabotaged through a failure to provide enabling conditions (Smyth and Henry, 1983). On these occasions, it has been convenient to label the *form* as having failed or as being unworkable, rather than looking in a critical fashion at the frustrating conditions and the nature of oppressive institutional arrangements. Clinical supervision is one such example.

We need, therefore, to look at some of the myths surrounding what it means to act 'clinically', as well as the origin of 'supervision' and stand off a little from attempts by others to redefine clinical supervision, and return to the essence of what its mentors had in mind. I also want to draw upon some ideas from critical social theory (Held, 1980; Bernstein, 1976; Habermas, 1973) and canvass a perspective from which to begin a rethink of the issues implicit within clinical supervision as a way of teachers working critically with other teachers.

Against this backdrop, and before I am accused of promising more than I can deliver, let me make the important disclaimer that I am not offering a step-by-step blueprint for the reconstruction of clinical supervision – that would be too ambitious, and probably ultimately self-defeating anyway. The argument I develop in relation to teachers examining their own (and one anothers') practice through clinical supervision applies equally to those of us who do research *with* teachers, and who collaborate *with* them in making sense of those practices.

Since its beginnings in the 1950s, supervision of the clinical variety has had a remarkable history. Described as a 'planned intervention into the world of the artificial' (Sergiovanni, 1976: 24), clinical supervision has as its prime objective bringing about improvement in classroom teaching, although it is concerned as well with 'the incompleteness with which most of us view our assumptions, beliefs, objectives and behavior' (ibid.: p. 24). Born in the real world of professional practice, clinical supervision arose in response to a concern that ways of working with teachers were ineffectual. The principles, procedures and philosophy of clinical supervision have been applauded by some as corresponding to 'best existing practice', described as 'the most sophisticated and concentrated program of supervision' (Weller, 1969), and labelled by its critics as 'unreal' and 'unworkable' (Curtis, 1975; Guditus, 1982; Harris, 1976). While I wince at the language used, I believe Wilhelms (in Cogan, 1973: ix) was accurate in describing it as 'a system of supervision with enough weight to have impact and with the precision to hit the target'. When compared to the alternatives clinical supervision represents, at best, 'a modest paradigm shift; one with the potential to change the practice of supervision substantially' (Sergiovanni, 1976: 21). We should, therefore, be less than perturbed too about the failure of the process to gain widespread acceptance. Propositions about clinical supervision being 'primarily a latent force for the improvement of instruction . . . [that] . . . has yet to be fully born to the world of public education' (Krajewski, 1976: 1) seem to be wide of the mark. They fail to acknowledge adequately the nature and importance of non-coercive and voluntary teacher involvement in processes like clinical supervision. I prefer to see this as a strength rather than a weakness, and relegate claims about the lack of universal appeal to the category of wishful thinking to which they belong. That it has a continuous history extending back some 40 years is evidence of the efficacy of clinical supervision. Indeed, chastened by first-hand experience, Goldhammer (1969: 368) seemed to have a more modest view of what was feasible and possible, than some of his critics when he said:

> I suspect that no one is more certain of clinical supervision's failure to represent an educational panacea than those of us who have practiced and studied it during the past several years. . . . Truly, there is nothing spectacularly new in this model. We do not offer it as a wonder drug.

That is just as true today, as it was then.

I believe we need to lay aside the negative connotations the label is supposed to conjure up of cold, formal, cut-and-dried procedures, with images of formica surfaces, unfriendly receptionists and needles ready to draw blood (Goldhammer et al., 1980) – I am not too concerned about those either. Kilbourn (1982: 2) was close to the mark in asking the question: 'when or under what circumstances supervision may correctly be called clinical'. Likewise, his answer makes good sense:

> One thing seems certain. There are features of the clinical process which cannot be absent without violating its spirit. I suggest, however, that articulating those features and detecting them in practice will depend largely on the wisdom gained from studying specific cases of clinical supervision since it is specific instances of clinical practice, complete with historical background, that give life and meaning to the process (ibid.: 2).

On this issue, the psychoanalyst Erickson (1969) provided what amounts to valuable insights into the origin of the term clinical that highlights the problems and prospects of using a clinical approach in teaching. As Erickson (1969: 721) put it:

> In the days when the church was the primary guardian of man's well-being, clinical referred to a priest's administrations at the deathbed – then the only gateway to true health, since all through life man owed a death. Later, the word was primarily applied to medical ministrations, as science and humanism joined forces in taking the short-range point of view that man owes himself a long and healthy life, or at any rate one free from disease. In our time and in the Western world, the word clinical is expanding rapidly to include not only medical but also social considerations, not only physical well-being but also mental health, not only matters of cure but also of prevention, not only therapy but also research. This means that clinical work is now allied with many brands of evidence and overlaps with many methodologies.

Erickson (1969) reminds those of us who use the clinical approach to supervision of three salient points. First, the fact that clinical pertains to rendering at the bedside – an obvious analogy for the fact that teachers stand to gain substantially from learning about their teaching in a job-embedded way 'in the clinic of the classroom' (Wilhelms, in Cogan, 1973: ix). Secondly, Erickson (1969) has noted how clinical encounters pave the way for an understanding of well-being, as well as being used for their accepted therapeutic or curative purposes. For those of us interested in better understanding how 'good' teachers work, this is significant. Thirdly, Erickson (1969) is expansive about what he considers count as methodology and evidence in clinical work. He goes beyond the purely empirical, observable, verifiable facts to include intuition, interpretation, emotion and the subjective as legitimate in the reconstruction and portrayal of case study accounts.

Emphasizing a 'holistic' view of the therapeutic aspect of clinical work, Erickson (1969) discusses the interrelated nature of the elements. There is a *complaint* (consisting of the description of circumscribed pain or dysfunction), *symptoms* (visible or otherwise localizable), *anamnesis* (the patient's reconstruction of the disturbance), an *examination* (through the clinician's senses and with instruments), a *prediction* (involving thinking about various modes and models of knowledge) and, finally, a *preferred method of treatment*. Erickson (1969: 722) contends that the complaint is more than the sum total of the symptoms, and that the subjective contribution of the patient is crucial:

> The treatment, thus, is not limited to local adjustments; it must, and in the case of a 'good' doctor automatically does, include a wider view of the complaint, and entail corresponding interpretations of the symptom to the patient, often making the 'patient himself' an assistant observer and associate doctor.

The argument, therefore, is that rather than striving for a state of 'objectivity' (and hence a false sense of security from scientism), the clinician works instead towards 'disciplined subjectivity'; that is to say, a circumstance in which he [sic] 'maintain(s) a constant inner traffic between his [sic] often dramatic observations and his [sic] conceptual models, however crude they may be' (Erickson, 1969: 723).

In the process of actively intervening into the life of another person, the clinician adopts a role similar to that of a historian 'in which the past, so far as it is historically known, survives in the present' (Collingwood, 1956: 226). The clinician's observations and interpretations involve him or her in portraying situations, while also working towards changing what he or she perceives as the circumstances that brought them about in the first place. In the sense that the clinician is both *making* and *influencing* history, the clinician is 'correcting events as he [sic] records them, and recording as he [sic] directs (them)' (Erickson, 1969: 723). While encouraging the client/patient to actively 'historicize his [sic] own position by thinking back to the onset of the disturbance', the clinician also ponders 'what world order (magic, scientific, ethical) was violated and must be restored before (the patient/client's) "normal" place in history can be reassumed' (ibid.: 723).

The point of this discussion about the function of clinicians is to dispel the myth that such people are concerned only with the pursuit of cold, hard facts. As Dunn (1982) has argued in relation to the policy sciences, the 'exceptional' clinician is overall concerned with the creative potential by which 'reason' can actively bring about concrete transformations of social situations. The problem Dunn (1982: 4) says:

> is one of discovering processes through which diverse forms of knowledge may be synthesized, since it is a presumed capacity for synthesizing scientific and experiential knowledge, and this alone, that distinguishes exceptional from unexceptional clinicians.

In related fashion, it is by assisting teachers to gain a more complete understanding of their own intentions and a sense of the discontinuities, stresses and tensions within their own practices (Giroux, 1982; Smyth, 1983b), that holds the greatest promise for clinical supervision to become an active force for transformation. As Kilbourn (1980: 174) has said, it is the knowledge forms generated 'from holistic interpretations of particular events and which depend on tacit understanding of the unique context (including the intentions of participants) of a given classroom situation', that makes clinical supervision an appropriate form by which teachers can transform their practice.

The term 'supervision' comprises an equally contentious part of the clinical supervision label. In common usage, it refers to the actions of a superior overseeing, inspecting, evaluating and prescribing the work of someone lower down the hierarchy. It is not surprising, therefore, that certified teachers have come to regard supervisory practices with a jaundiced eye, as Withall and Wood (1979) noted.

Cogan (1973: xi) clearly had in mind a less than prescriptive and a more liberating view of supervision that emphasized dialogue and interchange between professionals working together to improve the educational experiences of children when he said:

> Although supervision is part of the title of this book . . . clinical supervision is conceptualized as the interaction of peers and colleagues. It is *not* unilateral action taken by the supervisor and aimed at the teacher. On the contrary, the teacher is called on to assume almost all the roles and responsibilities of a supervisor in his interaction with the clinical supervisor. He initiates the action, proposes hypotheses, analyzes his own performance [and] shares responsibilities for devising supervisory strategies.

The way Cogan chose to construe supervision fits well with Erickson's portrayal of its original meaning – both are considerably more problematic than the definitive, sanction-ridden, hierarchical view conveyed by conventional wisdom.

This brief sojourn into the etymology of the separate lexicon of 'clinical' and 'supervision', taken in the context of what Goldhammer, Cogan and others were pursuing in the 1950s, serves to remind us that present-day applications of clinical supervision often fail to acknowledge the problematic nature of the original concept. In the next section, I want to pursue what clinical supervision might begin to look like if we engage in a concerted and critical return to what its mentors may have had in mind.

Bending the knees in piety

Goodlad (1978: 322) made an appropriate comment several years ago when he said: 'In education, it is a long time since we paid homage to the essence of our profession.' Despite the burgeoning literature and the increasingly wide-spread practice of clinical supervision in recent years (Snyder, 1981; Anderson and Snyder, 1982; Pavan, 1980), what is disturbing is the general absence of a serious questioning of the values, beliefs and assumptions of what we are about. Regardless of the frequent reference in the literature to claims that through clinical supervision teachers can improve their teaching, and thus the learning of their students, there has been little serious discussion about the efficacy of clinical supervision itself, or how it succeeds or fails to inform and enlighten.

The major point at issue seems to be whether supervision should be construed as a force for the preservation and maintenance of the status quo, or whether it should be an active force towards reform and change. These opposing views rest upon widely diverging assumptions and have quite different consequences. What I want to propose is that even though clinical supervision is couched in and spoken about in change-oriented terms, the rhetoric belies the reality. What clinical supervision amounts to in practice, is 'outsiders' ensuring that teachers do more of the same, albeit better. Much of what we allow to pass as clinical supervision in schools is not predicated on any critical questioning of the ends of teaching – it is means-oriented and con-cerned with the retooling of teaching skills. Construed in this way, therefore, clinical supervision becomes an essentially conservative practice. Untouched are the deeper social questions of the ends of education that have to do with truth, beauty, justice and equality. The tragedy is that rather than striving towards a circumstance of genuine participation in education, we have succumbed instead to asymmetrical and distorted forms of communication. We have allowed the expert to dictate to and dominate the inexpert, and above all have aided and abetted the consolidation of entrenched interests. In a word, we have failed to regard the content, processes and institutions of schooling as being in any way problematic.

To be more precise, clinical supervision tends to have been used as a subtle way of controlling and manipulating teachers and as an agency for endorsing and perpetuating existing curriculum and teaching practices. In becoming self-styled, 'itinerant clinical supervisors' (Garman, 1982) who have adopted the symbols and rituals of clinical supervision without incorporating the philosophy, we are guilty of tinkering with teachers. In this, Wilhelms (in Cogan, 1973: x) was accurate when he put it that, 'Teachers are better left alone . . . [rather] than merely tampered with.' What we need instead is to work *with* teachers to help *them* collectively transform their practice in the light of evidence generated about the goals and methods of their teaching. Adopting a more radical view of what clinical supervision might mean (Smyth, 1984d) involves asking questions about the *ends* as well as the *means* of teaching. In Mosher and Purpel's (1972: 110) words:

> Defined more broadly, clinical supervision . . . addresses itself to the enormous ongoing problem of curriculum development and the improvement of instruction. . . . To solve these problems requires radical and continuing change. Clinical supervision is one means by which teachers can confront and modify both the *content and the practice of teaching* [my emphasis].

Construing clinical supervision as a process with the capacity to enable teachers to undertake fundamental transformations of perspective goes to the very heart of the process. It is really a question of viewing clinical supervision as 'a process, a way of life, a cultural structure within which one works with teachers' (as well as having teachers work with one another), rather than as 'a technique that mechanically specifies a series of steps through which supervisor and teacher must travel' (Sergiovanni, 1982b: 69). This means moving outside of purely behavioural concepts (Eisner, 1982), lessening the concern with the process and procedural aspects (Goldhammer *et al.*, 1980) and deepening a commitment to tackling epistemological issues seriously (Garman, 1984). Furthermore, Retallick (1983) suggests that the *real* problems with clinical supervision have nothing to do with an alleged lack of time, money or trained personnel as sometimes suggested. Rather:

> the problems besetting clinical supervision are similar to those of most other current practices in teacher development and they cannot be further illuminated by continued investigation into the existing ideas and approaches. . . . We need to step outside existing conceptualizations and reflect on them from a wider perspective which may enable us to 'break out' and enter a new paradigm. . . . (W)hen looked upon from the 'outside', current practices in supervision and teacher development reflect an ideology of social control and psychological manipulation of teachers. The interests being served are largely those of the supervisors in their desire to maintain and extend control (ibid.: 3).

Ultimately, clinical supervision rests upon a fundamental set of beliefs about the nature of knowledge, how we acquire knowledge, and how we can use it to change quite complex educational phenomena (Smyth, 1983a, c). It is this issue I want to turn to now.

In the helping professions, generally, there is a crucial distinction to be made between creating dependence and fostering independence. Using clinical supervision as a strategy by which a more experienced 'practitioner' (even a specialist) diagnoses weaknesses and recommends (however benevolently) corrective action, constitutes the delivery of a service and has all the associations of powerlessness that accompany such a state of mind. For example, there are the feelings of docility and subservience we usually find between the rich and the poor, the young and the old, those who have 'problems' and others who are 'trained' to assess their needs and prescribe remedies. What action of this kind does is produce and legitimate a false dichotomy between the 'deliverer' and the 'recipient' (Fried, 1980a) that fosters passivity and dependence. This approach needs replacing by a view that endorses and encourages teachers to take control of their own strivings. Processes like clinical supervision *have* the capacity to provide teachers with collegial and collaborative ways of critically and consciously confronting their own circumstances (Smyth *et al.*, 1982b). Viewed as a form of empowerment, clinical supervision amounts to a way of transcending the technicalities of teaching, investing teachers with the capacity to explore, understand and transform their own thinking about both the means and the ends of teaching. More importantly, it has the capacity to enable them to examine, understand and challenge the institutional conditions and circumstances of their work. As Carr and Kemmis (1983: 180) express it, processes like clinical supervision become a medium for criticism and transformation as we:

> examine the socially given patterns of understanding (ideology) which have allowed [us] to take social conditions for granted, . . . as [we] examine the structures of institutions which codify and sustain these social conditions. In short, as [we] look beyond the inadequacies and contradictions of [our] own practices, [we] find ideological and institutional patterns which are to some extent responsible for maintaining these inadequacies and contradictions.

Accordingly, the aim is one of 'transforming ideological and institutional conditions which limit the capacity of practitioners to attain more rational and just social and educational arrangements' (ibid.: 180). For those of us who are 'teachers of teachers', the point is equally salient; we need to look carefully at ourselves and seek to locate where we are in our involvement in the process of formulating and articulating policy relationships.

Clinical supervision from a critical perspective

It is an intriguing question as to what the cultural habitus – the beliefs, traditions, myths, language and implicit conventions – of clinical supervision would look like if we adopted a more critical perspective; that is to say, if we were to view it as an agency through which teachers (ourselves included) could acquire an understanding of taken-for-granted assumptions, as a way of articulating the antecedents and social consequences of actions, and in the process formulating and implementing strategies for action. Adopting a critical stance does not, therefore, mean being negative; rather, it refers to analysing, reflecting on and engaging in discourse about the nature and effects of practical aspects of teaching and how they might be altered. It requires asking fundamental questions like those mentioned earlier: What am I doing? What are my reasons? What effects does my teaching have on my students?

According to Apple (1981: 3), being critical is a way of thinking and acting that 'seeks to illuminate the problematic character of the common-sense reality most of us take for granted'. Speaking of teaching, Sergiovanni (1976: 25) put it like this:

> We tend not to be aware of our assumptions, theories or aims and objectives. Sometimes we adopt components . . . that belong to others, that seem right, that have the ring of fashionable rhetoric, or that coincide with the expectation of important others. We may adopt overtly a set of aims and objectives, but covertly or unknowingly we hang on to contradictory assumptions and theories.

Being critical and acting in a reflexive way (Beasley, 1981) involves searching for meaning and patterns of thinking and acting normally taken for granted in acquiring, classifying and organizing knowledge about ourselves. Examining teaching in this way frees us intellectually 'not only from the domination of others, but from the domination by forces [we] do not understand or control' (Giddens, 1976: 60) and introduces into educational thought, discussion and action, moral and ethical considerations like 'justice' and 'equity'. Critical reflection opens up for consideration and dialogue the social consequences of what is being attempted in teaching. According to Zeichner and Teitelbaum (1982: 104), 'teachers begin to identify connections between the level of the classroom (e.g. form and content of the curriculum, classroom social relations) and the wider educational, social, economic and political conditions that impinge upon and shape classroom practice'.

This is not to suggest that the technical aspects of teaching should be ignored or rejected; rather, it is a plea to restore them to their rightful status, not as ends in themselves, but as important means to valued social purposes. An excessive concern with the instrumental and technical aspects of teaching gets in the way of asking questions about how schooling perpetuates injustices and in-equalities in our society, and actually prevents the asking of substantial questions. It is important to understand that reflectivity is not a synonym for passive contemplation either:

> Put simply, to act reflectively about teaching is to actively pursue the possibility that existing practices may effectively be challenged, and in the light of evidence about their efficacy, replaced by alternatives. Reflection,

critical awareness or enlightenment on its own is insufficient – it must be accompanied by action (Smyth, 1984d: 32).

In the broader context of social theory, Habermas (1978) argues that 'human subjects themselves must be able to appropriate the interpretations of their actions' (Bernstein, 1976: 202) in a way that enables explanations to be carried through into practical forms of action. It is this dialectical working out of the relationship between reflection, experimentation and action that enables us to engage in what Mezirow (1977, 1981) describes as 'perspective transformation' – changing, as it were, the frameworks with which we view our experiences, think, feel and behave. Actually penetrating practice in this way, and changing as a consequence, involves: 'a process that moves from experience to conceptualization, from conceptualization to practice, and from practice to an evaluation that produces the data necessary for the step back to experience' (Bagenstos, 1975: 233).

In these circumstances, we not only study experiences, but do so in ways that enable us to benefit from them. We ascribe meaning to experiences and use them as a way of viewing reality and as a basis upon which to transform reality. In a word, we 'intellectualize' our experience (Kohl, 1983) – not in an academic sense, but in terms of developing theories about our practice, questioning and reflecting upon those theories, and formulating alternative possibilities to be tested out in practice. Developing within us this capacity to intellectualize requires that we become aware of the fact that we are all 'caught in our own history and are reliving it, and [of] the cultural and psychological assumptions which structure the way we see ourselves and others' (Mezirow, 1977: 163). In the words of Bussis *et al.* (1976: 17):

> Simply having a new idea or feeling . . . is relatively inconsequential for effecting change. Translating an idea into action and experiencing its consequences counts for more and constitutes the basis for personal knowledge and learning. . . . [This] points up the obvious importance of experience in shaping personal constructs. If significant change is to occur, it requires a quality of experience that supports personal exploration, experimentation and reflection.

Much has happened since clinical supervision was conceived. What was fostered out of an intense sense of compassion for the dignity and human worth of teachers (Goldhammer, 1969) has come increasingly to be used in deterministic and manipulative ways. Where it is used as a 'refined teacher inspection technology' (Snyder, 1981: 221), and where it is used even more subtly as an 'instructional/performance delivery system' by which to pursue school goals and maintain teaching 'standards' and 'outcomes', there can be no doubt as to whose interests are being served – and they are not those of either teachers or children. If processes like clinical supervision are really teacher evaluation, then we should say it out loud and insist that those who profess to know about effective teaching be accountable for their expertise (Garman,

1986b). St Maurice (1987) put this most directly when he said that many teachers find clinical supervision to have become so tainted as to be avoided at all costs. For him, the reality is that 'the gaze is asymmetrical: the subject-as-object may seem powerless to gaze back and question its majesty and authority' (ibid.: 246). If the spirit and intent of clinical supervision are not to be distorted out of all recognition, then we need to endorse soundly the process as one of assisting teachers to discover ways of interpreting and radically changing what they do. We need to appropriate the sentiments and heed the warnings of Bernstein (1976: 229–30) about the nature of shared frameworks of meaning:

> Human action cannot be properly identified, described or understood unless we take account of the intentional descriptions, the meanings that such actions have for the agents involved, the ways in which they interpret their own actions and the actions of others. These intentional descriptions, meanings and interpretations are not merely subjective states of mind which can be correlated with external behavior; they are constitutive of the activities and practices of our social and political lives. If we are to understand what human beings are, then we must uncover those models, interpretative schemes, and tacit understandings that penetrate human thought and action. Any conceptions of what is 'strictly speaking' empirical or observable that excludes this dimension of human life, or simply relegates it to a realm of subjective opinion, is emasculated and epistemologically unwarranted.

Rather than condoning the use of clinical supervision as a way of cajoling, coercing and controlling teachers, we need to see clinical supervision as an agency by which to arrive at a greater awareness of what it is teachers do, why, with what effect, and how to act in teachers' interests to change existing power relationships that have become frozen or formalized and no longer subjected to questioning. In this we need to avoid becoming entrapped in our own rhetoric and incapable of seeing the assumptions behind the language we use. Stephens (1983: 3) put it neatly:

> We use words to describe and interpret our own experiences, to express our plans, to discuss proposals for common action, and to respond to the proposals and ideas of others. Nowhere more than in education – perhaps politics is the exception – are we so unrelentingly bombarded by words – spoken and printed. The words we use and hear envelop us in a rhetoric about education which we tend to accept as natural and commonplace. That rhetoric helps to shape our perceptions and to consolidate our assumptions in ways that we find very difficult to reflect upon.

The rhetoric of clinical supervision is compelling enough, couched as it is in terms of the 'improvement of teaching' through a collaborative process of consultation, observation, analysis and feedback. Terms like 'mutual trust', 'collegiality' and 'teacher autonomy' are seductive nomenclature. In using supportive language of this kind we need to be sensitive to the expectations that attach to it and avoid being branded as frauds by saying one thing while doing another. For example, the contradiction becomes apparent enough when we preach collegiality, collaboration and teacher autonomy, while imposing clinical supervision upon teachers. Similarly, using clinical supervision, however benevolently, as a method by which a person of superior status is able to diagnose and suggest remedies in the teaching of a subordinate, exposes a major contradiction that is not always apparent between what we espouse and what we do.

Adopting a critical approach towards the use of clinical supervision in teaching, is to do more than endorse a procedural orientation of a step-wise cyclical process aimed at describing and correcting problems within teaching. Certainly, that approach is useful under limited conditions. What is more important is the 'mental baggage' that accompanies the process; namely, a preparedness to reflect upon one's own history and practice, to speculate about the possibilities for change, and to actively follow through this commitment to change. In developing this orientation, participants in clinical supervision might ask themselves questions like:

- What are the taken-for-granted assumptions and values implicit in what we do?
- What contribution does historical knowledge about ourselves make towards understanding our present and future circumstances?
- How does knowledge of the present inform us as to the past?
- How does clinical supervision contribute towards maintaining 'good' professional relationships with our colleagues?
- What contribution does clinical supervision make towards articulating and clarifying our teaching intentions?
- Does isolating an agreed teaching focus beforehand contribute to the observation and description of our teaching?
- Is the information we collect about our teaching events and occurrences descriptive of what occurs?
- How do the descriptions of our teaching aid us in uncovering and discerning patterns and themes in our teaching?
- What evidence is there suggesting that we use these theories to discuss and portray hidden beliefs and taken-for-granted assumptions?
- Do our descriptions of our teaching and the discussions they generate actually lead to new ideas that we try out in our teaching?

Conclusion

I started this chapter by arguing that in order to qualify as a field of study, the area of supervision needs to be reconstructed in ways that enable taken-for-granted, even cherished, assumptions about the area to be challenged. This means developing reflexive capacities so as to transcend thought about supervision and develop in the process alternative – even oppositional –

possibilities of what it might mean to be involved in the theory and practice of supervision (Smyth, 1984a, 1985a, 1986c).

As a way of opening-up for discussion, dialogue and critique what those alternatives might look like, I pointed to the not so salubrious legacy of our area of inquiry. The point of my discussion was that the social order is not given but is deliberately constructed, and in order to understand the institutions, relations and practices of our daily lives in the area of supervision, it is prudent that a historical approach be adopted so as to reconstruct how it got to be the way it is.

The scene as I portrayed it was one in which the business management notions of accountability, inspection and quality control are still the dominant ones (Smyth, 1989a). The *real* question is whether the technical/rational view of knowledge as the basis for supervision, with its insistence on certainty, predictability and control, is really capable of delivering answers to the difficult ethical and moral questions that characterize teaching and supervision. Knowledge about ways of working with teachers, and indeed the very knowledge basis of teaching itself, is far more tentative and problematic. A more likely possibility was argued to lie in knowledge gained through intuition and reflection-in-action, which was more akin to the way skilful and artistic practitioners make sense of the confusing and contradictory circumstances of their work.

Based on these ideas, a more dialectical approach with its emphasis upon empowering teachers with ways of knowing that involve continually confronting themselves and searching for more responsive and less dominant educative practices, was proposed as an oppositional view to that of hierarchical scientific management of teaching. Through critical and reflective awareness of their own faculties, abilities and performances, teachers and those who work with them become capable of rescuing their practices from the dominance of experts and begin the important move towards being able to reform their own teaching.

The issues raised in this chapter have had to do with whether clinical supervision is a way of controlling, disenfranchising or pushing teachers around, or whether it is an emancipatory or liberating process through which teachers assist each other to gain control over their own professional lives and destinies. Although meanings and intentions can readily become distorted in the process of re-definition, I believe that Goldhammer (1969) and Cogan (1973) had the emancipatory view in mind in their original conceptualization. It has been in the processes of actually doing clinical supervision that the distortions I refer to have actually arisen.

The essence of the argument has been that there are two ways of viewing clinical supervision – as a delivery system through which to control teaching or, alternatively, as a form of empowerment by which teachers are able to gain tacit knowledge as a basis for transforming both their understandings and the debilitating aspects of their institutional lives. For those of us involved in clinical supervision, the crucial question that needs to be addressed relates to what it means to be engaged in the process of clinical supervision and of the circumstances that permit and constrain it. The meanings, interpretations and understandings vested in those of us who are actively *doing* clinical supervision, what we aspire to, what we gain, as well as our joys and frustrations along the way, remain sadly unexplored issues. There is a need to get behind the rhetoric of clinical supervision, to analyse the meanings that are actually embedded in what we do *with* and *to* teachers, so as to expose and begin to grapple with the contradictions of being human.

Note

1 The argument here follows Schön (1983).

3

A critique of top-down supervision[1]

Introduction

Having sketched out some of the arguments for a more educative approach in previous chapters, in this chapter I look at current widespread attempts to 'supervise' teachers (hierarchically) in the USA using a particular constrained model (the Madeline Hunter 'Teaching/Supervision Model'), and explore the implications of the extensive adoption of that model in a context of moves to effect wider school reforms. The fundamental point is that teachers' voices have largely been ignored and silenced in these reforms, and this is manifestly evident at the chalkface level when we look at what is happening to teachers through dehumanizing forms of in-class supervision being inflicted upon them. This systematic failure to adequately listen to teachers, to take account of what they have to say and to incorporate their views into the determination of educational policies that affect them, has palpable and far-reaching effects for all who are involved in educational policy making, wherever they may be located (Smyth, 1987b; Garman, 1986a). What I report upon here, are the unheard voices of the many teachers who have not been consulted in the wave of educational reforms and who feel justifiably confused and angry at having to accommodate to schemes and models that bear no relationship to the realities of schooling as they and their students experience them. The major point to be grasped is that current moves to 'reform' supervision (and along with it, teaching), are diametrically opposed to the kind of clinical supervision I have outlined so far in this book – notions that are based on ideals of reciprocity, democracy and education.

I employ the lens of 'critical pedagogy' (Simon, 1985, 1987; McLaren, 1988a, 1989) because it permits theorizing about the social practices of teaching and supervision as expressed through the comments of teachers, in a way that acknowledges the political and moral dimensions of both. The concern is not so much with teaching *per se*, which relies rather too much on the language of technique, 'and exclusive reliance on practical suggestions and the reduction of debate to questions of "what works"' (Simon, 1988: 2); rather, the focus is one that moves considerably beyond what teachers and supervisors actually do, to a discourse that is more politically informed and that draws attention to the potential for what Simon (1985) labels 'transformative critique'. He envisages this as involving three interrelated moments, that are worth briefly highlighting here (Simon, 1985: 1119):

> First, [it] views knowledge as socially produced, legitimated, and dis-
> tributed and seeks to make explicit the ways in which such production,
> legitimation, and distribution take place. Second, knowledge is ap-
> prehended as expressing and embodying particular interests and values,
> implicating issues of power and ethics in all expressions of knowledge.
> Third, seeking to negate the 'objective' nature of knowledge and forcing
> the educator to confront the relation between knowledge, power, and
> control, critique additionally requires the articulation and consideration
> of transformative action – that is, action that would alter the distribution of
> power and increase the range and scope of possibilities for individually
> and collectively defined projects.

To speak pedagogically (and politically) is, therefore, to ask questions about 'why things are the way they are and how they got to be that way' (Simon, 1988: 2). It is, after all, only by revealing how and in what ways particular teaching and supervisory practices – and proposals for their reform – have come about, that the constitutive interests can be unmasked, debated and transformed. Doing this within a critical perspective involves what Apple (1975: 127) describes as:

> a painful process of radically examining our current positions and asking
> pointed questions about these positions and the social structure from
> which they arise. It also necessitates a serious in-depth search for alterna-
> tives to these almost unconscious lenses we employ and an ability to cope
> with an ambiguous situation for which answers can now be only dimly
> seen and will not be easy to come by.

The purpose of this chapter is to show that alleged reform efforts involving supervising teachers so as to require them to conform to a particularly narrowly prescribed view of pedagogy, can be quite devastating for teachers as well as students. Using in-class supervision that espouses the benign language of 'improvement of teaching' actually ignores how such practices *are them-selves* deeply implicated in entrenching particular power relations, inequalities and injustices (Smyth, 1984b). The unspoken agenda is one of using power–coercive relationships as a way of getting one group (teachers and students) to act in ways that are not only palpably against their own interests, but which favour the material interests of another group (those who govern education). Supervisory practices are only morally and ethically sustainable as long as they are themselves open to the possibility of being turned back upon themselves so as to establish through dialogical means the efficacy of their own claims (Smyth, 1987a). As long as supervisory processes are construed as a bureaucratic means by which those deemed to know are able to exercise surveillance and invoke sanctions over another group deemed to be deficient, questions will continue to exist about the moral defensibility of what is being attempted (Smyth, 1985a). Such processes are not only disempowering in that they demand passivity and docility on the part of teachers who are prevented from actively participating in the determination of their own professional destinies, but, moreover, they are anti-educational in that they rely on the threat of brute force (or its metaphorical equivalent) rather than powers of reason, persuasion and argumentation.

Proposing a critical view of supervision means raising questions about the taken-for-grantedness and inevitability of the process itself (Smyth, 1986a, 1988a). Often what turns out to be the most interesting is not what we know, but rather what remains concealed and therefore undisclosed, and what we choose to treat as habitual and unproblematic. Adopting a socially critical view means looking at processes like supervision in terms of wider relationships and its implications for the economic, political and social structures of society. In other words, just as it is impossible to regard teaching and classrooms as neutral and value-free instructional sites that exist in 'antiseptic isolation from larger social and collective goals' (McLaren, 1988b: 2), it is not possible either to regard the supervision of teaching as being without quite specific notions of 'power, politics, history and context' (McLaren, 1988b: 1). We need to understand the role that supervisory processes play in linking knowledge and power, and how teaching and learning for 'self and social empowerment is ethically prior to a mastery of technical skills, which are primarily tied to the logic of the marketplace' (McLaren, 1988b: 1). But, we also need to understand how supervisory processes in schools might be otherwise.

Discussions of critical pedagogy tend rightfully to focus upon the interacting relations between teachers and students. Given the way both groups have been silenced in the stratified processes that pass for organization and administration in schools, it is not altogether surprising that there have been increased calls recently for teachers and students to find a voice. Yet, administrative and supervisory processes amount effectively to diverting attention and critique 'away from the economic, social, and educational institutions which organize class, race, and gender hierarchies' (Fine, 1987: 158) by fixating discussion on the technical and the instrumental. To redress this tendency, critical pedagogy:

represents an approach to schooling that is committed to the imperatives of empowering students and transforming the larger social order in the interests of justice and equality. [The] central task is to develop a language through which educators and others can unravel and comprehend the relationship among schooling [and] the wider social relations that inform it . . . (McLaren, 1989: ix).

Those who espouse critical pedagogy, therefore, generally tend to analyse schools in a two-fold way – as sorting mechanisms in which select groups of students are favoured on the basis of race, class and gender – and *as agencies for self- and social empowerment* (McLaren, 1988b: 1). The argument is that teachers must understand the role that schooling plays in joining knowledge and power in order to use that role for the development of critical and active citizens. The centrepiece for critical pedagogy is classroom social relations (Smyth, 1988b), and the way in which their theoretical meanings reside in the social consequences of classroom practice. It is classroom experiences that provide the major 'texts' for analysis as they are juxtaposed within a political/ social/economic context of schooling. My argument is that it is also important to consider the often neglected relationship between the supervisor (who could be a peer or colleague) and the teacher in unravelling the social relations of schooling. Teachers and students are not the only players in this game – there is another important educative act that goes on between teachers and supervisors that needs to be examined and transformed as well. In a literal sense, the supervisor (in the traditional hierarchical sense) represents the embodiment of the school's externally determined expectations; in the symbolic sense, the supervisor encapsulates the political/social values of the educational institution writ large. It is also clear in all of this that supervisors (like teachers) are the subject of increasing pressures that seek to limit and constrain their autonomy.

Supervisors and teachers manage schools in a very different qualitative sense, and students stand to gain when *both* work together to help students to become their own agents for self- and social empowerment. Supervisors in schools, like teachers, occupy what Wright (1980) describes in Marxist terms as a 'contradictory [social] class location' – they are on *some* occasions instruments of technical control, while on others they are the subject of the social relations of control. Supervisors display some of the features of a group who control the labour of teachers, but they are also excluded in many ways (by the very nature of hierarchical structure) from a say in the system that controls the way in which educated labour is used in schools. In Wright's (1980: 182) terms, supervisors are 'located simultaneously in two classes and share interests with both of these classes'.

But the issue is not one that can be easily contained to matters of social class, contradictory in nature or otherwise. At particular times and in specific contexts, questions of supervision are inextricably connected to matters of gender. It is clear that while teaching is construed largely as women's work (Apple, 1985), supervision is also seen predominantly as a male domain. As an expression of power relations, dominant forms of supervision therefore work to bolster and maintain the gender-constructed hierarchy. In other words, the entire process of supervision, far from being a neutral and value-free process as often espoused, is imbued with and predicated upon an undisclosed agenda of gendered oppression.

Supervision as the vanguard for school reform

Since the first wave of school reform initiatives generated in the early 1980s, administrators and policy makers have picked up on in-class supervision as a possible conduit for reform efforts by promoting elaborate 'instructional improvement programs' (Garman, 1987). The stated goal of supervision – the improvement of instruction – is part of the mental baggage of the taken-for-granted definition of supervision. Those teachers who have been able to see through the reform efforts have managed to defend their classroom autonomy by saying 'What does the supervisor know about teaching, anyway?' At the same time, entrepreneurs like Madeline Hunter in the USA have developed pro-grammes predicated on the reductionist assumption that it is possible to link a set of teaching behaviours to specific supervisory behaviours. Such pro-grammes and models not only make teaching appear uniform, but they actively encourage teachers to overlook diversity and background in their classrooms. Moreover, this model is sold to teachers on the basis of providing them with 'a common language of teaching', as well as being touted as having a research base to it (or as Hunter calls it, 'principles of effective teaching from psycho-logical tenets'). By invoking the research-based claim, supervisors appear to acquire a legitimate vehicle for being able to say that they know what constitutes good teaching. By marrying a standardized model of teaching with supervision, in-class supervision acquires a semblance of legitimacy it never had before.

While the aim of this chapter is not to provide any comprehensive discussion of the Madeline Hunter model itself, largely on the grounds that others have already done so (see Hunter, 1980, 1984, 1985; for critiques of Hunter's work, see Gibboney, 1987; Slavin, 1987; Costa, 1984; Garman and Hazi, 1988), for those not already familiar with the tenets of the Hunter model (and it is representative of similar ventures elsewhere in the world), they are high-lighted briefly below.

Hunter (1984: 170) herself sums up the essence of her work in terms of it being curriculum building involving: 'factor-analyzing . . . goals into depen-dent and independent sequences of learning, diagnosing students to deter-mine what each has achieved in that sequence, and employing psychological principles that contribute to the speed and effectiveness with which each student acquires new learnings in those sequences'. According to Hunter (1984: 170), teaching is a manifestation of science because:

1. Identifiable cause–effect relationships exist between teaching and learning.
2. Those relationships hold for all teaching and learning regardless of the content, age, socioeconomic and ethnic characteristics of the learner.
3. While many of these relationships were identified in the static purity of the research laboratory, those relationships seem to hold in the dynamics inherent in the vitality of a functioning classroom.

4. Those relationships are stated in terms of probability not certainty.
5. The deliberate, intuitive, or inadvertent use of those cause–effect relationships can be observed and documented in the process of teaching.
6. The principles derived from those relationships should also be incorporated in the process of planning and evaluation before and after teaching.
7. The science of teaching can be taught and predictably learned by most professionals who are willing to expend the required effort.

Despite its manifest limitations as a view of teaching, the Madeline Hunter model of instructional improvement has swept the USA in what Slavin (1987) has described as 'the Hunterization of American schools'. Any phenomenon as sociologically significant as this warrants further investigation, even though, as it turns out, most of the elements of the model are not new and have been around for some years; what Hunter has done is commodify and institutionalize the process.

The underlying logic behind the Hunter scheme goes something like this: (1) it is possible to provide uniform standards of 'good' teaching which are able to be isolated into essential elements; (2) that it is possible to articulate supervisory processes which enable judgements of these essential elements; (3) that it is possible to identify the sets of skills required for improvement; and (4) that it is possible to ensure such improvement. All of these assumptions are highly contestable, at each of these stages. It seems that by linking a standardized teaching approach to supervisory procedures, Hunter has given administrators the vehicle they need in order to respond to the political pressures generated by calls for school reform. For their part, teachers have been sold a quite different bill of sale – for the most part it has been presented to them as 'an inservice program for instructional effectiveness' (Davis and Odden, 1986). Very few teachers realize that the Madeline Hunter model is actually a model of supervision (and, in many cases, evaluation) (Garman, 1987). Hunter seems to sell the model differently depending upon the target audience – for teachers, it is a model of effective teaching based on research, while for supervisors and administrators, it is a model of supervision and evaluation (Hazi, 1987a). Major slippages of language like this can only be interpreted as being mischievous in the extreme, and the cause for some considerable concern.

The model is driven by the kind of fear mentality invoked by the populist writings of people like Bloom (1987) in *Closing of the American Mind* and Hirsch's (1987) *Cultural Literacy*, that schools/universities are the cause of the deepening social and economic crisis. The packaging and slick marketing of programmes like those of Madeline Hunter which promise to reintroduce rigour and respectability back into schooling through the prescription and close surveillance of what teachers do, is seen to be a rational response to the findings of the high-powered commissions of inquiry on what is wrong with US education. It is a rational response, because in many ways the Madeline Hunter model appears to have a modicum of respectability. It does, after all, allege to be based on solid research findings (although efforts to ascertain the nature of that research have been unsuccessful, since Hunter's materials are for the most part not subject to normal academic scrutiny). It does promise to deliver instructional improvement, and it does focus on teachers as the apparent weak link in the educational chain. In a strange way, the events surrounding the model even have appeal to certain categories of teachers – but more about that later.

It is clear through the data from teachers who have had the Madeline Hunter model of supervision inflicted upon them that this process is predicated on routinizing teachers' work (a fact that is not inconsequential given the largely female nature of the teaching force), that it structures collegial interaction in a way that precludes reflection and critique, and that the process itself relies for its existence upon a process of separating those who organize or 'conceptual-ize' from those who carry out or 'execute' pedagogical processes. None of these consequences are in any sense incidental or accidental – they are deliberately constructed so as to place constraints on teaching through enab-ling a technically oriented perspective to dominate 'and for the creative role of teachers to be sacrificed in the movement toward standardized curriculum' (Beyer, 1986: 229). As Beyer (1986: 229) points out:

> As a society we have embraced patterns of institutional and personal practice that de-emphasize participation and involvement in favour of efficiency, standardization, and control. The contradictions between crit-ical reflection and the ongoing patterns of school practice, thus, reflect other problems in American culture. In this sense we may say that the issues . . . have a social or ideological dimension as they are part of a more general phenomena whose reality we cannot afford to ignore.

Expressed in slightly different words, what this amounts to is a form of amputation in which teachers and students are required to be involved in forms of instruction that alienate them from their own cultures, judgements, experiences and histories. Giroux (1986: 35) claims that this less than creative way of treating teachers as civil servants 'dutifully carry[ing] out the dictates of others' is used 'to promote what is often euphemistically called "educational leadership"'. The presumption is that controlling the behaviour of teachers in this way (under the rubric of accountability) actually produces predictable student outcomes that *look as if* they are simple technical solutions 'to the complex social, political and economic problems that plague schools' (Giroux, 1986: 36). Relegating teachers to subordinate status and silencing oppositional discourse about the mission of schooling by positing in its place 'forms of methodological reification' (ibid.: 33) is no guarantee that the much vaunted cries for excellence in schools will actually come about. Treating teachers in instrumental ways may produce just the reverse. As one teacher put it, if teachers are treated as if they are 'hired hands' without any real stake in the educational enterprise, then we should not be too surprised if they react like hired hands (Levy, 1985).

In part then, what I have been doing here is to begin to dismantle the widespread view of supervision by challenging the dominant assumption that supervision is a neutral vehicle by which school improvement and wider school reform might be effected. We have to see the dominant notion of supervision itself as being constitutive of certain privileged interests that work against people in schools operating as 'active, critical, risk-taking citizens' (McLaren, 1988a: 2). Current technicist forms of supervision cause teachers to lose control over their jobs (Apple and Teitelbaum, 1985). Through a process of what can only be described as a degradation of labour, teachers are progressively denied the right to choose – curriculum, content, texts, pedagogy and, ultimately, the conditions under which they do their work. The long-term effect of this is that teachers lose the capacity 'to plan and control a large portion of their work, [and] the skills essential to doing these tasks self-reflectively and well, atrophy and are forgotten' (ibid.: 373). Processes of this kind that standardize and homogenize the curriculum and pedagogy itself, actually have the effect of alienating teachers and making them 'the executors of someone else's plans' (ibid.: 373).

The next section gives voice to the comments of teachers who have had first-hand experience of what it means to be involved in supervisory processes of the kind advocated by Hunter.

In the teachers' words

This section presents some of the more prominent themes that have emerged from interviews with some 200 teachers[2] who have been 'Hunterized' (Garman and Hazi, 1988) in Pennsylvania. The context in which the interviews were conducted, how the project was undertaken, and the nature of the database have been explained elsewhere (Garman, 1987); data are merely used illustratively here. The evidence speaks eloquently to teachers' problems with a single highly prescriptive model of in-class supervision. Even though there appears to be some initial support, this dissipates once more detailed reflection takes place. Teachers are focused on as distinct from supervisors, because they have been the *object* of the Hunter administrative model.

Talking about teaching and invoking the legitimacy of science

Teachers said loud and clear that the Madeline Hunter model and the staff development activity accompanying it provided them with an opportunity and a way of talking about teaching that was normally absent from their teaching. As one teacher expressed it:

> As I was going through the training I was really very psyched, not so much for the Hunter stuff, but for the camaraderie and getting away from teaching [and being with other teachers].

In the words of another, speaking of the training that came with Hunter:

> What I liked best was the interaction with different grade level teachers. I think that's one of the big things we miss in education. . . . At the end of the day I have 45 minutes in which I am to clean everything off and plan, and by that time I'm too tired to do anything. Essentially what happens in that time period is that when people do get together they gripe. They're tired. They don't discuss educational issues. So the best thing [of the training] was being able to get away together to discuss things. I wish we had more time for that, and less of Hunter.

It seems that many teachers like the discourse and staff development aspect attaching to the Madeline Hunter model and the manner in which they were able to work together as adults, even if they found the substance of what was supposed to be learned distasteful. One teacher summarized this sentiment thus:

> I don't really think it was the training I liked as much as I liked listening to the enthusiasm and complaints of the other teachers. I can't say it was Madeline Hunter or the staff development that excited me, as much as being with those people and getting a little more insight into what they do, and sharing what I do.

This tells us something important about the intensified nature of teachers' work (Apple, 1986) which leaves them no opportunity for adult dialogue, and the insular ways in which schools are organized that actually exacerbates such dialogue. Comments like 'At school, it's not considered very fashionable to talk about teaching' and 'We are getting a common language for what teaching is', disclose something important about what is not happening in the normal course of events in some schools.

Being couched in the language of science, the Madeline Hunter material acquired a mystical kind of legitimacy that was comforting to some teachers. Sometimes, getting legitimacy of a general uplifting kind, for what they were doing, was important for teachers. Like the teacher who said:

> It was a boost for me because as we went through the model, there were some things that I could see that I was already doing with the kids, and it made me feel as though I was doing my job because I fit in.

What is disturbing because of its inaccuracy *in fact* (a viewpoint actually built into the Hunter model), is that the research is actually capable of saying what teaching *should* look like. One teacher who was prepared to accept Hunter's research-based claim at face value, said: 'I think it's nice to know what [the research says] an ideal lesson should be like, even if you're not in the situation where you can use the format all the time.' But there were other teachers who were much more sceptical about the alleged research basis of the Madeline Hunter model and the reality of what they experienced in the workshops. A typical comment was:

Well, about the model and research in general, they keep saying 'the research shows, the research shows' but I have seen very little of the research that supports their allegations. Some of it is common sense, and I suspect the research does show that. But it appears to me that they are taking an inch of research and developing a yard of educational theory! I don't think we should accept the statement that 'research shows'.

Other teachers struggled to reconcile how best to balance off the competing claims of wanting to be autonomous professionals (if that term any longer has meaning in contemporary education systems), with what they saw as the need to be accountable for public monies being spent. One teacher summarized the accommodation in these terms: 'Since we've had Hunter I think our image has changed for the better, so we put up with the inconvenience. . . . It has us on our toes, and I think that's what the public wants.'

What teachers were saying, then, was that the existence of the Madeline Hunter model provided them with a renewed vigour to talk with one another about the dailyness of their teaching. They saw too, in the language of the model, a form of legitimacy in 'science', that they felt squared with the way the general community wanted reassurance about the quality of schooling, even though some of them were distinctly nervous about the supposed research-based claims of the model.

There is actually quite a fine line being pursued here. Breaking the 'culture of silence' (Freire, 1972) that exists among teachers in schools will be embarked upon by some teachers even when that means working in ways that are patently not in their own best interests – the cycle of isolation is broken, but only at a very considerable cost. But what is problematic about having a particular model (in which teachers exercise no choice as to its selection) imposed upon them, is that some teachers are readily prepared to jettison their own language and ways of making sense of things, in favour of the lexicon of an alien model. Typical of this position was the teacher who seemed to be captivated by the pragmatism of the model, even to the extent of being blinded. In the teacher's words: 'I think the biggest advantage of the Hunter model is the terminology that's used. It's very easy to find out exactly where you're at in a particular part of the model . . . it makes an evaluation or observation very easy.'

Hunter's approach, with its apparently ready-made language of teaching, has the effect of separating students and teachers from their own language, customs, rituals, experiences and histories. What is most worrying about such technologized approaches is that they have the potential to detach students and teachers from their own ways of construing teaching and learning, by positing in their place, forms of discourse that are alien to the cultural lives of people in schools (Smyth, 1987c). Ironically, some teachers saw in the Hunter language, confirmation for what they were already doing; they interpreted this as absolving them from having to engage in any change at all:

The only thing I had to learn out of it [Hunter] was the names they gave to the different stages. They were familiar, but its just new names. I didn't have to change my teaching technique at all. I just had to get to use the jargon.

One teacher quite candidly admitted to feeling 'nervous' at the start, but found that Hunter was no different in substance to what she had been taught in college: 'I thought I would have to completely redesign the way I teach, but I didn't have to. I was doing all those things automatically: I just didn't know what they were called.' It was also true that some teachers were much less prepared to be compromised on the issue of a 'common language' for teaching implied in the model. One teacher saw this as far too constraining:

This idea about the common language of teaching. I don't know that you need to have a universal language. I'd rather just talk . . . in my own language. I don't know why we have to channel it into narrow terms. I don't like reducing teaching to the lowest common denominator. I don't like that. I don't want the job simplified. I don't want it standardized.

Because of the power of language, the legitimacy of teachers' own lived practical experiences becomes subservient to externally imposed 'management pedagogies' (Giroux, 1985). For some teachers, the fact that the Madeline Hunter model enabled administrators and supervisors to capture and monopolize the language of teaching was nothing short of a naked grab for power. As one teacher cryptically noted:

When the supervisor told me about not having 'closure', it was like a slap on the hand. By being able to give me a slap, by being able to hold the stick, kind of gives them the sense of feeling powerful as far as being able to use the jargon and talk in educational terms.

For another, the knowledge/power nexus was not insubstantial, and very difficult to accept:

I really feel that this is just a way of empowering administrators. They like to throw around the jargon and it gives them a sense of power, and I'm beginning to think that's the game we're playing now. [I] found it frustrating to have to keep justifying what you're about, to people who really don't understand what you are about.

Clearly, the imperative behind the language-as-power game being played out in these management pedagogies, becomes: the reduction and standardization of knowledge; the measurement of attainment against arbitrarily determined objectives and standards; and the allocation of teaching resources so as to maximize output. Because the discourse of management pedagogy is located in the lexicon of the technocrats, and not that of the value-laden experiences of classrooms, teachers and students have continually to struggle against the goals and objectives set by others outside of classrooms. Ryan

(1982: 30) claims that the technocratic view has an air of pseudo-respectability about it, 'its scientistic language, reflecting an instrumental orientation to carefully-defined and measurable goals, gives the perennial politics of control a gloss of sophisticated modernity'. As Ceroni (1987: 9) (herself a teacher) put it: 'Hunter's language is clearly the language of technology.' Lying behind endeavours of the Hunter type, is the kind of legitimacy summed up by Buchmann (1984: 431), when she said:

> the public accepts scientific findings not because it shares the scientific conception of reality but because of the social authority of science. Scientific knowledge and judgement are opaque and indisputable for most people.

Stratification through division of labour

In talking with teachers about their experiences in using the Madeline Hunter model, it became clear that the model was based upon a notion of enhancing and rewarding individualism. Individual teachers were given the opportunity to get away from their schools and go to 'swanky places for lunch or dinner' during training, and generally to obtain relief from the tedium of normal classroom demands. Such a short-range view turned out to have much more serious long-term implications, as this form of preferential treatment began to create categories of teachers and barriers between them. Being trained in the Madeline Hunter model meant career enhancement (Garman and Hazi, 1988), especially in situations where school systems display preferential treatment for recruiting teachers who are familiar with the model. Those who acquiesce by demonstrating a preparedness to accept the model, move into the fast lane, while others are left behind. For some, this took the form of being clear about the rules of the game being played between teachers and administrators: 'It's given teachers a framework so that they know what they're expected to do . . . [and administrators] are less likely to come in and look for silly things – at least you know what they're looking for.' For others, it meant going along, at least for the time being, with the game-like atmosphere: 'I will do the dance for them. I like teaching too much to get raked over the coals. I don't know how long I can play the rebel role, but I guess [acquiescing] is a small price to pay.'

This kind of elitism also produced another form of hierarchy in the form of a mindset that says that there are those who 'know about teaching', and they are qualitatively different and better from those who 'do teaching'. A common expression of the kind of resentment created by this artificial separation of expertise came in the form of: 'I just resent being forced to participate in something, by people who know less about teaching than I do, [and] being forced to participate in a program . . . [which] is anti-educational.' The kind of intellectual imperialism behind this separation is not only arrogant, but it also produces a kind of fracturing and fragmenting of knowledge about teaching that further legitimates the separation of the 'knowers' from the 'doers' – a dichotomy that is highly questionable in teaching. An artificial pecking order about whose knowledge is of most worth is thus created and sustained, with the result, as one teacher put it: 'It's very clear that my ideas aren't worth anything.'

Some teachers saw the standardization of teaching implicit in the model as a way of distinguishing committed teachers from the apathetic ones. It was a way of helping to 'pull the lazies into line' and arresting 'apathy that has gone on for too long – the malingerers are finally getting what they deserve'. Sentiments like these, while laudable in the current climate of accountability and efficiency, largely miss their mark. Diagnosing deficiencies in individualistic and atomistic ways, when the malaise may lie in the institutional and social conditions within teaching, is to ignore totally the managerial and bureaucratic circumstances that cause teachers to become that way. Mandating a model that implies a certain view of teachers, actually serves to produce a mood of a particular kind. One teacher in a school where the Hunter model had been introduced said:

> The attitude is very negative . . . not so much that teachers are resisting or rebelling, just that there is a feeling of a lack of professionalism, that they are really not a part of anything. It's a helplessness that converts itself into anger, and that anger converts itself into being obstinate. So, then, the attitude gets interpreted by the administration that 'Ahh, these teachers are really bitter and angry, and what kind of people are they who are teaching our children'. Yet, in fact, it's the system and the circumstances that have made them this way.

In other words, the behaviourist victim-blaming rhetoric (Ryan, 1971) that surrounds schemes like the Madeline Hunter model may actually deflect attention away from the factors that place unrealistic demands on teachers in the first place, and that make them seem incompetent. McLaren (1988b: 5) put it nicely when he said:

> Too often when analyzing teaching, the oppressive institutional fabric of the school and the social practices and discourses it legitimates are ignored in favour of evaluating teaching as if it took place in a social vacuum devoid of power relations. . . . The isolated individual thus bears the burden of the contradictions inherent in the educational system. It is a logic that conceptualizes . . . teacher behavior as an ensemble of personal attributes and deficiencies without realizing that character traits are created, in part, by the contradictory configurations of the capitalist social structure. Individual interests are constituted by structural arrangements – demands which we, of course, reproduce in the course of manufacturing such individual interests.

What McLaren is highlighting is that causation in social actions like teaching is much more complex than schemes like the Madeline Hunter model allow us to believe; indeed, they may even be pointing in the totally wrong direction. Teachers who opted to become involved in the Madeline Hunter model (through attending training workshops) frequently reported feelings of having 'sold out' on their colleagues, and of having great difficulty in trying to co-opt colleagues into the scheme upon returning to school. Notwithstanding, there was also a lot of sensitivity as colleagues worked out how best to maintain the respect of one another, in circumstances not of their own making. As one Hunterized teacher said of the generosity of her colleagues: 'We were all teachers . . . and even if they were opposed to the program as a whole, they were very gentle with us. They knew how awkward a position it was for us . . . .' At another level, driving wedges between categories of teachers so that some are stigmatized as being 'deadwood' or 'incompetents', may serve certain rhetorical interests, but it does not address the deeper underlying processes that result in teachers becoming that way, or resolve the issue in any other than an ephemeral way.

Furthermore, extending and entrenching the hierarchies between teachers by forcing them to compete against one another for spurious rewards, produces nothing more than an ungainly scramble; personal gain comes to outweigh the criteria of collaboration in a work setting that desperately needs high levels of teacher-to-teacher dialogue just to make sense of what is occurring. This put-down of teacher-generated knowledge, by requiring strict adherence to a seven-step model, produces what Apple and Teitelbaum (1985) call 'de-skilling', as teachers' capacities to make autonomous decisions atrophy as a consequence of dependence on the outside 'expert'. Slavin (1987: 57) calls this the 'deprofessionalization of teachers' brought about, as he sees it, by the institutionalization of Madeline Hunter-type models with their removal of teacher pedagogical choice.

Separation of 'means' from 'ends' through homogenization

The view that knowledge about teaching can be standardized, commodified and packaged for speedy and effective delivery – and its corollary that everything is known by an elite – is predicated on a view that splits the *ends* or valued social purposes of teaching from the *means*. According to one teacher, the Madeline Hunter model is an 'affront to dedicated professionals'. Another who had been through a 4-day training workshop in the model described it as 'the most anti-intellectual exercise I ever encountered. What it felt like was analogous to bringing all the great chefs of the world together and teaching them how to boil water' (Gondak, 1986: 4). In Gibboney's (1987: 49) words, the model is 'managerial not educative' and displays all of the characteristics of what Dewey labels a 'mechanical woodenness view of teaching'. From a teacher's perspective, the Madeline Hunter model has nothing going for it pedagogically – it is a way of getting administrators off the hook of being seen to be evaluating teachers. As one teacher put it: 'The only advantage I can see is for people administering it. It's simple to do. It's simple to teach people to do.' The effect is a form of surveillance that focuses exclusively upon the extent to which teachers exhibit behaviour that meets up to certain predetermined standards. What such tactics do, of course, is prevent serious analysis of the 'rightness' of questions about particular educational practices. By limiting the focus to the means of teaching (which are themselves unable to be questioned by virtue of their having been legitimated by the canons of 'science'), any discussion about the moral or ethical worth of teaching is pushed off the agenda. Construed in this way, teachers become technicians concerned with implementing the ideas of others, rather than intellectuals involved in questioning and interrogating their own teaching and the contexts in which it occurs.

Mischievous distortion of 'voluntarism' and 'rewards'

It is an interesting question, then, as to how teachers become involved in schemes like the Madeline Hunter model that are clearly not designed to serve either their interests or those of their students. The answer to that question is by no means simple or straightforward and is bound up with the complex political processes that go on within schools and educational systems. From the interview data it seemed that teachers became involved in the Madeline Hunter scheme by means of various forms of coercion. Sometimes it was quite overt:

> The administrators committed us to this program, and as a result of committing us, if a teacher refuses to go along with the model, then it works against him when it comes time for evaluation.

At other times, the strategy was altogether more subtle:

> What they did in our district was that the superintendent, the two principals, and four teachers received the training first, and they became like the facilitators for everyone else. Little by little they've been presenting it to the rest of the staff. I feel uneasy about the teachers 'selling out' to the administration.

It was also clear that teachers were frequently given a partial and misleading impression of what was involved. Teachers reported being 'lied to' and being told that the process was not to be used for 'evaluative' purposes, after which the entire process was then mandated upon them.

Add to all of this teachers' own aspirations for career advancement, the considerable media hype about what is good for schools and for the nation, and what we have then is a powerful amalgam of inducements and blunt instruments designed to convince teachers that they cannot opt out of being involved. None of this is to suggest that teachers are somehow easily duped; rather, it points to the carefully contrived way in which the Madeline Hunter model has been perpetrated upon teachers in a climate of school reform which is supportive of the tenets of the model.

Pennsylvania is an interesting – but by no means isolated – example of how the process has worked. The governor's 1983 White Paper (Thornburgh and Smith, 1983) had as its ultimate goal the 'rewarding of good teaching' – a laudable goal, and one no doubt designed to be attractive to teachers. After all, who in their right mind could possibly be opposed to such a motherhood ideal? Where the slippage has occurred is in respect of the pursuit of that praiseworthy goal. From its initial beneficent ideal, the Madeline Hunter model has come to not only be 'official' policy in some school systems, but adherence to its principles is also used as a way of screening applicants for selection to teaching positions (for example, in Lincoln, Nebraska) and as a basis upon which teachers can be reprimanded or even dismissed. One teacher who received her training in the Madeline Hunter model, while working as a substitute teacher, reported her principal as saying that if she ever applied for a job then she could 'use some of the terminology'. Other teachers reported a fear of being penalized in various ways, if their teaching did not conform with the model.

Funding that was supposed to be used to reward good teaching and outstanding classroom performance, has finished up being used to pay consultants and to train teachers in the use of the model (Garman and Hazi, 1988: 670); a far cry from what teachers were led to believe was the case at the beginning. Where rewards are offered and inducements given, it is always on the conditional basis of slavish adherence to the model. It becomes a *de facto* form of compulsion in which there are strong ideological pressures to conform. In the wider world, such terms like 'fraud' and 'misrepresentation' would be used to describe what is occurring here.

All of this is fairly consistent with the way in which the state operated in the UK in the 1970s with the establishment of the Assessment Performance Unit within the Department of Education and Science. While it was allegedly set up to diagnose student under-achievement so it could be remediated, it quickly turned into an organization that was more concerned with 'enhanced managerial control, under the convenience flag of "accountability"' (Simon, 1979: 10). In the UK, Hartley and Broadfoot (1986) have documented the manner in which the government has been committed to a strategy of replacing what has historically been a high degree of teacher autonomy with forms of teacher appraisal that amount to 'increasing tight central control over education' (p. 49). Elliott's (1989) work has also exposed the increasingly instrumental manner in which the culture of teaching is being eroded in the UK by formal appraisal of teachers, but as he argues, this is not all bad in that out of this teachers can develop counter-hegemonic forms. In Australia, precisely the same kind of situation is being rehearsed too (Ashenden, 1987), in order allegedly to address questions of social inequality in schools – the real agenda is that of monitoring school performance through 'performance indicators' that are inextricably linked to teacher appraisal. Frank Smith (1986), through the title of his book, *Insult to Intelligence: the Bureaucratic Invasion of our Classrooms*, summed up the essence of this quite nicely.

At the classroom level, Pennsylvania teachers resist schemes like the Madeline Hunter model by responding to it in a game-like way. For many, it was easier to accommodate to the rules of the game than to overtly oppose them. 'It's just easier to go along with the [Madeline Hunter] program and not be identified as a malcontent by the administration', was the way one teacher put it. Or as another put it: 'I can do a 45 minute dog and pony show twice a year. . . . Then I close my classroom door and do what I know is good for the children.' Another teacher who had been Hunterized described her own performance as 'the Madeline Hunter tap dance'. Yet another indicated that: 'If my supervisor walked in unannounced I would switch into Hunter. I tend not to follow the model exactly, but if she walked in I'd change. In fact, I keep a lesson in my top drawer for just that reason.' Through actions and comments like these, teachers are not only being candid, but they are actively demonstrating that oppressive regimes are only always partial, at most. Power is not monolithic and unidirectional – it has a dialectical aspect to it that takes expression in a variety of forms of resistance. As Giddens (1979) put it:

> all social actors, no matter how lowly, have some degree of penetration of the social forms that oppress them (p. 72).

> Power relations . . . are always two-way, even if the power of one actor or party in a social relation is minimal compared to another. Power relations are relations of autonomy and dependence, but even the most autonomous agent is in some degree dependent, and the most dependent actor or party in a relationship retains some autonomy . . . (p. 93).

Wearing T-shirts and badges that say 'I've been Hunterized' (Garman and Hazi, 1988), while an uncharacteristically outward manifestation for teachers, reflects something about the passion with which some teachers (at least) are prepared to develop forms of solidarity with others who feel similarly aggrieved. In a work situation that is not known for its extensive group contact, displays like this amount to more than symbolic expressions of discontent – they are ways of saying 'I am prepared to go public about an issue I feel strongly about.'

Having seen something of the way in which teachers have responded to these initiatives, it is apposite to conclude this chapter by looking at the way in which supervisory practices have been accorded legitimation by the 'school reform' movement.

Countering dominant views of 'in-class supervision'

Schemes like those described above are, of course, part of a much larger scenery. The plethora of reports on schooling over the past decade (Cross, 1984) make it clear that the USA is experiencing a military and economic decline, in which schools are simultaneously regarded as a major cause of this deepening crisis, as well as the vehicle through which the hoped-for restoration is to occur (National Governors' Association, 1986). This phenomenon of a resurgence of interest in teachers as the targets of reform, after a long period of benign neglect (Giroux, 1983), is not altogether altruistic. Giroux (1987: 5) claims that official reports on education encapsulate a 'studious refusal to address the ideological, social and economic conditions underlying poor teacher and student performance'. Instead of an analysis of the deep-seated underlying causes of this perceived malaise, what there is instead is a rehearsal of responses that amount to worn-out and bankrupt solutions to the alleged problems of schools. As Charles Breinin (1987), a science teacher asks, 'why is the first response to school reform always "get the teacher"?' There is a seemingly endless parade of calls for a return-to-the-basics, demands for an increase in academic standards, an extension of testing and moves for the removal of incompetent teachers. But, the argument being put here has been that the culprit is not so much a crisis of *competence*, but rather a crisis of *confidence* with its roots in the social and cultural dimensions of what schooling and learning are about. While the official reports on school reform affirm that 'good' schooling depends on 'good' teachers, what they fail to be clear about is 'that what makes most teachers good is not a mystical talent to rise above adversity, but the ability to shape the conditions and the consequences of their work' (Bastian *et al.*, 1985: 47).

In-class supervision is clearly an aspect of general school supervision which espouses supervision as a means to professional progress. Currently called instructional supervision, in-class supervision has a long tradition as look-alike teacher evaluation. In recent times, there have been attempts (at least on paper) to promote in-class supervision as a vehicle 'for the improvement of instruction' (Smyth, 1986c). There has even been some suggestion that such in-class supervision might serve two divergent but mutually exclusive purposes:

> The supervisory process must reflect the basic purposes that it is designed to serve. Effective supervisory processes must accommodate at least two major purposes: the development and improvement of teacher competencies and the evaluation of teachers. The development and improvement of teaching competencies is a formative process that provides supervisors with the opportunities to help teachers grow professionally and to develop and refine effective teaching skills. The evaluation of teachers is summative requiring a supervisor to reach an overal summary judgement of a teacher's performance for the purpose of making some type of personnel decision. These two purposes require distinct approaches to the process of supervision, and each must be considered explicitly in the development of a supervisory process for local schools (New Jersey State Department of Education, 1986: 5–6).

The above statement couches the supervisory process in terms that appear to encapsulate two different approaches to supervision. In reality, these are two different approaches to *evaluation* that have been co-opted by supervisors to obscure the real intent of the evaluative approach. At some point in history, the articulated goal of teacher evaluation began to be 'for the improvement of instruction' instead of 'for performance appraisal'. This slippage of language came to be incorporated into state school codes, and into textbooks as well. Supervision thus became a euphemism for evaluation, as supervision 'for the improvement of instruction' served to further entrench, confuse and obscure the real meaning of supervision, while sowing the seeds of pretence and self-delusion among supervisors themselves. In-class supervision, usually carried on through observation, judgement and prescription, has been associated with teacher evaluation in the public schools since the turn of the century.

Specifically, there are three major difficulties with supervision for appraisal purposes, when it is allowed to masquerade as a form of teacher improvement. First, the *ritualistic quality* that has come to prevail as a major feature of dominant forms of in-class supervision, is patently inadequate and teachers are deserving of better. Secondly, and related to this, the *episodic nature* of in-class supervision and the reductionist nature of what occurs, actually has the effect of separating teachers from thinking about and analysing their own personal and professional histories, and how these impact on their present practices. And, thirdly, it is difficult to accept the *purportedly neutral* and value-free approach implicit in the dominant view of how supervisory processes work as a form of surveillance. There is a political agenda in what is attempted, but it is undisclosed and should be unmasked.

Each of these concerns needs to be looked at in turn, if a thorough-going critique is to be mounted of some of the more particular variations of supervision, like the Madeline Hunter model. These are discussed briefly below.

Promoting ritualism

There is a ritual nature to in-class supervision required by mandate which involves giving teachers a once yearly appraisal of their performance through visiting their classrooms. Teachers have strong images and perennial doubts about the supervisor's visitation, echoed in sentiments like: 'What does the supervisor know about teaching and the way I'm supposed to teach kids on a day-to-day basis? One or two visits won't tell anything.' At the same time, this is tempered by 'good feelings', in the form of affirming gestures that 'At least someone in the front office will see what I'm doing!', or 'somebody cares about my classes'. Seasoned teachers often report that good ratings gave them a sense of esteem, even though in-class visitation was still largely ceremonial and didn't much change the way they taught their students. The ritual of the visitation is clearly recognized by those who have been part of the school culture, with teachers tolerating and accommodating to being scrutinized and judged. For their part, supervisors adjust to their sense of uneasiness as they pretend to know what good teaching is, and prescribe future improvements accordingly. The whole experience is made tolerable because of its ritual nature, and is not taken too seriously in its literal form, since ritual has a figurative meaning ascribed by the culture. What remains unquestioned throughout, of course, is the common-sense, naturalness or inevitability of the process of supervision itself. As long as it remains at this performative level, each of the parties is able to go through the motions of the game-like process without bruising either themselves or each other too much.

Concealing history

As long as in-class supervision remains fixated at the level of the 'merry pop in' (Crane, 1975) ritual, then teachers and those who purport to assist them, are destined to remain amputated from the burgeoning personal and professional histories which both bring to the teaching process. Dropping in on teachers on an isolated or episodic basis means that supervisors have no real way of intersecting with the rich personal histories of teachers and their students, or indeed, of gaining a sense of where teachers have come from pedagogically or where they might be headed. In Simon's (1988) terms, they are never able to develop a real sense of where things came from, how they came to be that way, or what sets of constitutive interests causes them to be and remain that way. Without being inscribed with a sense of history, teaching (and the concomitant process of surveillance) remains fixated at the level of unconnected bits of behaviour that can at best be picked up like pebbles on a beach and looked at, but which are put back in pretty much an undisturbed form. Instead of a progressive and collaborative unpicking of a stream of lived experiences of teachers and students, what we have instead is supervision that amounts to a reductionist process of enacting some kind of quality control audit in which discrete pieces of behaviour are held up against the micrometer of externally determined standards of what is deemed to be 'good' teaching.

Denying the political

Allowing in-class supervision to be construed only as a process of mechanically checking on the presence of certain teaching skills (and which relies on the separation of facts from values), is to ignore the reality that all teaching no matter what its espoused intent, has an agenda (disclosed or otherwise) of shaping and moulding the extent to which students are equipped and prepared to accept as unquestioned, or to challenge, the existing social order. At issue, then, is the deliberate process of separating those who 'know about' teaching from those 'who do' teaching. It amounts to a separation between those who 'conceptualize' from those who 'execute' (Braverman, 1975). As Berlak and Berlak (1981: 253) put it, whenever this occurs (as in the case of traditional forms of supervision), then a '*de facto* political position [is] taken'. Like teaching itself, which is a political act, the supervision of that teaching also has political consequences in either preserving or challenging the existing state of affairs. Moreover, as long as teachers are treated as if they are technicians or minor partners adhering to the directives and orders of others, then they are restricted in the extent to which they are free to reflect upon, to theorize about and to re-shape the immediate and wider social setting in which they work. Where there is an undisclosed agenda of maintaining the status quo with its preservation of existing power relationships, this is not a situation of neutrality – it is a denial of the politically charged nature of the situation. In seeking to make teachers conform to a particular view of the way teaching should be, in-class supervision is a political act.

Conclusion

In this chapter, the case has been argued that educational reform needs to be studied from 'below', in terms of being cognizant of the lives, feelings and aspirations of teachers. Furthermore, top-down educational reforms that translate into dominant forms of supervision that amount to checking up on fragmented aspects of teacher behaviour, are not accidental occurrences. Models of supervision, like those exemplified in the work of Madeline Hunter, draw their pseudo-legitimacy from the broader inquiries into education that support a narrow 'how to' view of schooling, instead of a critical or questioning one. Such forms of intellectual bullying can only succeed as long as teachers continue to refrain from asking questions to do with the moral and ethical rightfulness of what they do.

The major claim of this chapter has been that current top-down rationalist attempts at educational reform have failed because the definition of reform they present is a standardized one that is fixed and determinate and is construed as being translatable into practice in an unproblematic fashion. Such endeavours are also fundamentally flawed because teachers as the major 'actors' have been largely excluded from the action, except as benign respondents to the agendas formulated by others (Smyth, 1987d). Teachers have had a long history of being treated as the objects of other people's supposed reforms. Answers are seen as lying in measures aimed at increasing the rigour of teachers' work, in testing them more, in sending them 'back to school', and requiring that they work longer hours. In locating and addressing the real issues, little is said, for example:

> regarding the fact that public school teachers constantly confront conditions such as overwhelming emphasis on quantifying tasks, the growing lack of control over the curriculum, little or no input into the decisions that critically affect their work, isolation from their peers, and the often condescending treatment they receive from school administrators (Giroux, 1987: 5).

What the data presented in this chapter show is that teachers, even in the face of such oppression, have very effective ways of opposing and subverting those forces that would standardize and control what it is they do. As Beyer (1989: 1) put it, teachers are being focused on as 'the primary cause of . . . [the crisis] and the best hope for its eventual resolution'. While focusing on teachers 'has a plausible ring to it' (Beyer, 1989: 1), what it does is pinpoint the culprit in a way that is unfair, misleading and ultimately unhelpful. Teaching is not something that occurs in isolation from, nor is unaffected by, wider economic, political and social structures. As Beyer (1989: 2) put it, even

> everyday, seemingly commonsense practices, ideas and values in schools have been shaped, even constituted, by perspectives that have social,

political, and ideological frames of reference. These frameworks are woven into the very fabric of schooling and our conceptions of teaching.

In Fine's (1987) terms, what we have witnessed in the current wave of educational reforms (and exemplified in the teachers' reactions to the Madeline Hunter model), is that teachers are silenced so that certain things don't get talked about; particular topics are off limits, labelled as 'undesirable', are 'subverted', and ultimately are 'exported' (p. 157). As Fine (1987: 157) put it, silencing amounts to a process of:

> institutionalized policies and practices which obscure the very social, economic, and therefore experiential conditions of [teachers'] and students' daily lives. . . . Silencing constitutes the process by which contradictory evidence, ideologies, and experiences find themselves buried, camouflaged, and discredited.

Processes of supervision like those hawked about by people like Hunter, that make extravagant claims to being 'scientific' and 'research-based', are really nothing more than ways of bolstering corporate, institutional and bureaucratic interests. By concentrating exclusively on the 'technique' aspects of what constitute 'good' teaching, they divert attention away from an analysis of the economic, social and political hierarchies that maintain and perpetuate in-equality and injustice. Schemes like these, and the ideology they endorse, are sustainable only as long as the technical and instrumental myth about teaching is believable by the majority of teachers. Its continuance is by no means a foregone conclusion!

Notes

1 I wish to express my considerable appreciation and gratitude to Noreen Garman who co-authored the paper from which this chapter emerged. Fazal Rizvi also made helpful comments on an earlier draft.
2 The interview data cited in this paper was derived from two funded research projects: Garman (1987) and Hazi (1987b). A re-analysis of the data from the above two projects was made possible, in part, by a research grant from the Research and Graduate Studies Committee, Deakin University, Australia, for a collaborative project entitled 'School reform in the U.S.A. and their effects on the professional lives of teachers: An Australian/American critique'.

4

Developing an educative agenda

Introduction

I am not sure that continuing to dwell at any further length on the moribund
nature of past or present supervisory practices is that helpful. Others have done
so, as have I in the previous chapter. My purpose here, rather, is to adopt a
somewhat more proactive stance by suggesting what a revamped, more
liberating view of supervision might be. I envisage this view as a major shift in
perspective – not a change of style or behaviour, for that would be too shallow.
I have in mind what MacDonald (1988) calls a revelation of our 'passion', our
'values' and our 'justifications':

> What we must ask ourselves then is to really profess; to reveal and justify
> from our own viewpoints what we believe and value. . . . We are asking
> persons to transcend the limitations and restrictions of their social
> conditioning and common sense and to venture beyond by seeing and
> choosing new possibilities (ibid.: 163).

I believe we need to challenge extant views of supervision for four cogent
reasons:

1 Current practices lock us into technical rationality that demands that we
  instrumentally separate our thinking about the 'means' of supervision from
  the ethical, moral and political dimensions whose 'ends' they are supposed
  to serve – the effect is a narrow concentration on *how-to questions*, rather
  than on *what* and *why* questions.
2 Bureaucratically and hierarchically construed structures that separate those
  who 'know about' teaching (supervisors) from those who 'do' teaching

(teachers), amount to a form of *institutionalization of technical rationality* with origins deep in its own unquestioned ends.

3 These approaches do not have centrally built into them a concern about the *rightness of action* and how we treat others: MacDonald (1988: 166) says we 'park the Bill of Rights at the front door when we enter school'.

4 Supervision's current concern with pragmatic aspects of teaching technique does *not encourage or even permit questions to be asked about structure*; for example, our schools are organized and run in ways that closely approximate a factory model, and this has profound implications for what is learned, how it is learned and how knowledge itself is treated.

These are not mere omissions nor oversights from current forms of supervision – they come about because the social relationships that exist in traditional forms of supervision militate against these views surfacing as issues.

Supervision for liberation

To shift supervision from its current oppressive managerial preoccupation with accountability, quality control, efficiency, effectiveness and sanction-ridden forms of surveillance, we must begin to embrace more robust possibilities that question the presumed supremacy of the technocratic-mindedness of what now passes as supervision in our schools. We need, for example, to raise the issue about whether 'competent practice' (Greene, 1986a: 70) is sufficient on its own to drive discussions about teaching and supervision. Following Greene (1986a: 70), we need to be better prepared to ask moral and ethical questions about what valued social purposes teaching is directed towards and why prevailing practices actually exist.

By continuing to pursue our current reductionist conceptions of supervision in which teaching is broken down into smaller and smaller observable and measurable fragments of behaviour (see the Florida Coalition for the Development of Performance Measurement Systems, 1983, with 121 separate behaviours that a supervisor is required to search for), we are unwittingly endorsing a view that says a person can develop 'intellectual, emotional and interpersonal ability in much the same way as one develops muscles' (Barrow, 1987: 195). Hargreaves (1988: 216) claims that teachers 'are not just bundles of skill, competence and technique: they are creators of meaning, interpreters of the world and all it asks of them'. Because teachers interact with the world around them, and make sense of it, adapt and refocus what it is they do, we can no longer defend definitions of teaching that are expressed solely in terms of competence in prescribed skills, pedagogical or otherwise. As Hargreaves (1988) says, asking why teachers fail 'to do X' does not advance matters much – in his view, asking why teachers 'do Y' and how on their terms they 'cope', 'adapt' and 'reconstruct their circumstances' is more revealing (p. 216). To continue to see the issue of teaching quality from a deficit point of view that presupposes that poor-quality teaching 'results from deficiencies in personality, gaps in learning, or weak matching of competencies to tasks', is to continue to ignore the fundamental point that 'teacher quality (or its absence) actually results from processes of a social nature, from teachers actively interpreting, making sense of, and adjusting to, the demands and requirements their conditions of work place upon them' (Hargreaves, 1988: 211). Of course, the proposition that teachers be 'respected as active and rational interpreters' (Hargreaves, 1988: 216) of their own work, has its own set of policy implications for those who 'manage' educational systems.

The kind of alternative vision that I, and people like Hargreaves, have in mind, insists on teaching as having an *empowering* agenda – one that enables teachers, as well as students, to 'become different, to think critically and creatively, to pursue meanings, to make increasing sense of their actually lived worlds' (Greene, 1986a: 72). As Greene points out, this deliberate, mindful, and action-oriented process involves 'provoking persons to get up from their seats . . . [and] say something in their own voices, against their own biographies and in terms of what they cherish in their shared lives, what they authentically hold dear' (ibid.: 72). Greene argues for a form of freedom, not so much from physical or psychological oppression, but from 'complacency' and 'taken-for-grantedness' that produce palpable forms of paralysis. Overcoming the uncritical, passive acceptance of the world means that teachers (and supervisors) have to work consciously towards a state of 'disequilibrium' which sees through the apathy and indifference of the natural and the taken-for-granted. Greene argues against knowledge about teaching that is regarded as 'privileged' (in the sense that supervisors prescribe research, lesson plans, objectives and curriculum guides) and against teaching that amounts solely to a form of technical literacy for students.

To speak about supervision in empowering terms is to endorse a view of supervision that amounts to reflection-in-action (Schön, 1983), in which the agenda is not one of standardization and homogenization of pedagogy against some artificially constructed standards, but rather one of deliberate attempts to situate teaching in its theoretical, historical and political context that will enable those participating in it to share in a particular lived reality. Of course, this means departing dramatically from the posture that somehow supervision is a non-political, neutral, value-free activity. Supervision of the kind being suggested here is, therefore, much more person-, context- and situation-specific; its agenda is to help teachers and students in the sense-making process. Supervisors in this scenario are not engaged in rating teachers' performance against external standards or indicators, nor are supervisors in the business of enforcing schemes of external compliance. In this alternative, the sole reason for supervisors' existence (as distinct from teachers') is to ensure that the necessary physical, intellectual and emotional resources are available to help teachers make sense of their pedagogy. This enabling function amounts to cultivating ways of working that increasingly allow teachers to understand *their own* personal and collective histories and to work *collaboratively* at unravelling the culture of their own teaching. In this context, 'teachers-as-workers' can indeed be their own inspectors (Halberstam, 1986). Viewed from this vantage point and at a more practical level, supervision has several dimensions:

- Less measurement against standards of performance, and more activity of an ethnographic, biographical and autobiographical kind that allows (even demands) that teachers connect with their students' personal and social lives.
- Better ways of helping teachers to recognize and counteract the bureaucratic intrusions (Smith, 1986) into their classrooms that have no educational foundations.
- Helping teachers to see how their voices are being progressively silenced in the debates about school reform (Fine, 1987), and how the media hype about accountability is being used as a device for legitimating anti-educational forms of managerialism.
- Equipping teachers to describe and analyse the pedagogical imperatives of their work (Smyth, 1984a, 1986c), so as to expose and ultimately transform the authoritarian hierarchical structures that have come to captivate their professional lives and those of their students.
- Assisting teachers to counteract 'negative pedagogy', and the kind of cultural illiteracy that is fostered by mindless measurement-oriented forms of teaching (Johnson, 1982; Hirsch, 1987; Bloom, 1987).
- Encouraging teachers to judge the 'political correctness' of what they do, case by case, not according to the neatness-of-fit with some long-range goals or nebulous national priorities (MacDonald, 1988).
- Devising better ways of helping teachers to celebrate what it is they do in their teaching, as a means of developing robust self-images of themselves (Boomer, 1985).
- Engaging teachers in the 'study of the academic culture of teaching' to shift teachers from being 'passive, manipulated and silent', to being able to provide an active, informed commentary on one anothers' teaching (Traver, 1987).

In a very real sense, Hult (1979) captures the essence of these points when he speaks about 'pedagogical caring'. For him, caring amounts to a 'concern and appreciation for the special uniqueness and circumstances of the person' that involves 'overcoming obstacles and difficulties' (pp. 238–9). At the same time, however, it involves more than a concern for the *individual*. That which is cared for may be an idea as well as a person or a plurality of ideas or persons:

> Pedagogical caring refers to the careful . . . manner or style by which a teacher operates. In doing his [*sic*] professional job with due care, the teacher demonstrates serious attention, concern, and regard for all his [*sic*] duties. And what is especially ingredient to pedagogical caring is the teacher's commitment to develop and maintain his [*sic*] style throughout his or her professional career, even under conditions of adversity (Hult, 1979: 243).

Traver (1987: 436) summarized this metaphorical tilting of the world on its head when he spoke about the glaring omission from the scholarly wisdom of what we think we know about teaching:

What we think we know about teachers results from concepts and methods that are not primarily authored and owned by teachers. To the extent that we believe that understanding people requires first that they speak with their own words, we must admit that we know very little. We must, therefore, think about ways to make it possible to listen to teachers, to respect their intelligence, ethic, and emotion, to ask them to keep journals and memoirs, to share classes and meals, and to help them to write and speak. What this means is that we must seek teacher empowerment within the academic culture of the study of teaching.

This situation is certainly no less true for the research and practice of supervision. We must have parallel ways of working that amount to a 'new consciousness about the intelligence, ethic, and emotion of teaching' that respect and acknowledge the worth of teachers' knowledge about their work (Traver, 1987: 434). This view is not, unfortunately, widely shared in the field of supervision now.

Typical notions of supervision which are encased in a patriarchial and managerial view of how schools and teachers should be organized need to be supplanted and informed instead by the ideas of feminist writers (Noddings, 1986; Gilligan 1982; Walkerdine, 1986; Lather, 1984, 1986; Williamson, 1981–2), who not only understand the gendered nature of teaching but who can articulate what a feminist pedagogy might look like within an educative agenda for schooling. This alternative perspective – which has a lot to do with an 'ethic of caring' (Gilligan, 1982) and the development of distinctive relationships that are characterized by 'reciprocity' – is so novel that it creates an entirely different moral attitude towards what is meant by supervision. Noddings (1986) speaks about the need to develop 'fidelity in teaching', a simultaneous concern about a faithfulness to ideas and ideals, alongside the concern for a high degree of exactitude and accuracy. As Noddings (1986: 496) says, we have a high degree of faithfulness:

When we know to what or whom we are faithful, when we have reflected on the reasons and emotions involved in our faithfulness, and when we are committed to fresh affirmations of faithfulness at ever finer and truer levels. . . . Fidelity to persons does not imply that academic excellence, the acquisition of skills, of the needs of contemporary society should be of no concern.

Noddings (1986: 499) notes the ultimate tragedy:

This way of thinking and speaking has almost disappeared from formal educational discourse. It occurs on the fringes of the educational research community, in almost embarrassed whispers. While there is a growing reaction against single-minded calls for excellence and technical proficiency, it is a disgruntled response cast largely in the language of liberal ideology.

It is those alternative ways of thinking, speaking and acting in supervision that I want to revitalize in the next section.

An 'educative' view of supervision

The American social philosopher Fay (1977, 1987) is important in this discussion because his altered concept of the relationship between theory and practice serves as a corrective to present dominant (i.e. instrumentalist) views. The essence of Fay's (1977) argument is that instead of one group or class being subservient to or beholden to another because of status or position, relationships ought to prevail in which *all* members can arrive at new self-understandings that empower them to 'reduce their suffering by creating another way of life that is more fulfilling' (p. 204). What Fay proposes is an agenda on how those who have been excluded for whatever structural reasons from a say in determining their own professional destinies, can arrive at new levels of collective self-understanding as a basis for action. His argument, when applied to supervision, amounts to abolishing privileged, elitist forms of supervision and replacing them with forms that stimulate dialogue about teaching and learning in schools. Fay is on about a discourse that sharply contrasts the pedagogic with the managerial in schools.

This notion of supervision is, therefore, fundamentally to do with teachers' ability to acquire an understanding of how the social and institutional circumstances of their school lives causes them frustration and how the anxiety ultimately detracts from self-fulfilment. This educative (or 'transformative') perspective rests on the assumption that by assisting teachers to understand themselves and their world, we make it possible for them to engage in the radical changes necessary for them to overcome the oppressive conditions that characterize work patterns and social relationships. Knowledge becomes a means for teachers to arrive at self-understanding and self-awareness of disabling conditions – not a means by which those in dominant positions acquire power and exert control. Knowledge about pedagogy is no longer, therefore, a set of prescriptive procedures construed as something to be 'applied' to teachers and students. Rather, knowledge becomes their means for jointly identifying their social and institutional constraints and working for change. To the extent that ideas and knowledge emerge from and help to sustain certain social conditions, those ideas can now take on a dialectical relationship contributing towards changing the social structure that spawned them in the first place. If we are not to stagnate, it is only healthy that this should occur.

More inclusive forms of supervision, therefore, involve teachers (as well as students) in coming to see how, through their own actions, they are 'unwitting accomplices' (Fay, 1977: 205) in perpetuating 'self destructive patterns of interactions that characterize their social relationships' (ibid.: 204). All social practices, including those within schools, are created and sustained by certain interests, and when participants unknowingly collude with those who hold power, they frustrate even their own interests. If supervisors in school settings have any legitimacy at all, then their function must be to reduce the way in which teachers are systematically unclear about what it is they do and how and why teachers continue to have unfulfilled ambitions and aspirations in working with students. Helping students, teachers and members of the wider community to unveil or unmask self-understanding that conceals how they unwittingly collude or 'participate in their own misfortune' (ibid.: 205), is what the *sine qua non* of supervision should primarily be about. A supervisor, therefore, 'sparks . . . [teachers] into changing the way they live and react to others' (ibid.: 206).

Noticeable by its absence from this conception of supervision is any mention of the imperative to define schools and what they do in terms of attaining and maintaining 'standards', or pursuing ill-defined systems or nationwide goals. Calls to instrumentally and unquestioningly follow the objectives laid down by others (even if the goals happen to be in the 'national interest') is to acquiesce to a thinly disguised attempt to manipulate schools to satisfy narrow sectional economic interests. To continue to allow prevailing corporate models of supervision to masquerade in the guise of attempting to improve teaching is to do nothing more than 'evacuate politics from the agenda' (Hextall, 1984: 254) by having school participants believe that schools should be left in the trusted hands of a disinterested civil servant class who operate according to value-free managerial principles of accountability, efficiency and effectiveness. These procedures in these hands are far from disinterested. Their undisclosed and conservative politics is to maintain existing power relationships within the rigidly defined limits of the status quo.

We need to take care, however, in espousing an alternative that an educative view of supervision in schools is not seen as merely *involving* those who have previously been *uninvolved* in school matters. To have involvement or participation *per se* as the agenda is to miss the point of how school structures themselves are systematically distorted, sustained and textured by the misunderstandings school people hold. As Fay (1977: 205) says, structures and beliefs are dialectically related, in that 'ideas are a function of social conditions, but . . . they [in turn] . . . play a causal role in creating and sustaining particular social structures. [The educative model] tries to see the relation of conditions and ideas as a dialectical one.'

The educative view reveals to school participants the nature and extent of their misunderstanding and that their ignorance was not accidental, but has its roots deeply embedded in the layered, stratified and supposedly objectified social order of the society of which they are a part. Once school participants can begin to see the interpenetration of structures and beliefs, they can challenge and question the constructed and taken-for-granted way schools are portrayed.

This approach is essentially optimistic and empowering, not moribund and pessimistic. It elevates school people, so that they are seen (and see themselves) as having the capacity to understand how their schools as institutions came to be the way they are. The educative model, therefore, takes seriously the need to 'change people's basic understanding of themselves and their world as [a] first step in their radically altering the self-destructive patterns of interaction that characterize their social relations' (Fay, 1977: 204).

Change in an educative model of supervision requires that teachers (as well as students and parents) have an opportunity to decide for themselves 'on the basis of lucid, critical self-awareness, the manner in which [they] wish to live' (Fay, 1977: 207). In Kant's terms, they emerge from a state of immaturity that involves accepting someone else's authority to a situation that calls for using reason. This model implies a view of autonomy in which participants' rational thinking becomes the major source of what happens inside schools, rather than the dictates of those who operate at a (physical or psychological) distance from classrooms.

The point of departure for the educative approach lies in the different view it espouses of teachers. Instead of regarding teachers as untrustworthy and in need of tight bureaucratic control an educative view of supervision starts from the presumption that teachers are 'conscious of themselves as active deciding beings, bearing responsibility for their choices and able to explain them by referring to their own purposes, ideals and beliefs' (Fay, 1977: 229).

Reclaiming control through reflection based upon rationally informed discourse is the major difference between the educative and corporate models of supervision. Acting rationally, according to Fay (1977: 229), amounts to groups and individuals changing their self-understandings on the strength of 'the force of the argument and not [because] some extraneous factor . . . leads [them] to adopt a new viewpoint'. In this scheme, 'persuasion, argumentation, debate, criticism [and] analysis . . . are [at] the heart of the educative model' (ibid.: 229). To that extent, it does not involve replacing one form of dogma with another; rather, change is rejected on the basis of reason.

The educative approach to supervision is, therefore, primarily concerned with power. It is concerned with how self-knowledge can enable people to see how the conditions that constrain them are created and sustained by elites. But, knowledge made possible through the educative mode will not, in itself, lift people out of situations that caused them to be constrained in the first place. Rather, the intent is to develop a capacity for critical self-reflection that reveals to those relegated to subservient roles how they came to be deprived of the power of self-determination. People who were previously objects in the world are transformed into active, self-determining subjects.

What educative possibilities might look like?

Surprisingly, there is no shortage of evidence of teachers working with one another in more collaborative and 'critical' ways. Describing several such projects of the North Dakota Study Group, Perrone (1988: 5–6) cites a monograph, *Speaking Out: Teachers and Teaching*, that captures what teachers themselves think about the merits of thinking and talking together about their work:

> This monograph is about our teaching practice – what it is and what it could be. It is about teachers – what we do and how we think and learn from what is done. It is an exploration of a set of ideas about teaching – ideas which have a long history – which are made particular by our current, lived experience. Finally, and most importantly, it is about having a voice in what we do.
>
> Having a voice is critical and political. We create, share, and change our world with and through language. Recognizing that day-to-day experience is a powerful source of understanding and knowledge which, when articulated, can be fed back into the quality of work is critical for teachers in gaining a voice. Recognizing knowledge and voicing it is basic to changing the ways teaching is thought about and enacted.
>
> Voices, of course, need to be cultivated and supported. About 15 years ago, groups of teachers across the country started creating varying opportunities to lend each other the kinds of support needed to make themselves heard. For teachers participating in this project, collegial groups . . . have been particularly important. They allowed teachers to talk about their practice and the children they teach, to describe both in some detail, and to help each other find the patterns and relationships, and thus meaning, within the wealth of detail of their teaching lives. These groups created space and time within which teachers could do this important thinking.

In the contemporary climate of paranoia about the importance of technique, the actual reflective procedures used by these teachers emerged as much less important than what they gained from the process of dialogue.

To take another illustration. Acting as a 'critical friend', McDonald (1986) describes the story of a group of high school teachers (of which he was a part) who met regularly (mostly outside of school hours) to reflect on their practical knowledge as teachers and of the insights, uncertainties and paradoxes that emerged from these discussions. Given the power to determine their own agenda and to explore the role of academic theory in their teaching lives, these teachers found that they were able to stay in charge of the knowledge-creation process, instead of being subjugated by the ideas of others. From an initial concern about how to work as a group (or 'collegiality for collegiality's sake'), McDonald (1986) reports teachers' increasing interest in gaining policy power over their teaching, culminating in an increased confidence and realization that they can claim that power based on knowledge generated about their own teaching.

Duckworth's (1986) experience of working with teachers in 'sense-making' ways also points to the particular importance of how teachers think about the ways in which they work with their students. Her experience suggests that if understanding practice is the intent, 'then the way to gain insight is to watch [what students] do . . ., and try to make sense of what happens' (Duckworth, 1986: 490). First, teachers engage with the phenomena of teaching by closely observing what happens in their own teaching. Secondly, students 'explain what they mean' so that they can make things clearer for one another, determine what they want to understand, and thus become more dependent upon their own judgements while taking one anothers' ideas seriously (ibid.: 490).

Arguably, the most insightful accounts of what teachers can achieve through discussions and support groups have come out of the writings and activities of the Boston Women's Teachers' Group. Their accounts (Freedman et al., 1986) perceptively analyse how teaching affects teachers' personal and professional lives. The group's focus on the need to locate discussions about teaching within wider considerations of institutional structures amounts to a much-needed radical shift in the nature of teacher-initiated discourse about schooling (Freedman et al., 1986). Deflecting the spotlight away from the alleged deficiencies in schooling that attach to individual teachers' presumed inadequacies, as the Boston Women's Teachers' Group did, permits and requires a different set of questions – ones that have more to do with the oppressive way schools are organized and administered. This move away from the victim-blaming rhetoric (Ryan, 1971) opens up a form of debate that has largely been stifled by educational reformers and policy makers who presume to know about teaching.

Emerging from the writings of the Boston Women's Teachers' Group (Freedman et al., 1983a,b) are what Kanpol (1988) identifies as forms of 'group solidarity' – the metaphorical equivalent for teachers of the 'macho militancy' portrayed by Willis's (1977) 'lads' in Learning to Labour. While Kanpol's (1988) critical ethnography of a group of eighth-grade middle-school teachers is an important start in that direction, we are in need of more accounts documented by teachers themselves of how the process occurs. We need to know more about how teachers develop collaborative and counter-hegemonic alliances based on dialogue.

Examples that constitute a basis for a departure from the narrow accountability ethos can be found in the work of various writers, e.g. Strieb (1985), Raphael (1985), Goswami and Stillman (1987), Ayres (1988), McTaggart et al. (1988), Nixon (1981), Hustler et al. (1986), Grundy (1987), Gitlin and Smyth (1989), who although they are not all classroom teachers, have written about teaching from the vantage point of teachers.

Conclusion

Clearly, the meaning attached to supervisory practices that amount to forms of quality control and inspection of what teachers do has out-lived its usefulness (despite those who continue to argue consistently the accountability line). We would do well to take Grumet's (1979) point seriously about what it is that supervision purports to do, and ask whether we can any longer afford to live with the moral and ethical consequences of the metaphorical equivalent of supervision as some kind of skilled copy-reading of the surface content of others' teaching. Although using supervision as a way of hierarchically shafting teachers (in the guise of accountability) may have limited appeal in some quarters, even the medieval monks approached their task of scanning liturgical texts for errors, omissions and deviations with much less certainty and faith in either their theory or their authority.

Although I have sketched the broad outlines of more educative possibilities here (an approach that is consistent with the tenets of clinical supervision as articulated in the Introduction to the book), teachers themselves have much more to do as they give expression to what working with one another means in more authentic, responsible, critical and enlightening ways. It makes a good deal of sense for teachers to pick up on those initiatives already started, and to run with them.

5

Teachers as collaborative and critical learners

Introduction

The question of how to bring about lasting, significant and meaningful change in schools is one of the most enduring, confusing and perplexing issues currently confronting us. Seemingly endless amounts of money, time and effort have been invested in tackling the question from a planned, rational change perspective of developing research agendas, pursuing answers to those research questions, and then disseminating and implementing policy based on those findings.

Contrary to this view, the argument of this chapter, and indeed of the second half of this book, is that schools are not tidy rational organizations, and that change as a consequence is an *ad hoc* piecemeal process. Because of the unique culture of schools, there are severe impediments to the way teachers respond to supposedly rational change processes orchestrated from outside. Teachers' own interpretations and theories about what works in classrooms *can* and *should* constitute the basis of change strategies in schools. Teachers themselves have the capacity to engage in practical reflection (Elliott, 1976a) through the development of collaborative alliances that not only enrich their sense of what is feasible and possible, but transform as well their understanding of those realities. In initiating and carrying out this process of critical reflection about their own teaching, teachers clearly require various forms of assistance; however, more about this shortly.

The rational, planned or linear model of how to implement change has suffered because, as Carnine (1981: 23) has noted, 'Those most interested in improving school practices often lack a healthy respect for hidden impediments.' It is not that there is any lack of knowledge about what *should be done*; rather, it has to do with a failure to appreciate the enormous chasm between *knowing something* and being able to *initiate action*. Carnine cites from a consultant engaged by the US Army during the Korean War to train soldiers in ways of avoiding trenchfoot and frostbite – greater sources of casualties than gunshot wounds:

> I did my eager best to develop the finest six hour course possible, but I soon saw that something was wrong. The entire subject matter could be stated in a single sentence: 'Keep Your Socks Dry!' For the first time I saw the difference between deficiencies of knowledge and deficiencies of execution. Even after watching movies of toes falling off, soldiers simply wouldn't go to the trouble to keep their socks dry (Carnine, 1981: 23).

Without being trite, the message is clear: when speaking about schools the factors that inhibit change are pervasive, deep-seated and embedded in the nature of schools and classrooms as workplaces. To make inroads into the problem of bringing about change in the direction of improving the quality of what occurs in classrooms will require peeling back the layers and uncovering those deeply ingrained impediments to change. Some significant work has already been done along these lines (Jackson, 1968; Lortie, 1975: Sarason, 1982; Lieberman and Miller, 1979; Lieberman, 1982).

The kind of realities of teaching that Lieberman and others allude to are both sensible and 'grounded' (Glaser and Strauss, 1967) in teachers' own conceptions, experiences and theories about teaching. There is considerable tension between the way teachers experience schooling and the way policy makers and others perceive that reality. Lieberman (1982), for instance, portrays an inherent tension in teachers' need to continually move back and forth between a concern for the idiosyncrasies of pupils, while attending to and acknowledging the existence of group norms in classrooms. In this process of vacillation, teachers continually accommodate to the need for rules and regulations in the knowledge that these stifle individualization and innovation. Although they are self-confessed pragmatists, teachers' work styles are characterized by concerns for practicality and immediacy, in which they have daily to contend with community expectations and demands that take little account of the ambiguity and uncertainty surrounding much of what transpires in classrooms. To the outsider, 'All you have to do is teach those kids' (Lieberman, 1982: 256). Outsiders fail to appreciate the highly personalized artistic nature of teaching, the endemic uncertainty of the linkage between teaching and learning in the absence of an established knowledge base, and the absence of goal specificity. There is an insensitivity to the fact that control of classroom norms is a matter of survival in a context characterized by isolation, and in an absence of a strong professional culture based on shared experiences.

While it is true that schools have a bureaucratic face, and there are therefore grounds to regard them as rational, there is also a widespread presumption that what appears rational and logical can become the basis for action. Wise (1977) described as the 'hyper-rationalization hypothesis' the tendency by policy makers to formulate and implement change on the presumption that schools are rational, ordered organizations: 'What appears logical may or may not have a connection to reality. Where the connection to reality is absent, a policy intervention will fail' (ibid.: 44). Wise points to a marked disjuncture between the rational model and school reality, concluding that 'the rational model does not seem to have become the dominant framework for teachers' discourse on teaching, schooling and education' (ibid.: 50).

At the level of individual teachers and classrooms, Floden and Feiman (1980) claim that the answer does not lie *either* in simply exhorting teachers to act in 'more rational ways' (whatever that means!). Considered in context, teachers and the theories they hold about what they do, why and with what effects, may be eminently reasonable and perfectly rational:

> Although teachers do not engage in conscious and systematic delibera-
> tion, they still have good ways of thinking about what they are doing, even
> if those ways do not approximate the *a priori* models. Teachers develop
> heuristic strategies for dealing with the fast-moving complexity of the
> classroom; some of these shortcuts are better than others. Teachers are
> rational in their actions, not as defined by *a priori* models of action, but as
> defined by choosing appropriate means to reach their goals (Floden and
> Feiman, 1980: 3).

The changes most likely to succeed are those that acknowledge the practicality and immediacy of classroom issues by starting from where teachers are
at in their understanding of themselves, paying due regard to their own
histories and their particular work contexts. An important reality is the way
teachers learn. There is evidence that teachers do not learn, by and large, from
scholarly journals (Little, 1982), research reports (Stenhouse, 1978) or even
pre-service courses (Hogben, 1980). Rather, they are influenced most by
precept and example, especially role models held of their own teachers.
Research on adult learning (Knowles, 1978; Sprinthall and Sprinthall, 1980;
Bents and Howey, 1980) suggests that adults learn in situations where they are
provided with an opportunity for continuous guided reflection based on 'lived
experiences'. Sprinthall and Sprinthall (1980) believe that even though the
research on adult development is still in the formative stages, the type of
explanatory framework required may well develop out of practice. They argue
that since theory and practice are really different sides of the same coin, valid
theory can be derived from careful and systematic analysis of practice. They
suggest a number of elements as being important in adult learning:

1 *Role-taking experience*. This involves the performance in a direct and active
   way in situations involving new and more complex interpersonal tasks. For
   example, teachers may act as observers and counsellors for each other, or
   demonstrate to colleagues new teaching models or methods.
2 *Qualitative aspect of role taking*. Recognition is given to the capacities of
   individuals and the complexity of new tasks and roles. There needs to be a
   matching of experiential background and new role expectations.
3 *Guided reflection*. This acknowledges the importance of not only providing

adults with new and real experiences, but also the need to assist them in making sense of those new experiences. Educational institutions are generally notoriously bad at teaching people to do this.

4 *Continuity*. Brief, episodic learning encounters as experienced in one-shot professional days are ineffective in facilitating change. Periods considerably in excess of 1 year are necessary.

5 *Personal support and challenge*. Giving up old habits is a painful process, a bit like 'grieving'. During the transition phase, where old behavior is being replaced, careful and continuous support is necessary.

On the basis of what we know about adult learning, Willie and Howey (1981) present an argument that the cornerstone of effective staff development should be a knowledge and understanding of adult development, and that this should be reflected in the in-service education of teachers. They argue that as adults mature, there is an increasing life-time *search for intimacy* – a search for relationships in which one individual is able to confide in another, talk about self, and disclose problems without fear of threat or recrimination. Willie and Howey argue that the nature of human relationships and issues of reciprocity and trust should lie at the heart of what teachers do among themselves as professionals. Unfortunately 'most of what we currently refer to as in-service is characterized by sterility and lack of personalization' (Willie and Howey, 1981: 38). What is required instead is that small groups of teachers, who trust one another, work together on an extended basis to deepen that sense of trust and respect by providing each other with 'accurate, precise, and humane feedback about their behavior in the classroom' (ibid.: 38).

A second central aspect is adult *interaction with life's work*. Willie and Howey stress the importance of self-esteem in the workplace. They note, however, that the diminished status of teachers brought about by unreal public expectations, has been met by a form of in-service education that assumes a reactive, teacher deficit stance, with the teacher being viewed as some kind of 'reservoir of techniques and in-service as an additive process through which the number of techniques is increased' (Willie and Howey, 1981: 41).

A third element in adult development, according to Willie and Howey, is the *quest for meaning*. All adults, in varying degrees, seek to uncover purpose or meaning in what they do. The extent to which individuals are introspective about life generally and the world they inhabit, holds important implications for the way they work and the satisfaction derived from it.

The implicit assumption in all of this is that adults learn by doing and benefit most from those activities that combine *action* and *reflection*. Although this revelation comes as no surprise to those who have worked closely with teachers in their own contexts, it is comforting to note, as Berlak and Berlak (1981: 246) do, that 'We have some evidence that teachers learn their craft largely from one another.' Summarizing some of the work that has been done, Blumberg (1980: 231) claims that 'the number of times teachers call upon one another for help or assistance far outweighs the number of times they call upon their formal supervisors or consultants'. Blumberg (1980: 231) suggests that this provides a valuable, albeit often overlooked, potential for a range natural forms of teacher socialization:

> Teachers who interact with their peers learn and practice many of the interpersonal skills and develop the repertoire of tactics they are likely to require for effective supervision. This informal learning situation can present them with the opportunity to engage in the process of identity bargaining, so necessary to developing a working consensus conducive to helping another teacher . . . to develop a capacity for empathy . . . to acquire a sensitivity to knowing which lines of action are most appropriate for a given interpersonal situation; and to become more skilled at employing the interpersonal skills needed to develop a mutual definition of the situation that facilitates one teacher's ability to influence another.

Galloway and Mulhern (1973) carry this point even further by arguing that for far too long school authorities have undersold the potential of teachers as a valued resource for each other in learning about teaching, and in fact by their inaction have unwittingly endorsed a policy of secrecy and defensiveness among teachers. Alfonso and Goldsberry (1982) claim that failing to acknowledge the reality of teachers using each other as resource persons even in the absence of well-articulated and well-endorsed strategies, is paramount to denying teachers the opportunity to develop professionally. In Alfonso and Goldsberry's (1982: 106) words:

> Colleagueship among teachers is typically ignored and often inhibited, by the school's formal organization; consequently, teachers are frequently isolated from their colleagues. This isolation, combined with the dearth of supervisory support, drastically impedes the professional development of even the most conscientious and dedicated teachers. Despite a paucity of research, evidence indicates that systems of intervisitation or colleague consultation seem promising and valued by teachers. . . . It is clear that if supervision is to be improved, its base must be broadened. It is simply not possible for those who carry the formal title of supervisor to have any direct impact on large numbers of teachers.

There seems to be some empirical support for these claims. The research on staff development, so far as it applies to teaching, reached similar conclusions. Joyce and Showers's (1980) analysis of 200 studies found five consistent themes characterizing programmes that were 'effective':

1 Presentation of theory or description of skill strategy.
2 Modelling or demonstration of skills or models of teaching.
3 Practice in simulated and real classroom settings.
4 Structured and open-ended feedback.
5 Coaching for application (hands-on, in-class assistance with transfer of skills and strategies).

Despite difficulty in reviewing the actual research on teacher development because of the lack of rigour for what passed as 'research', Joyce and Showers

important points from their survey of the research. First,
quire new repertoires of classroom practices and, secondly, for
is necessary that a number of distinct elements be present in any
ment strategy. They found, for example, a compelling case for the
n of a theoretical component or the description of a skill strategy for
t was necessary that this be accompanied by a demonstration of the
teac... strategy, followed by extensive practice by teachers in actual classrooms. Above all, they found a need for teachers to be assisted in making the
transfer to the classroom situation, especially through the use of open-ended
feedback about the in-class performance of the strategies being trailed.

Having established that the school site should be the focus, McNergney and
Carrier (1981) have used Hunt's (1975) research to emphasize the importance
of the context in which teachers' development occurs – the specific school, the
specific classroom, the specific concerns of the teacher, and the specific
relationships among the people involved. McNergney and Carrier propose a
personalized teacher development model which recognizes the needs and
abilities of teachers and acknowledges the *interactive* effects of teachers'
histories and learning environments in which they work. They offer a *development* model in that teacher growth is seen as occurring over time, with a
predominant focus on *contemporaneous* issues, or those of interest and
immediacy to teachers. Above all, their model stresses *practicality*, so that the
lives of students and teachers within classrooms can be enriched, and *reciprocity*, or the process of teachers assisting each other to identify individual
strengths and limitations.

Research by Little (1982) concluded that while the common-sense notion
that people learn by experience is hardly new, much less is known about
how this occurs. Little (1982: 331) found that continuous job-embedded
professional development was most likely to occur when:

> teachers engage in frequent, continuous, and increasingly concrete and
> precise talk about teaching practice (as distinct from teacher characteris-
> tics and failings, the social lives of teachers, the foibles and failures of
> students and their families, and the unfortunate demands of society on the
> school). By such talk, teachers build up a shared language adequate to the
> complexity of teaching, capable of distinguishing one practice and its
> virtues from another, and capable of integrating large bodies of practice
> into distinct and sensible perspectives on the business of teaching. Other
> things being equal, the utility of collegial work and the vigor of experi-
> mentation with teaching is a direct function of the *concreteness, precision*,
> and *coherence* of the *shared language*.

Teachers-as-critical-inquirers

The notion of teachers being critical, reflective and responsive to their own and
each other's teaching, is also not new. Since the writings of Dewey (1933),

people have been struggling with feasible ways of actually doing this. There are a plethora of apparently plausible reasons why teachers do not engage in systematic analysis of their teaching – the isolated nature of classrooms, the complexity of classroom life, inadequate time, a lack of observational prowess, anxiety at having their teaching observed, as well as a belief in the craft-like nature of teaching learned largely on the job by processes of trial and error. This reticence on the part of teachers, has been aided and abetted by an educational system that believes standards of teaching should be ensured through externally imposed minimum standards and mechanisms of inspection, accountability and quality control.

That some researchers have been less than charitable in speaking of teachers' self-monitoring capacities is evident in comments by writers such as Jackson (1968) and Lortie (1975). Berlak and Berlak (1981) indicate that educational scholars like Lortie and Jackson do not appear unsympathetic to teachers, yet their comments about teachers' 'conceptual simplicity', 'avoidance of elaborate language', their 'uncomplicated view of causality', their 'unquestioning acceptance of classroom miracles' and their 'intuitive, rather than a rational, approach to classroom events', sound suspiciously like a hegemony in which a low-status group (i.e. teachers) are subordinated and dominated by others (i.e. researchers and administrators). Like Berlak and Berlak (1981: 235), I reject the notion that 'the experts in teaching are not the teachers but scientifically-trained administrators, or educational scholars who study schooling scientifically'. The idea that teachers are only capable of dispensing the 'soft human virtues of patience, understanding and idealism' (ibid.: 235), and are incapable of rigorous and disciplined thinking about their own teaching, is an attitude bordering on the arrogant. As Elliott (1976a: 55) noted:

> The fact that any genuine accountability system embodies the view that teachers are able to identify and diagnose practical problems objectively is very important because it indicates a respect for the teacher as an autonomous person who is capable of improving his own performance in the light of reflection. The fact that this view is not implicit in many current accountability systems is indicative of the low esteem in which teachers are held.

Reticence among teachers towards being reflective and analytic is an indicator of the complexity of the process, and the absence of clearly articulated paradigms and frameworks within which to undertake the task. Speaking of the notion of 'teachers-as-reflective spectators' in their own classrooms, Beasley (1981: 9) put it that:

> because of the complexity of their situation, the end result (of observing their own practice) may have an amorphous quality that makes reflecting on what has occurred very difficult. Teachers and students may at the end of a lesson, for example, have a feeling that it went well or badly but discussing why this was so may remain largely at the level of intuition.

Rather than being despondent because teachers have not acted reflectively in the past, we should speculate instead about possibilities and prospects for the future that may help teachers gain greater control over their own teaching. When teachers do adopt a reflective attitude towards their teaching, actually questioning their own practices (Holly, 1982), then they engage in a process of rendering problematic or questionable those aspects of teaching generally taken for granted. As Dewey (1933) put it, to be reflective was to look back over past experiences, extract their net meanings, and in the process acquire a guide for future encounters of a similar kind. Implicit in Dewey's view was an open-mindedness towards the acceptance of facts from multiple perspectives, a willingness to consider the possibility of alternative (even competing) realities, and the realization that cherished beliefs and practices may have to be challenged and even supplanted. Elliott (1976b: 2) expressed the sentiment of this when he said:

> changes in classroom practice can be brought about only if teachers become conscious of theories and are able to critically reflect about them. Teachers would then be encouraged to reflect about the theories implicit in their own practices and cease to regard them as self-evident.

Put simply, to act reflectively about teaching is to pursue the possibility that existing practices may effectively be challenged, and in the light of evidence about their efficacy be replaced by alternatives. Reflection, critical awareness or enlightenment on its own is insufficient – it must be accompanied by 'action'. The intent is that teachers reach a point where 'the teaching act itself [is seen] as a source of knowledge' (Devaney, 1977: 21).

In recent times, there has been an encouraging growth in field-based studies that focus upon in-class observation and analysis by teachers of their own and each other's teaching (Smyth, 1982). This is possibly in part attributed to a growing realization by school practitioners that they *can* participate as full, active and purposeful agents in the improvement of their professional lives. They are no longer totally dependent on the goodwill and resources of outside experts. It has to do, as well, with the fact that there has been enhanced activity involving teachers in becoming more deliberately reflective and analytic about their teaching through a variety of supportive 'action research' projects (Nixon, 1981; Holly, 1982; Little, 1982; Beasley, 1981; Borthwick, 1982).

There has also been an upsurge in interest among teachers choosing specifically to take up and use the Cogan/Goldhammer model of clinical supervision in a non-hierarchical manner. Cogan (1973: 30) summarized the possibilities for developing insights and understandings when he said 'the teacher should not only learn new behavior but he [*sic*] should understand why he [*sic*] does what he [*sic*] does and why it is better or worse than other things he [*sic*] might do'.

The investigation by Mohlman *et al*. (1982) of the in-service education of secondary teachers using peer observation through clinical supervision found this element to be a 'resounding success'. Teachers were enthusiastic in their sharing of ideas derived from observation of each other's teaching. This squares with similar findings by myself and colleagues. One of the experienced teachers we worked with summed it up when she said of her involvement in clinical supervision, 'it was gratifying to me to find another staff member who was willing to work in partnership with me, and help me in my professional development, and allowing me to participate in a similar manner' (Smyth, 1983a: 18).

The idea of teachers as clinical inquirers in their own classrooms (Smyth, 1982) has a good deal more currency today than a few years ago (Alfonso, 1977). From pessimism about the possibility of peer supervision, albeit still 'a disturbingly slippery concept' (Alfonso, 1977: 595), we seem to have reached the point where teachers are finding it both a workable practice (Goldsberry, 1980; Smyth et al., 1982b) as well as a salutary experience (McCoombe, 1984; Robinson, 1984). They are sufficiently convinced of the value of their 'lived experiences' while experimenting with clinical supervision actually to commit themselves to writing about those experiences for the benefit of other teachers (Beasley and Riordan, 1981; Beasley, 1981).

Notwithstanding the isolationism that still characterizes schools (Flinders, 1988), the persistent shortage of time (Giroux, 1987) and the continuing air of competitiveness among teachers, they have begun to internalize the rationale and intent of mutually supportive processes like clinical supervision by moving beyond the rhetoric and actually adopting action – this is an enormously encouraging sign. When this happens we get closer to the ideal espoused by Eisner (1978: 622) when he wrote:

I would like one day to see schools in which teachers can function as professional colleagues, where part of their professional role was to visit the classrooms of their colleagues, and to observe and share with them in a supportive, informative and useful way what they have seen. Less professional isolation and more professional communication might go a long way to help all teachers secure more distance and hence to better understand their own teaching.

Becoming critical

Being critical in the sense in which I use that term here does not mean being negative but refers rather to the stance of enabling teachers to see their classroom actions in relation to the historical, social and cultural context in which their teaching is actually embedded. This means creating conditions under which teachers, both individually and collectively, can develop for themselves the capacity to view teaching historically; to treat the contemporary events, practices and structures of teaching problematically (and not to take them for granted); and to examine the surface realities of institutionalized schooling in a search for explanations of its forms and thereby to clarify for themselves alternative courses of educational action that are open to them. Acting critically, therefore, refers to 'collaboration in marshalling intellectual capacity so as to focus upon analyzing, reflecting on, and engaging in discourse about the nature and effects of practical aspects of teaching and how they might be altered' (Smyth, 1985a: 9). As Apple (1975: 126) has put it, a socially critical perspective amounts to 'the emancipation of individuals from lawlike rules and patterns of action . . . so that they can reflect and act on the dialectical process of creating and recreating themselves and their institutions'.

Becoming critical and acting reflexively involves developing a realization that 'persons are both the products and the creators of their own history' (Berlak and Berlak, 1981: 230). In practical terms, this means teachers engaging themselves in systematic individual and social forms of investigation that examine the origins and consequences of everyday teaching behaviour, so that they come to see those factors that represent impediments to change. Comstock (1982: 371) summarized it when he said:

> The function of a critical social science is to increase the awareness of social actors of the contradictory conditions of action which are distorted or hidden by everyday understandings. It is founded on the principle that all men and women are potentially active agents in the construction of their social world and their personal lives: that they can be the subjects, rather than the objects, of socio-historical processes. Its aim is self-conscious practice which liberates humans from ideologically frozen conceptions of the actual and the possible.

Placing aside momentarily the rhetoric of 'critical theory', the issue to be addressed now is: what clinical supervision with its commitment to collegiality and collaboration might look like 'on the ground' if it were to be transformed in the way being suggested. This will involve canvassing some of the notions from within critical social theory and suggesting how they may be used to better inform, and hopefully transform, an already existing way of working with teachers.

As a starting point in understanding our teaching actions and those of others, we may need to consider the nature of our 'speech acts' (Habermas, 1979) and the way these ordinary actions have subtle communicative effects that are often characterized by mistrust and distortion. As Forester (1980: 276) put it:

> Such distortions of pretense, misrepresentation, dependency-creation, and ideology are communicative influences with immobilizing, de-politicizing, and subtly but effectively disabling consequences. To isolate and reveal the debilitating power of such systematically distorted communications, Habermas seeks to contrast these with ordinary, common sense communication of mutual understanding and consensus which makes any shared knowledge possible in the first place.

What is essentially at stake here is enabling teachers to move beyond being ignorant of the traditions of their own teaching, to a position in which they are able to understand how communicative structures of schooling are systematically but hierarchically distorted. To use Forester's (1980: 277) words again: 'They are able to see how existing social and political-economic relations actually operate as distorted communications, obscuring issues, manipulating trust and consent, twisting fact and possibility.'

As we saw earlier, an exclusive concern with the technical act of teaching can prevent more important questions from being asked. An example, taken from the area of curriculum improvement, may serve to illustrate the point about how to shift the analysis of teaching to a different plane. In an Australian study by Cooper and Meyenn (1984), a group of staff developers embarked on a 3-year programme aimed at bringing about educational change through assisting a school and its community to develop and implement an alternative elementary school mathematics curriculum. The aim was to refocus the schools' mathematics curriculum and to help teachers to change their orientations. To all intents the facilitators appeared to have the interests of teachers, children and the local community very much in mind as they carefully negotiated all aspects of what was involved. Substantial changes did in fact occur. At the conclusion of their work, the facilitators reflected on what had been achieved. While they had got the technicalities of curriculum development and improvement right, they considered that they failed dismally to change any of the social relationships in the school. Cooper and Meyenn (1984: 143) put it as follows:

At the beginning of a project an incident was observed that was very important to one of the author's motivation to become involved. While supervising student practice at a preschool next to the project school, he observed a 'bright eyed' five year old girl, who seemed to exhibit an eagerness for learning, perform mathematically above her peers. It was winter. The preschool was not well heated. The young girl was poorly and very lightly dressed. She was shivering. The teachers said she came irregularly and was often 'blue' with cold when she arrived. She seemed to come from an environment which, to the teachers, appeared quite deprived. The whole meaning of the project was encapsulated for this author in doing something to the school so children like this could, if they wished, use the school to improve their life chances. When the project ended over two years later, one of the last classes observed contained this child. She was still poorly dressed and still appeared as eager to learn and please as before. The teacher of this class had changed his approach to mathematics over the years of the project. He now used more materials and tried to get children actively involved. The class sat in a circle and discussed measurement. Children were selected for tasks. But not all. Time passed. This child, so eager, was left doing nothing but watching others. The class broke up in disarray as others, who had also been left out, began to wander and play. The teacher was too involved with those who were on tasks to supervise. This child did not join with the others. She waited to be noticed, quietly, where she had been told to stay. In the end she started, for something to do, to stack material left out in neat piles. She had been given no mathematics that would widen her life chances but had been given another lesson on her place in the world. How much longer could her eagerness remain? The author was devastated. After hours of talking, planning and acting, there could, it seemed, be no more savage indictment of the project's failure to come to grips with what was supposed to be its central aim.

And so, too, it should be with processes like clinical supervision. We need to sharpen our focus on the significant and avoid what Murray (1975: 8) describes as 'getting permanently lost in the Pedagogical Provinces while the Province itself flounders'.

Through his discussion of a 'method for critical research', Comstock (1982) provides some 'pointers' as to how we might reconstrue clinical supervision so that the unexamined and taken-for-granted become a prime focus. The critical approach begins, Comstock (1982: 378) says, with the 'life problems of . . . individuals, groups or classes that are oppressed by and alienated from the social processes they maintain or create but do not control'. Given the long history of various forms of inspection, teacher evaluation and quality control that have gone under the guise of school improvement, it is not difficult to cast teachers in the oppressive role Comstock envisages. For example, the effective control of curriculum, pedagogy and evaluation are increasingly coming to be orchestrated beyond the classroom door.

Working critically with teachers requires a 'facilitator' or 'critical friend' (i.e. colleague) assisting them in uncovering the understandings they hold about the social dynamics of their own settings, and how these came about historically. This involves, first, developing a dialogue through and by which teachers are able to see contemporary events that constrain them, but to view them against the historical legacy that spawned them. Although Comstock (1982) had in mind an 'outsider' enacting this facilitating role, what I am suggesting here is that by using teaching colleagues, 'insiders' can use forms like clinical supervision to effectively challenge and change the status quo. Secondly, it involves enabling teachers to see themselves as potentially active agents who have a stake in altering the oppressive circumstances in which they are technicians implementing somebody else's curriculum, pedagogy and evaluation. The following sections identify several stages in this process.

Enabling teachers to see the nature of ideological domination

Strategically, this involves teachers in helping other teachers to render an account of their contemporary situation as a basis for an ideology critique. The agenda, in Comstock's (1982: 379) words, is to provide a dialectic by which 'micro-analyses of particular struggles will serve to modify and elaborate macro-theories. Critical micro- and macro-analysis thus proceed in dialectical tension and unity.' For clinical supervision, this means developing and fostering extensive group-based dialogue well before the commencement of the four-stage cycle of clinical supervision itself outlined in the Introduction. A broader question to be focused on would be the contemporary and historical place of teachers in controlling the evaluation of their own practices. For example, teachers might begin collectively to reflect upon why it is that bureaucratized educational systems have been able so successfully to control their lives and work, effectively keeping them in their institutional places. They may speculate on how this form of control has had practical consequences for what transpires within schools, and how this orchestration has affected students. Teachers might also examine the extent to which they are the originators of their own actions, versus pawns in working through somebody else's agendas. Connections need to be made between the local scene, in which teachers are embedded, and actions occurring at regional and national levels that have the effect of keeping teachers in their places.

Uncovering the interpretive understandings teachers hold of their world

How teachers account for their own actions and how they condone and rationalize the actions of others, such as administrators, is central to what Comstock labels the search for 'differentiated meaning'. The attempt for teachers is to ascertain through dialogue with other teachers, how and in what ways their meanings are differentiated among themselves, and how these can provide a basis for pointing up contradictions and ideologically distorted self-understandings. It is through beginning to engage in dialogue with colleagues about the intersubjective meanings they hold about the nature of teaching and learning, that teachers come to see the structural basis of the meanings, values and motives they hold. They come to see the essentially historical nature of human action and of how those actions 'take place within a context pre-conditioned by the sedimentations of the past' (Piccone, 1973: 141). The kind of questions that might be included here are:

- What does it mean to be a teacher?
- What is the nature of knowledge about teaching; who creates it, who holds it, and whose interests does it serve?
- In what ways can self-evaluation of the clinical supervision kind uncover myths about teaching and contradictions between intent and action?
- How can teaching result in changing the life chances of children?

Historical conditions that constrain and shape teachers' understandings

It is important that teachers be assisted to see through investigation and analysis that control over the generation of knowledge about teaching has in the past been vested in the hands of non-teachers. For example, there has been a deliberate and thinly veiled policy in educational systems, aided and abetted by universities and educational research and development agencies, that teachers be kept in positions of subservience. This has been reinforced by the bureaucratic ways in which schools are organized so as to perpetuate the myth of accountability to outside constituencies, and results in the further oppression of teachers by the degrading processes of supervision, evaluation and rating.

Teachers need to be encouraged to undertake investigations that allow them to see clearly for themselves how these circumstances came to be in their own particular context. Teachers have to be able to see how conditions are not the 'consequences of immutable laws, but ... structures and processes constructed by elites with specific interests and intentions' (Comstock, 1982: 382). Indeed, these investigative undertakings need to be sufficiently plausible for teachers to be able to see in the accounts they uncover, events, issues and processes that will enable them to readily identify areas to be targeted for change.

Linking historical conditions with the contemporary forces that maintain them ·

Having considered and described the social processes and structures that caused particular circumstances to come about in the first place, teachers need assistance in seeing how contemporary practices serve to reinforce and maintain the legitimacy of those conditions. It is, after all, only by engaging teachers in a dialectic between 'their historically created conditions' (Comstock, 1982: 383) and their current situations that it becomes possible to see present relationships for what they are.

A controversial example may serve to make the point. In recent times, we have seen a flurry of rhetoric on school improvement and effective schools aimed at requiring schools to 'lift their game' and remedy the alleged failure of schools to meet the technical and scientific needs of industry. This is in effect a human capital view of schooling that has its wider origins in the relationship between labour and capital. Shapiro (1984: 12) put it this way:

> While improvements in scientific and technical training are high on the list of educational proposals as the means to improve productivity, it is possible to detect slightly more old-fashioned means to increase industrial output. While it is clear that such suggestions concern only the behavior of adolescents in schools, not adult workers, it is probably not too fantastic to believe that there is in these recommendations some implicit statement concerning the need to ensure a less lackadaisical, more disciplined work force, better prepared to accept long hours of labor and less prone to tardiness and absenteeism. Thus, there are . . . frequent statements of the need to lengthen the school day and the school year; the need to implement attendance policies with 'clear sanctions as incentives' to reduce absenteeism and tardiness; the need for increased

homework assignments and a more rigorous regimen of testing. For both teachers and students there is a common message – one which in the name of higher productivity insists on the increased scrutiny of individual performances, a more thorough system of monitoring skill levels, and a more pervasive use of ranking in order to maximize output. While there is no simple one-to-one correspondence between what happens in schools and in industry, the accelerating obsession with output, performance and productivity in both places, is surely part of the accelerating zeitgeist of our time.

Shapiro's (1984) thesis is that the rush of reports on schooling that portray the USA as a nation at risk amount to no more than 'business as usual'. What is being proposed is nothing profoundly new but rather a reaffirmation of what already exists – all in the interests of exhorting schools to meet industrial needs, to pursue scientific preparation to counter the Soviets, Japanese or whoever, and for forms of socialization within schools that guarantee discipline in the workplace. In similar vein, Braverman (1975) portrays contemporary economic conditions with jobs becoming increasingly fragmented and subdivided so as to cause a growing gulf between those who conceptualize tasks and those who execute them. Whereas this used to be restricted to factory-type occupations, this fragmentation is coming increasingly to characterize white-collar and office jobs as work becomes 'measured, monitored for cost effectiveness, and minutely regulated' (Shapiro, 1984: 14). The reality is that people are becoming:

> locked into situations of intellectual and spiritual starvation, condemned to hierarchical settings in which workers' responsibilities are minutely circumscribed, capacities restricted and narrowly defined, and ability to make judgements replaced by authoritarian control (Shapiro, 1984: 15).

Little wonder that schools have come to reflect the emptiness and alienation of society generally. To quote Shapiro (1984: 16) again:

> The ability to penetrate, critically analyze and apprehend the false and distorting messages of the dominant ideology leave us helpless in a world where human experience is so often misrepresented or mystified by those who provide us with the shared meanings of our culture.

The dialectic between the macro and micro becomes evident enough when we observe how the struggles are actually played out in the school setting. Cooper and Meyenn (1984: 143) took mathematics as their example:

> It became clear that there was a considerable 'hidden curriculum' and that mathematics was used as a convenient vehicle to inculcate attitudes and values seen as appropriate by the social structure. For most children, mathematics is boring, poorly understood, usually pointless and very repetitive. Children who receive high marks for mathematics can be considered to have proved to the world, and to prospective employers,

that they can put up with boring work (and even find some satisfaction in it) and that they can get on with tasks they do not really understand or see any relevance for. It is easy to argue (as do Bowles and Gintis, 1976) that these are the types of people, rather than those who challenge and question, that society wants schools to produce.

Assisted forms of self-evaluation like clinical supervision enable teachers to collect the evidence on issues like this necessary for them to analyse their contexts and to reveal how organizational practices and structures reproduce and reinforce the status quo.

Isolating the contradictions in current actions

So much of what teachers do in schools appears to be habituated and originates from social conditions over which they are effectively prevented from exercising deliberate control. Because they are embedded in their actions, while they are enacting them, teachers are often blinded to the kaleidoscope of events and issues and may become unaware of many of the unintended consequences that arise from these ideological distortions. It is in uncovering the fundamental contradictions within their practice that it becomes possible for teachers to see how their intentions are thwarted and unrealizable.

Berlak and Berlak (1981) provide the very interesting and illuminating example of Mr Scott, a grade 4 elementary teacher in a British school, as an instance of how teachers live with incoherence and contradiction not of their own making, and of how they seek to cope. Mr Scott has a particular point of view that endorses the importance of mathematics for elementary students. On a particular day, from his vantage point in the middle of the room, Mr Scott scans the classroom, his eyes resting upon individuals, pairs and trios some of whom are working, while others are engaged in extraneous conversations. On this occasion, his eyes rest momentarily longer on Steven and Bruce who are sitting together; yesterday they had been on opposite sides of the room. They are intently examining football cards and deep in conversation, their mathematics exercises cast aside. Mr Scott chooses to ignore Steven and Bruce and goes to assist Mary who has her hand raised. Mr Scott's action of ignoring Steven rests somewhat uneasily with his subsequent indication to Steven that he must correctly solve a minimum number of mathematics problems or be deprived of a sporting privilege.

Snippets of conversations with Mr Scott on these events are insightful (Berlak and Berlak, 1981: 126–7):

> Steven is a very creative boy and he can't settle down to work; he's got to be left alone before he produces his best work . . .
>
> I separated the football fanatics and they became miserable, so I let them sit together again. I don't want them to be miserable . . .
>
> I have yet to come to grips with myself about what a child should do in, for

instance, mathematics. Certainly I feel that children should as far as possible follow their own interests and not be dictated to all the time, but then again . . . I feel pressure from . . . I don't really know how to explain it, but there's something inside you that you've developed over the years which says that children should do this. . . . I still feel that I've somehow got to press them on with their mathematics.

Berlak and Berlak (1981: 129–31) seek to analyse critically the contradictions that appear to be implicit in what Mr Scott has done in the contemporary circumstances and how past events live on into the present:

Mr. Scott this morning walks past Steven rather than telling him to get back to work. One could view this as a non-event since Mr. Scott did not do anything to Steven. However, this 'non-event' stands out for several reasons – because he treats Steven somewhat differently than the others and differently than he did yesterday. It also stands out because Steven isn't doing his maths, and Mr. Scott, in word and deed, considers maths an especially important part of the work of the school. How can we make sense of this non-event? . . . [A]s Mr. Scott tells us about Steven's 'creativity', about the misery of the football fanatics when they were separated from one another, about the pressure he feels to get the 'fourth years' to progress, as he tells us what in his view lies behind what he did, we discern his response to Steven as part of a pattern. This pattern includes both his bypassing of Steven and his later confrontation of him . . .

As Mr. Scott talks to us and as we watch him teach, it becomes apparent that he is responding with some degree of awareness to a wide range of contradictory social experiences and social forces, past and contemporary, both in his classroom, his school and beyond him in the wider community. He has internalized these contradictions and they are now 'within' him.

Implicit in Mr. Scott's responses over the course of any period of time are alternatives he perceives that have arisen from previous social experience with others, encounters with his wife, children, friends, former teachers, parents, his present colleagues and superiors, children in his classes now and over the years, and indirect encounters – watching and/or listening to people via the media, or reading fiction, biography and the daily press. The past that is in the present situation includes . . . Mr. Scott's reconsideration of Steven's talents and weaknesses only yesterday when he for a moment recalled one of his own painful school experiences . . .

As Mr. Scott directs Steven back to his mathematics work, what we observe may be the manifestation of a continuous tension within him that includes both 'beliefs' and values; for example he may believe that if Steven (and boys like him) do not 'buckle down' they are destined for second-class citizenship, . . . or that if . . . the Head sees the boys messing about with trading cards during maths, he will lower his estimation of Mr.

Scott's professional competence – hence influence the recommendation he receives when he applies for a headship to which he . . . aspires. The dialectic may be said to include what are commonly termed 'values' – his unexamined and frequently expressed commitment to the 'work ethic', the importance of making it in a society which he believes rewards mathematics competence. . . . The dialectic cannot be said to be a process that is either engaged in freely or shaped entirely by outside circumstances; it is both. Both Mr. Scott's 'beliefs' and 'values' have been shaped by social, political and economic circumstances . . .

Although Mr. Scott's perspective on 'getting ahead' may have been profoundly shaped by his history, it may also have been influenced by his reflections upon history, by his self-conscious observations that the competitive and individualistic culture has shaped his teaching but in ways he does not presently approve and will attempt to alter . . .

As he goes about teaching at any given moment, Mr. Scott is pulled and pushed towards numbers of alternative and apparently contradictory behaviors. One set of alternatives is whether to allow Steven to discuss the football cards – or to chastise the child, or in one way or another remind him that he must complete his maths – but at any given moment Mr. Scott cannot both remind and overlook.

In this instance, one pair of conflicting tendencies underlying the observable behavior is, on the one hand, toward allowing Steven to enjoy the present, and on the other, insisting he forego the pleasure of the present in order to be prepared for the future.

In circumstances such as those portrayed about Mr Scott, the attempt is for teachers working with other teachers to begin to see how while it may be impracticable to reclaim the past, a knowledge of the past nevertheless points to breaks and discontinuities that cause ideological distortions and contradictions in the present. The real challenge lies in teachers coming to work with colleagues like Mr Scott in educative ways that enable them to develop strategic forms of action. This is not to suggest that through this means that teachers will be offered 'the means to freedom in the sense of lifting them out of the causal realm altogether, thereby making their feelings and actions in some sense uncaused' (Fay, 1977: 212). Rather, what is being suggested is the notion of using processes like clinical supervision to allow them to become autonomous agents capable of reflecting on and acting upon their work settings.

When not construed as a way of tinkering with the technical skills of teaching, clinical supervision has the potential to enable teachers to collect and analyse data about equity, gender, class and race issues in their teaching and to challenge and supplant many of their taken-for-granted assumptions about these issues. Teachers *can* collaboratively move beyond the 'surface' curriculum to search out and begin to alter the 'hidden' curriculum. An illustration may serve to make the point:

A physical education teacher was concerned about her feelings that she held quite different standards and expectations for boys and girls. When she had her colleague conference with her, collect information on a particular lesson, and analyze it afterwards, the situation was as she had suspected. Her directions to students revealed a different set of expectations based on sex stereotypes. What puzzled teacher and colleague was what 'caused' her to be the way she was. Discussion and reflection on the issue led them to conclude that there were strong historical, rather than personal forces, at work. The teacher's action was, in a sense, shaped by the cultural expectation that boys are stronger, more agile, and display greater physical aggressiveness than girls; this was a cultural image that was powerfully reinforced by the media. Having attained this kind of consciousness about her own actions, the teacher was able to begin operating in different ways (adapted from Berlak and Berlak, 1981).

Using educative and empowering forms of action

Fay (1977) speaks of the critical perspective in the 'educative' sense as enabling teachers to problematize (i.e. problem posing rather than problem solving) the settings in which they work, so as to remove the blinkers that have blinded them from seeing and acting in alternate ways. In his words (Fay, 1977: 210):

> The point . . . is to free people from causal mechanisms that had heretofore determined their existence in some important way, by revealing both the existence and the precise nature of these mechanisms and thereby depriving them of their power. This is what is meant by aid[ing] people who are objects in the world in transforming themselves into active subjects who are self determining.

For Fay (1977), the first step in this educative process of teachers altering the patterns of interaction that characterize and inhibit their social relationships, comes when teachers work with one another in ways that amount to changing their understandings of themselves. By this he means from one of dependence to one of autonomy and responsibility. Through dialogue between themselves, teachers can problematize issues they want to work upon in their own practice. Having grasped a historical understanding of how their frustrating conditions came about in the first place, teachers are able to initiate and sustain a collaborative process of planning, acting, collecting data, reflecting and reformulating plans for further action. Having initiated this process for themselves, teachers might seek the aid of an outside 'facilitator' *only* when they feel it might be helpful. For example, they may see it as useful for an outsider to assist as they struggle to generate accounts of their actions that reflect the problematizing process and its concomitant dialogue and collaborative reflection.

It is at this stage that the cycle of clinical supervision becomes indispensable as a method by which teachers confer, problematize, act, collect data and reflect on actions prior to reformulating plans. Using clinical supervision in this way, teachers not only change the technicalities of their teaching, but begin to transform the conditions, the structures and the practices of their teaching. What is significant about clinical supervision used in this problem-posing way, is that it is part of a much wider generative process of examining teaching, uncovering issues, and working to reconstrue them in fundamentally different ways. Viewed thus, clinical supervision is not something 'tacked on' at the end, but rather part of a continuous cycle of critical analysis, education and action (Comstock, 1982).

For processes like clinical supervision to work in ways that foster genuine collegiality and enable teachers to take charge of their individual and joint practices, we need social relationships that permit this to happen. While blueprints are not readily available on how this might happen, the Boston Women's Teachers' Group (Freedman *et al.*, 1983b) made some insightful comments when reporting on work they undertook into contradictions within their own practices. They concluded:

> Teachers frequently expressed a general sense of efficacy in their class-rooms, amply documented by anecdotes . . . , that was lacking or allowed to go unnoticed in the area beyond the classroom. . . . It was in their attempt to extend the discussion into the areas outside the classroom walls that teachers experienced the greatest resistance – whether this referred to community meetings with parents, whole-school discussions of school climate, or attempts to link one teacher's issues with another's. Pressure from outside support groups, and federal and state programs mandating teacher involvement, afforded the few possibilities for lever-age teachers experienced in confronting systemwide reforms (ibid.: 297).

What Freedman *et al.* (1983b) were arguing for was a sense of being a professional that meant a lot more than 'facing the issues alone' – a situation that frequently culminates in the unrewarding consequences of 'bitter self-recrimination or alienation from teachers, parents and students' (ibid.: 298). They were concerned about moving beyond the bankrupt solution of blaming the victim, namely, disaffected teachers. Rather, they saw the problem as one of working on the contradictory demands made on teachers and the institutional structures that create and prevent their resolution. In the words of Freedman *et al.* (1983b: 299):

> Teachers must now begin to turn the investigation of schools away from scapegoating individual teachers, students, parents, and administrators towards a systemwide approach. Teachers must recognize how the structure of schools control their work and deeply affects their relation-ship with fellow teachers, their students, and their students' families. Teachers must feel free to express these insights and publicly voice their concerns.

Conclusion

In this chapter, I have highlighted the view that school change is not the rational deliberate process that some people would have us believe. One of the realities of schooling is that teachers possess their own theories about what they do, what is reasonable, feasible and possible in classroom teaching. This is invariably knowledge based upon lived experiences, rather than the wisdom of outside experts. Far too little regard seems to have been paid in the past by school authorities and policy makers to workable ways in which teachers *can* and *do* use colleagues as important and valued resource persons. Recent studies suggest that teachers *do* learn from their individual and collective experiences, and are able to share their expertise among themselves when they engage in 'frequent, continuous, and increasingly concrete and precise talk about teaching practice' (Little, 1982: 331). The idea of teachers acting in critical, reflective and responsive ways about their own teaching is gaining increasing acceptance as teachers begin to see the inherent possibilities in developing shared or collaborative frameworks of meaning about teaching.

In the current context of moves in some quarters towards teachers acquiring increasing control over their own classroom practice, clinical supervision is increasingly being seen as a viable means. The non-judgemental and genuinely collaborative intent of clinical supervision enables teachers working together in a consultative relationship to gain data-based insights that were difficult, if not impossible, under normal conditions of classroom isolation, and certainly impossible where the strategy was used as a thinly disguised form of inspection and quality control. While clinical supervision will no doubt continue to be used in some quarters as a way of not so subtly controlling teachers, the most exciting possibilities are likely to occur in those situations where teachers are able to use the process to gain a window on their own teaching and in the process to arrive at an understanding of what it means to engage in truly emancipatory learning.

I pointed to how clinical supervision arose in response to the need to provide teachers with ways of working with other teachers that were directed towards enabling them to control their own professional development. In that it had a democratic intent, clinical supervision was seen to be dramatically different from hierarchical, managerial and manipulative forms of supervision which rely on inspection, quality control and administrative sanction. Historically, these oppressive forms of supervision were necessary as a way of restricting entry into the teaching force, but they came to be forms of endorsement for particular views of teaching. These managerial forms with their primary emphasis on standardization, efficiency and control came also to be ways of legitimating a form of social engineering that was linked to a meritocratically organized social and economic class system.

Goldhammer's attempt, therefore, to free supervision from its 'watchdog origins' was far more than an attempt to move it into the fashionable 'human relations era'. What he had in mind was a systematic data-based way of teachers working with other teachers that dispensed with judgemental preconceptions and emphasized the personal empowerment of teachers to understand the wider social contexts of teaching and learning through collaborative and collegial alliances.

As with so many good ideas in teaching, the well-intentioned notion of clinical supervision has become distorted through the process of redefinition as vested interests have worked to reconstrue clinical supervision in the image of the inspectorial mode. While these moves have been malevolent in some cases and amount to openly espousing the use of clinical supervision to evaluate and rate teachers, on other occasions the effect has been far more subtle but no less devastating. Those who propose clinical supervision as an instrumental form of fine-tuning teaching so teachers become better at doing more of the same, are pushing a conservative line that effectively forces teachers to think about the means of teaching, rather than focusing on the more important ends.

What I am suggesting is that if we build upon clinical supervision, as originally conceived, then we move in the direction of a process that has the capacity to enable teachers to question taken-for-granted assumptions about their own teaching, and that furthermore, has the potential to allow them to challenge the structures and constraints within which that teaching occurs. Viewed in this way, teachers can become enamoured with a way of genuinely reforming teaching, not just with a technique to remedy perceived deficiencies.

My thesis in this chapter has been that through collaboration and non-evaluative dialogue, teachers can employ clinical supervision as an educative way of uncovering the historical antecedents of actions that live on in the present as contemporary contradictions that impede and frustrate change. Seeing how the particular struggles in which they are involved are not isolated aberrations but inextricably linked to processes that have deeper social origins, is a crucial part of being a teacher. In order to succeed in bringing about reforms that have any chance of making schooling more practical, realistic and just, teachers also need to see how existing practices reinforce and legitimate those conditions. By isolating these kind of tensions and seeing them for what they are, teachers are not only able to see the discrepancies that exist between the actual and the possible, but they are able to work towards the kind of collaborative involvement necessary to change that state of affairs.

6

Developing and sustaining the critical

Introduction

It is interesting to speculate on what lies behind the recent surge of interest in what might broadly be described as a reflective approach in the continuing professional education of teachers (Erickson and Grimmett, 1988). While there is a good deal of contention at the moment as to precisely what this means, it is clear that we have been down a very similar track before, most notably with the work of Dewey (1965) earlier this century. So what makes the current revival, if that is what it is, so significant? For an answer to that we have to look carefully to the social, economic and political times in which we live, and at the way in which the emphasis on reflective approaches represents something of a calculated response to the prevailing views about the nature of schooling and knowledge. There can be little doubt that as we rush headlong into this era of neo-conservative ways of thinking and acting educationally, the reflective approach represents an interesting and challenging counter-discourse to the ensconced technicist views. At the same time that we are being increasingly courted and urged by technologically minded policy makers and educational reformers (the 'can do men') into believing that all our social and economic ills will somehow magically dissolve if we place our faith in their capacity to get the mix of techniques right, significant questions are being asked as to whether the applied science mentality that lies behind their thinking and their strategies has the efficacy to resolve the complex issues in the ways being suggested.

In this chapter, I want to make a crucial theoretical and practical advance on the work of Schön (1983) discussed in Chapter 3, by pointing to some of its major limitations and by offering an alternative that has potential for teachers in their work as reflective practitioners in clinical supervision. In particular, I want to propose that in order to develop and sustain a critical form of pedagogy, teachers need to be concerned with four forms or moments; namely, those of:

- describing . . . (what do I do?);
- informing . . . (what does this description mean?);
- confronting . . . (how did I come to be like this?); and
- reconstructing . . . (how might I do things differently?).

It is clear that the work of Schön (1983, 1987), spoken about at length in Chapter 3, has been important. Indeed, it seems that Schön's work has come to be something of a significant rallying point for besieged liberal progressive educators who are under tremendous threat at the moment as a consequence of the new ice age of educational conservatism. Connelly and Clandinin (1988: 1) regard as quite remarkable 'the speed with which Schön's . . . recent works [have] penetrated the reference lists of teacher education writers'.

I have argued so far in this book that Schön's work provides a useful focus with which to reinforce and keep alive the tradition of experiential knowledge, but it is his substantive arguments that I see as being of major importance. In the face of widespread and continuing demands for technocratic ways of operating, he argues that proposals for more stringent forms of accountability based on research evidence (in teaching or wherever), are entirely wrongheaded. The problem has more to do with a deep-seated 'crisis of confidence' (as distinct from 'competence'), that amounts to a manifest inability of the professions to deliver solutions on the environmental, economic and social problems of our times. As we have seen, his claims are rooted in the argument that those who persist in presenting the view that professional practice should have a demonstrated 'scientific' basis to it, and that it should adhere closely to prescriptions deriving from large-scale, objective, outsider-initiated research, ignore the extent to which *practitioner-derived knowledge* is, in fact, trustworthy and relevant in and of itself (see Smyth, 1987d). By choosing to focus exclusively on the 'products' of other people's research at the expense of the 'process' by which understandings are reached, proponents of such views actually misconstrue the value of research which lies not in it being definitive, but rather in the tentativeness of research as something to be explored, confirmed or rejected in the light of experience. All of this is by way of countering the point that continuing to seize upon the instrumental applicability of other people's research findings about professional practice, is tantamount to placing a level of certainty on research that social scientists themselves would deny. For Schön (1983), shifting from 'problem solving' to 'problem setting' (or problem posing) involves fundamentally rethinking how we view professional practice and the relationship between theory and practice. Increasingly, professionals of all kinds (teachers included) are being confronted by situations in which the tasks they are required to perform no longer bear any relationship to the tasks for which they have been educated: 'The situations of practice are not problems to be solved but problematic situations characterized by uncertainty, disorder and indeterminacy' (Schön,

1983: 15–16). Teachers, in particular, are becoming increasingly engulfed in wrangles over conflicting and competing values and purposes and are often 'faced with pressures for increased efficiency in the context of contracting budgets, demands that they rigorously "teach the basics" exhortations to encourage creativity, build citizenship, [and to] help students examine their values' (ibid.: 17).

However, having acknowledged the importance of Schön's work and its contribution to the education of teachers generally, there is a very worrying aspect to his work that makes it problematic. What is missing from his conceptualization is any acknowledgement of the socially constructed nature of knowledge. His notion of the reflective appears to remain trapped within a psychologistic framework that regards knowledge as being acquired solely through the systematic application of cognitive skills to particular situations and contexts. There is an extensive body of literature extending back to the seminal work of people like Mills (1959) and Berger and Luckman (1966) to mention a few, that suggests this is a limited interpretation. We fail to get a strong sense in Schön's writing that 'problem posing' is a form of social reflection that involves people in undertaking dialogue about concrete experiences, and about how they can support one another in overcoming the constraints that cause them to accept extant structures of power. In other words, there is a political dimension to Schön's work that is totally missing. For example, there appears to be no understanding that in order to replace dominant forms of discipline-based knowledge with more informative practitioner-derived alternatives, we need processes that involve 'forms of critique which [are] relentless in the task of unmasking the lies, myths, and distortions that construct . . . the basis for the dominant order' (Giroux and Freire, 1987: xii). Fay (1977: 221) summed up what I am getting at when he spoke about the need to move the idea of reflection outside of 'the relatively individualistic world of psychological rehabilitation into the wider public world of concerted social and political action'. Drawing upon the ideas of Freire, Fay argues that educators need to see their social settings as offering 'limit situations' to be transcended. Fay's (1977: 224–5) fundamental point is that:

> What matters is not only the fact that people come to have particular self-understanding, and that this new self-understanding provides the basis for altering social arrangements, but also the manner in which they come to adopt this new 'guiding idea'.

Challenging practices as a consequence of national self-understanding is one thing, but it is insufficient for any kind of lasting change because all of the preconditions for recidivism remain intact. It is only through reason and the force of argument which occurs in an environment characterized by 'persuasion, argumentation, debate, criticism, analysis [and] education' (ibid.: 229), that people are able to see how they have become 'unwitting accomplices' in sustaining forms of knowledge that actually work against their own best interests. For Fay (1977: 230), this educative mode of reflection occurs in specific kinds of situations:

> These settings are groups that are relatively small, relatively egalitarian (in the sense that no member has command over another without another's approval), relatively free of recrimination between members, relatively committed to rationally discussing its members' situations and experiences, and relatively insistent that its members take responsibility for whatever claims, decisions, or actions they undertake to make. Only within settings like these can 'consciousness raising' based on rational reflection apparently take place.

The kind of theorizing that Fay has in mind is 'essentially a subversive activity' (ibid.: 233) because of the way it is directed at those who benefit from arrangements the way they currently exist.

We get no indication from Schön's writing of the importance of this discursive and dialogical dimension. Maybe there is a reason for that – perhaps he also regards it as a subversive activity, and to be avoided, in which case there are some questions that could be raised about whether he is genuinely concerned about authentic liberating change, or whether he has a more cosmetic view of what should happen. It is an intriguing question as to whether examining how people 'think in action', has the kind of ingredients necessary to enable them to break outside of the causal conditions that made them that way in the first place.

Impediments to empowerment

While it is true that the largely undefined call for a reflective approach within teaching has occurred as a consequence of moves to empower teachers, particularly in a climate characterized by centralized authorities acting in ways to reduce teacher autonomy, many of these calls are remarkably unreflexive of their own agenda. Indeed, the way the term is picked up and used on some occasions, itself generates major problems. Liston and Zeichner (1987: 2) argue that reflection is becoming something of an 'educational slogan . . . that lacks sufficient conceptual elaboration and programmatic strength'. As Gore (1987) points out, what happens in circumstances like these is that people like Cruickshank (1985) are able to use it as a way of appearing to give legitimation to a focus on the pedagogical and behavioural skills of teachers (or the means of teaching), to the exclusion of the ends or valued social and moral purposes to which teaching is (or should be) directed. For example, while Cruickshank and Applegate (1981: 553) define reflection in terms of 'helping teachers to think about what happened, why it happened, and what else they could have done to reach their goals', it is clear that their conception of the reflective amounts to nothing short of prescribing what teachers ought to teach within tight guidelines, while co-opting one another into policing the implementation of predetermined goals. Activity of this kind, gives the reflective approach a bad name!

Whether we are speaking about a reflective stance for experienced teachers or neophytes, it is important that the process be clearly seen to be based on moves that actively recognize and endorse the decidedly historical, political, theoretical and moral nature of teaching. When teaching is removed from an analysis of contextual determinants like those within which it is located, it comes to take on the aura of a technical process. The notion of reflection is not, therefore, related at all to passive deliberation or contemplation – a meaning which is sometimes ascribed to reflection in everyday life. What I am arguing for here is a notion of the reflective that is both *active* and *militant* (Mackie, 1980; Shor, 1987), and that is concerned with infusing action with a sense of power and politics, and which reintroduces into the discourse about teaching and schooling a concern for the 'ethical, personal and political' (Beyer and Apple, 1988: 4). Beyer and Apple (1988: 4) put this succinctly:

It involves both conscious understanding of and actions in schools on solving our daily problems. These problems will not go away by themselves, after all. But it also requires critically reflective practices that alter the material and ideological conditions that cause the problems we are facing as educators in the first place.

Clearly, the major impediment (but at the same time the major challenge) to the reflective approach have been recent attempts to 'reform' schooling in the direction of harnessing schools to the requirements of the economy by ensuring that what goes on *inside* schools is directly responsive to the economic needs *outside* of schools. In large measure, this has meant deliberately constructing the mythology that somehow schools and teachers are the cause of the economic failure, but if certain narrowly prescribed forms of action (a return to the teaching of basic skills; better teacher appraisal schemes; tighter classroom discipline; longer school days; more sophisticated performance indicators; state-wide testing; performance budgeting; and other cost-efficient and cost-effective measures) are adopted, then schools can be magically restored to their rightful role as servants of the economy (Walker and Barton, 1987). The claim of the policy-making technocrats is that it is just a matter of entrusting schools to them so that they can come up with the right mix of variables to be prescribed for teachers to follow in achieving the required strategic, economic and social goals. It is precisely this kind of 'common-sense' thinking which is in fact imbued with all manner of undisclosed political agendas that ought to be the object of discussion about teaching and teacher education, more generally. To paraphrase a comment by Dippo (1988: 486), teachers as practitioners ought to be provided with

the tools and resources they need to recognize, analyze, and address the contradictions, and in so doing open-up the possibility that conditions in schools . . . can be different. . . . [S]uch empowering educational goals

[are] clearly linked to the larger political project of redefining existing social and economic relations.

Tom (1985) also points out that while always a minority viewpoint, the reflective (or inquiry-oriented) approach to teaching goes back a long way, but that the confusion arises is in respect of what is defined as the 'arena of the problematic'. As Tom (1985: 37) puts it, while there is a view that 'to make teaching problematic is to raise doubts about what, under ordinary circumstances, appears to be effective or wise practice', the object of that problematizing (or reflective action) is by no means agreed upon. According to him, 'the objects of our doubts might be accepted principles of good pedagogy, typical ways teachers respond to classroom management issues, customary beliefs about the relationship of schooling to society, or ordinary definitions of teacher authority – both in the classroom and in the broader school context' (ibid.: 37). Reflection can, therefore, vary from a concern with the micro aspects of the teaching–learning process and subject matter knowledge, to macro concerns about political/ethical principles underlying teaching and the relationship of schooling to the wider institutions and hierarchies of society. How we conceptualize teaching, whether as a set of neutral value-free technical acts, or, relationally, as a set of ethical, moral and political imperatives, holds important implications for the kind of reflective stance we adopt.

For myself, I am of the view that focusing on the reductionist aspects of the teaching–learning process that have a technocratic orientation to them, in the absence of the wider ethical and political scenery, is to fail to make the crucial linkage between issues of agency and structure and to relegate teachers to being nothing more than 'a cog in a self-perpetuating machine' (Tom, 1985: 38). Teaching, and reflection upon it, has a lot more to do with intentionality and the way in which teachers are able to be active agents (Ross and Hannay, 1986) in making the linkages between economic structures, social and cultural conditions, and the way schooling works.

Countering the dominant view that educational phenomena are natural and capable of detached analysis, requires a viewpoint that embraces the essentially political, historical and theoretical nature of teaching. Such a socially constructed view, which regards teaching as serving certain human interests, posits the entire educational system as potentially part of the arena of the problematic (Tom, 1985: 42) and incorporates reflection that focuses primarily on the way in which schooling contributes (or not, as the case might be), to the creation of a less oppressive, more just, humane and dignified society.

The idea that teaching is a political process serving certain interests in demonstrable ways, while actively excluding and denying others, is not a notion that has general acceptance either among teachers or the wider community (White and White, 1986; Stevens, 1987; Lightfoot, 1973). To some extent, this is understandable given the often technicist ways in which the teacher education enterprise trains teachers (and school systems support the view that teachers ought) to engage in the transfer of knowledge to students, rather than to question the notions of power and ideology behind that knowledge (Freedman, 1986). Only rarely have teachers been required (or indeed permitted to) confront the knowledge/power issue. Teachers struggle hard, therefore, to see the importance of looking at the manner in which the system in which they work increasingly demands that schools be responsive to the needs of the economy. Because of the way in which capitalist systems in general have been able to ascribe the causes of our economic ills to the personal inadequacies and failings of individuals (illiteracy, lack of incentive and poor work habits among students), rather than deficiencies of the system itself, it has not been difficult to link this with the systematic failure of schools to meet the needs of industry. The argument is such a compellingly simplistic one that it is proving extremely difficult to dislodge – get students in schools to conform through more compliant forms of education, and all our economic woes will disappear. The kind of position represented by these ideas needs to be challenged and roundly critiqued through the kind of reflective process being spoken about here.

Requiring that teachers develop a sense of personal biography and professional history, is one way for them to begin to overcome their inertia and unwillingness to question where particular teaching practices came from, and to that extent to accept teaching actions as natural or common sense and unquestionable. It is to attune them to the fact that silences on these matters are perhaps not accidental at all, but may be socially constructed responses to a wider societal agenda. As Gadamer (1975) argues, understanding practice involves coming to grips with the way in which beliefs and values (which are themselves historical constructions) amount to powerful forces that enable us to ascribe particular meaning and significance to events. Put another way, our experiences as teachers have meaning for us in terms of our own historically located consciousness; what we need to do is to work at articulating that consciousness in order to interpret meaning. Failure to understand the breaks and the discontinuities in our history, makes it difficult for us to see the shifts in the nature of power relationships, with the result that we end up denying their very existence. Elsewhere (Smyth, 1984e: 63) I have put it in these words:

> Reflection, critical awareness, or enlightenment on its own is insufficient – it must be accompanied by action. . . . [As Freire so aptly put it] reflection without action is verbalism; action without reflection is activism. . . . [What we need to do is to open up] dialogue between teachers about actual teaching experiences but in a way that enables questions to be asked about taken-for-granted, even cherished assumptions and practices, the reformulation of alternative hypotheses for action, and the actual testing of those hypotheses in classroom situations.

It is to the relationship between reflection and action that I want to turn to now.

Confronting the cultural dispositions of schooling

The notion of empowerment (even if it is becoming an overused term) has to do with teachers taking charge of aspects of their lives over which they have been prevented from gaining access in the past (Fried, 1980a). The intention is to critique and uncover the tensions that exist between particular teaching practices, and the larger cultural and social contexts in which they are embedded. Willis (1977) expressed it in terms of the social actors themselves reflecting upon, challenging and refuting, rather than accepting, the structural conditions which envelop their lives. There is a sense in which people who do this embark on a process of *becoming different*, by thinking critically and creatively, to pursue meanings that enable them to make increasing sense of the world in which they live. As Mishler (1986: 119) put it, empowerment entails a shift in the balance of power as participants move *beyond* the description of the 'text' of their teaching, to embrace possibilities for action, 'To be empowered is not only to speak one's own voice and to tell one's own story, but to apply the understanding arrived at to action in accord with one's own interests.' It means a preparedness to no longer accept things the way they are, but to see instead, 'patterned inequalities, institutional power, ideologies [and] . . . the internal dynamics of how a system works, and for whom the system is not functional' (Everhart, 1979: 420). My argument is that teachers are only able to reclaim the power they have lost over their teaching if they place themselves in critical confrontation with their problems.

Thus, empowerment through reflection has less to do with 'a handing down of knowledge . . . [and is more like] a partnership, a mutual sharing of ideas, intuitions and experiences' (Fried, 1980b: 30). In Greene's (1986a: 73) terms, this means 'a sense of agency is required of . . . teacher[s]' in which they can 'become challengers, when they can take initiatives' and in which schools 'become places in which spaces are created in which worthwhile questions can be asked'. For most teachers, this is in stark contrast to the 'delivery of services' mentality created by centralized bureaucratic educational authorities which insist on presenting the educational world in terms of 'one rank of people (service delivers) who have been trained and hired to treat the rest. They diagnose our problems, assess our needs, and then provide us with anything from a prescription to an entire program to fix what's lacking, or leaking, in us' (Fried, 1980a: 4). Simon (1987: 374) expressed the way in which teachers become empowered through reflection, when he said:

it literally means to give ability to, to permit or enable. When we hear the word empowerment used in education, it is usually being employed in the spirit of critique. Its referent is the identification of oppressive and unjust relations within which there is an unwarranted limitation placed on human action, feeling and thought. Such limitation is seen as constraining a person from the opportunity to participate on equal terms with other members of a group or community to whom have accrued the socially

defined status of 'the privileged', 'the competent'. . . . To empower is to
enable those who have been silenced to speak.

According to Anderson (1987: 14), there have been few indicators as to how
teachers themselves 'can reflect on the structural conditions that inform their
practice'. What becomes crucial in addressing Anderson's (1987) concern is
the stance taken towards knowledge about teaching; who has the right to create
it and under what circumstances; and the implications of that on the working
lives of people in classrooms. If teachers are denied the opportunity to
articulate, critique and culturally locate principles about their own (or one
anothers' teaching), then politically speaking, such teachers are being treated
no differently to disenfranchised workers who have historically been oppressed and denied access to power over their work.

If consciousness-raising is in fact about teachers coming to recognize the
nature and sources of the forces that keep them subjugated, then as Harris
(1979) says, this has to start with *them* sketching out the contours of actual lived
situations, and posing problems about those concrete situations. As I have
alluded to already, this process of distancing themselves from classroom
events and processes can be difficult and perplexing for teachers (Pollard,
1987), because classrooms present such a kaleidoscope of events that it is
difficult for teachers to obtain a stable image of themselves and of the
interactive part they play in the creation of those events. Before we can engage
teachers in untangling the complex web of ideologies (Berlak, 1987) that
surround them in their teaching, they first need to focus on those manifestations of their teaching that perplex, confuse or frustrate them; that is to say,
the practicalities of the here-and-now that teachers pride themselves in being
so vitally concerned about.

If teachers are going to uncover the nature of the forces that inhibit and
constrain them, and work at changing those conditions, they need to engage in
four forms of action with respect to their teaching (each of which have their
origins, broadly speaking, in the work of Paulo Freire). They can perhaps be
best characterized by a number of moments that can be linked to a series of
questions:

1 Describe . . . what do I do?
2 Inform . . . what does this description mean?
3 Confront . . . how did I come to be like this?
4 Reconstruct . . . how might I do things differently?

Describing

Starting with the hermeneutic notion that teaching is a form of text (Gordon,
1988) to be described and then untied (Young, 1981) for the meaning it
reveals, provides a form of accessibility which has a lot of appeal to teachers.
Because teaching is the kind of activity that can only be adequately explicated
and critiqued in a post-factum manner, Elliott (1987: 151) argues that 'rational

action is logically prior to rational principles'. The latter, he says, 'are the result of reflection on the former' (ibid.: 151) and any critique of teaching must, therefore, be in the context of practice if it is to go beyond being partial. In essence, the claim is that to articulate adequately the principles that lie behind teaching, teachers must start with a consideration of current practice as the way of gaining entry to the 'knowledge, beliefs, and principles that [they] employ in both characterizing that practice and deciding what should be done' (ibid.: 151). Both Harris (1986) and Bonser and Grundy (1988) claim that written codification can be a powerful guiding device for practitioners engaging in reflective deliberation.

As teachers reflect about their own (or one anothers') teaching, they describe concrete teaching events. The teachers I have worked with (Smyth, 1987e, 1988c) use a journal or diary (Holly, 1984; Tripp, 1987; Holly and Smyth, 1989) as a way of building up an account of their teaching as a basis for analysis and discussion with colleagues. Having to write a narrative of what was occurring in confusing, perplexing or contradictory situations helps them to organize an account of their teaching in a way which is crucial to them finding and speaking their own voices (McDonald, 1986). These descriptions do not have to be complex or in academic language – on the contrary, if there is to be any genuine ownership by teachers, it is important that such descriptions be in their own language (cf. Lortie, 1975). The rationale is that if teachers can create a text that comprises the elements of their teaching as a prelude to problematizing it, then there is a likelihood they will have the basis upon which to engage in dialogue with one another so as to see how their consciousness was formed, and how it might be changed. Creating personalized narratives are also a way of guarding against the rampant 'intellectual imperialism' (Harris, 1979) so prevalent in teaching, whereby outsiders provide the packaged and commodified answers to the issues that are non-questions for teachers. In Shor's (1980) terms, when teachers keep journals they are able to 'extraordinarily re-experience the ordinary' in a way that is clearly based on a sense of the concrete in their working lives, but in a manner that enables them to see how the elements of particular situations alienate and confuse them, and impose real 'limit situations' (Fay, 1977) on what it is possible for them to do.

Informing

When teachers describe their teaching, it is not an end in itself; it is a precursor to uncovering the broader principles that are informing (consciously or otherwise) their classroom action. As Kretovics (1985) put it, it is a way of beginning to confront the 'structured silences' that abound in teaching. Developing narratives are a way of uncovering what Argyris and Schön (1974) called 'theories-in-use', what Hirst (1983) labelled 'operational theories', or what Tripp (1987) has characterized as 'local theories'. By whatever term we choose to describe them, when teachers engage in the activity of unpicking descriptions of their teaching in order to make a series of 'it looks as if . . .'

statements, then they are really recapturing the pedagogical principles of what it is they do. For example, on the basis of descriptions of the way a teacher treats children, it could be said that such a teacher holds a view of classroom management that says 'the extent to which a teacher is going to have discipline problems is related to factors like the consistency and firmness of his or her reactions to breaches of classroom rules, the types of punishment he or she metes out, and their severity' (Gordon, 1988: 431). In trying to work out their operational theories, teachers are in effect seeking to develop defensible practical principles 'grounded in a largely tacit knowledge of complex and particular situations' (Elliott, 1987: 152). Such theories or thematic representations may fall well short of being generalizable, but the contradictions they contain may nevertheless be highly significant in explaining the nature of idiosyncratic work contexts. It should be said that what teachers are trying to do in this process is to move their teaching out of the realm of the mystical, as it were, to a situation in which they are able to begin to see through discussion with others, the nature of the forces that cause them to operate in the way they do, and how they can move beyond intellectualizing the issues to concrete action for change.

Developing short-range theories or explanatory principles about practice, is not without its own set of complex problems and impediments, a major one being the generally enforced separation of theory from practice. Most educational research assumes that theories about teaching are developed by people outside of classrooms and then transfused into classrooms to be applied by teachers. Such an applied view of the nature of research is, to say the least, highly problematic, in that it takes no account of the extensive experiential wisdom possessed by most teachers. Carr (1982: 26) speaks of the prevalent but quite erroneous view of educational theory as being akin to a collage of 'maps, guides, itineraries and rule-books produced in some far off land and then exported to the "world of practice" so that its inhabitants can understand where they are, what they are doing and where they are supposed to be going'. The problem, then, is primarily a political one of who has the legitimate right to define what counts as knowledge about teaching. While teachers may have been reluctant in the past to be seen to be publicly exercising that claim, others outside of classrooms have been far less reticent. As Kohl (1983: 30) aptly put it:

> Unless we [as teachers] assume the responsibility for theory making and testing, the theories will be made for us by . . . the academic researchers and many other groups that are simply filling the vacuum that teachers have created by bargaining away their educational power and giving up their responsibility as intellectuals.

Confronting

Theorizing and describing one's practice is one thing, but being able to subject those theories to a form of interrogation and questioning that establishes something about their legitimacy and their legacy, is altogether another matter.

Yet, if we are to be clear about what it is that we do as educators, and why we do it, then it is imperative that we move to this stage. Above all, we need to regard the views we have about teaching not as idiosyncratic preferences, but rather as the product of deeply entrenched cultural norms that we may not even be aware of. Locating or situating teaching in a broader cultural, social and political context amounts to engaging in critical reflection about the assumptions that underlie those methods and classroom practices. Regarded this way, teaching becomes less of an isolated set of technical procedures, and more of a historical expression of shaped values about what is considered to be important about the nature of the educative act. When teachers write about their own biographies and how they feel these have shaped the construction of their values, then they are able to see more clearly how social and institutional forces beyond the classroom and school have been influential.

As a way of providing some structure, it is possible for teachers to approach the confrontation of local theories of teaching through a series of guiding questions, that might include the following:

- What do my practices say about my assumptions, values and beliefs about teaching?
- Where did these ideas come from?
- What social practices are expressed in these ideas?
- What is it that causes me to maintain my theories?
- What views of power do they embody?
- Whose interests seem to be served by my practices?
- What is it that acts to constrain my views of what is possible in teaching? (Smyth, 1987e)

In Freire's (1972) terms, this amounts to a way of problematizing teaching by asking poignant questions about the 'social causation' (Fay, 1977) of those actions. Untangling and re-evaluating taken-for-granted (even cherished) practices requires breaking into well-entrenched and well-constructed mythologies that may not always be easily dislodged.

Reconstructing

Being able to locate oneself both personally and professionally in history so as to be clear about the forces that have come to determine one's existence, is the hallmark of a teacher who has been able to harness the reflective process so as to begin to act on the world in a way that amounts to changing it. This amounts to being able to see teaching realities not as immutable givens but as being defined by others, and as essentially contestable. If teachers are to experience their lives in authentic terms, then they will have to expel the internalized images that researchers, administrators and policy makers are so deft at perpetuating. By constructing portrayals of their own teaching that are embedded in the particularities of that teaching, they are able to gain a measure of control through self-government, self-regulation and self-responsibility that will enable them to trumpet the virtues of 'what's best in teaching'. Adopting this kind of perspective towards reflection is to deny the artificially constructed separation of thought from action, of theory from practice, of mental from manual labour and, ultimately, to jettison the false and oppressive view that people outside of classrooms know what is 'best' about teaching. Put quite simply, the people who do the work of teaching, should be the same people who reflect upon it.

When teachers are able to begin to link consciousness about the processes that inform the day-to-day aspects of their teaching with the wider political and social realities within which it occurs, then they are able to transcend self-blame for things that don't work out and to see that perhaps their causation may more properly lie in the social injustices and palpable injustices of society – which is to say, deficiencies in teaching can be caused by the manner in which dominant groups in society pursue their narrow sectional interests. Although teachers are by no means a numerically small group in society, it is becoming increasingly clear that they are being acted upon by educational systems and governments in ways that bear an uncanny resemblance to the oppressive treatment meted out to minority groups. Indeed, only when teachers take an active reflective stance (see Freedman *et al.*, 1983b) are they able to challenge the dominant factory metaphor of the way schools are conceived, organized and enacted. Being reflective, therefore, means more than merely being speculative: it means starting with reality, with seeing injustices, and beginning to overcome reality by reasserting the importance of learning.

Conclusion

To adopt the more expansive and politically informed kind of reflective pose being argued for in this chapter, is to proceed in a mutually reinforcing direction so that teachers are able to support one another in the effort to reclaim the classroom (Goswami and Stillman, 1987). To argue, for example, that such a reflective process is only possible for experienced teachers who have a lifetime of teaching behind them, is to deny a long and sometimes harsh history that inexperienced teachers (themselves products of the education system) bring with them to teaching. These histories are most decidedly worth unpicking in some considerable detail, for the more just and humane alternatives they will reveal. Adopting an exclusionist policy over matters like this is only ever justified in a context that construes teacher education as a narrow process of infusing skills. Besides, to operate otherwise is to ignore what we already know about the powerful socializing effect of the profession on neophyte teachers.

Reflective practitioners and non-reflective practitioners are not two fundamentally irreconcilable groups. Rather, they are at different points in working to overcome the social, cultural and political amnesia that has come to grip the entire teaching profession in recent times (McLaren, 1987). To be sure, there are problems with the reflective approach, but they are not of a kind that have to do with developing a formula and having everyone march in the same direction to the sound of the same drum. The problems are not about ensuring neat and system-wide uniform dissemination of packaged arrangements, but rather have to do with winning the hearts and minds of people committed to a common struggle (Spring, 1977). There are other problems too because of the in-built presumption that teachers will necessarily want to become self-aware and act in ways that promote their own interests and those of their students, in preference to the forces of dogma and irrationality that blind them to the nature of reality. This, of course, may be quite an erroneous presumption and one which Elbaz (1988) is right to point to as a persisting dilemma. But none of these are adequate justifications for not embarking on the process, for as Rudduck (1984: 6) put it: 'Not to examine one's practice is irresponsible; to regard teaching as an experiment and to monitor one's performance is a responsible professional act.'

In the final chapter, I deal with some actual examples of teachers who have employed the general principles spoken about here, as they moved down the track of becoming more reflective critical practitioners of their teaching and its institutional context.

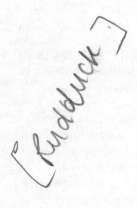
[Rudduck]

7

Critical pedagogy of supervision

Introduction

This concluding chapter discusses the experience I had recently with a group of Australian primary and secondary teachers (and I include myself), who tried to implement the ideas spoken about so far in this book.[1] I have chosen to write the chapter from a 'jointly authored' sense because it represents the collective experiences all of us had in this project as we experimented with a way of *describing*, *theorizing* and *confronting* our teaching, as described in the previous chapter. What is written is a particular view as seen through the eyes of one writer; to that extent, it is only a partial account, albeit one that attempts to draw upon the wider perspectives and experiences of others who were involved. In the opening parts of the chapter, where the context and rationale are being sketched out, I take a major role as the narrator. Much of the justificatory rationale, its rhetoric and its location in a field of study was mine, and mine alone. I make no apology for that. As the chapter develops, and as the intent of the project becomes a little clearer, I hope that the voices of my co-participants become louder. Well, at least that is the intention, anyway. It is true that in the very nature of the activity there were limits too to the extent of collaboration. But at the same time, while I was acting as the instigator and the spokesperson for the activity, it was equally true that working in the ways described actually touched and changed the lives of the people involved in important ways. I hope that this comes through as well. Not everyone was of the same mind at the beginning, nor was there anything like unanimity at the end; indeed, for some, the whole project proved difficult for them to take. Nevertheless, despite these differences in viewpoint, everyone involved was chastened by the experience of having tried an alternative approach to making sense of their work and their context, and of having developed informed opinions and some first-hand evidence as to what it meant to experiment with an alternative.

The project had its genesis in an uneasy feeling I carried with me as a high school teacher over a decade ago, and which was shared by others around me. The source of my unease was the skills-related way in which most in-service teacher education was conceived and enacted, seemingly for and on our behalf. It seemed to me that there had to be an alternative to the widely held view that teacher improvement meant a form of intellectual re-skilling. It concerned me that even though the skills-related approach had repeatedly been shown to be educationally bankrupt, it was still by far the most extensively used mode of teacher development and renewal.

What follows is an attempt, therefore, to develop a politicized counter-discourse to the desultory experiences I and others have had as classroom teachers. Confronting and reconstruing teaching so as to contest the deficit skills model, seemed to be as good a way as any of doing that. The experiences of the classroom teachers who worked with me on this project and what it meant to them, as well as my reflections on the actual process of working with them, are documented. To minimize confusion, I have used the term 'we' to describe the collective experiences of the group, and 'I' to refer to my own predelictions and reflections on events and activities as they unfolded.[2] On the occasions where I am describing the actual experiences of my co-participants I have persisted with the use of the term 'we', because to have detached myself completely by talking about the 'teachers' would be to introduce an element of the artificial that was not present, as well as to deny my own implicatedness in the project.

The central construct behind what was being attempted in this in-service-cum-supervision activity had to do with challenging the myth that somehow classroom teaching is or should be a detached, neutral, objectivist and value-free activity. We were concerned with contesting the purist view that political matters have no place in schools. The endless calls for a return-to-the-basics, demands for an increase in academic standards, an extension of testing and moves for the removal of incompetent teachers were, to our way of thinking, all highly political activities. As teachers we are required to suffer increasing forms of degradation in the nature of our work as a consequence of these supposed educational reforms. Yet, in the guise of accountability and measures designed to achieve improved quality control, efficiency and effectiveness in our classrooms, what is really occurring, as Elliott (1979: 67) argues (at least in his context of England), is a legitimation of the transference of power over educational decision making from teachers to groups outside of schools. It is equally apparent that none of these technical solutions address the *real* problem in our schools, which is not a crisis of *competence* but, rather, a crisis of *confidence*.

From our vantage point of teachers, current attempts at educational reform seem to have failed because as the major 'actors' we have been largely excluded from the action, except as benign respondents to the agendas formulated by others. As an occupational group, teachers have had a long history of having been treated as the 'objects' of other people's supposed reforms (Karier *et al.*, 1973; Lawn 1987): the stereotypical answer now, as always, to the perceived teacher malaise, is seen as lying in measures aimed at increasing the rigour of our work, in testing us more, in sending us 'back to school', and requiring that we work longer hours. The problem with such simplistic approaches is that while they aim to produce material improvements that appear to be possible in perplexing, difficult and uncertain times, what they fail to disclose is how small improvements leave untouched the political, economic and social structures which gave rise to the difficulties in the first place. What these cosmetic changes fail to attend to are the deep-seated sources of power and exploitation that lie in the structural arrangements that gave rise to them. What this project was committed to was a form of educational reform that hinged around empowering teachers in ways that would enable them to open up and create spaces in schools through which it would become possible to ask worthwhile questions. As Greene (1986b: 441) put it, this involves inspiring 'hitherto unheard voices . . . [to] . . . rediscover their own memories and articulate them in the presence of others, whose space they can share. [This] demands the capacity to unveil and disclose.'

On what was being attempted

In the context of the previous chapter, we set out to 'describe', to 'inform', to 'confront' and to 'reconstruct' our teaching.

Describing: 'What do I do?'

As we read the burgeoning literature on teachers reflecting on their own practice (Bonser and Grundy, 1988; Gore, 1987; Liston and Zeichner, 1987; Pollard, 1987; Tom, 1985), it became clear that if we were to be at all analytical about our teaching and begin to locate it sociologically speaking, then we first had to be able to describe at least some 'critical incidents' of that teaching. We were impressed by the idea of using a journal or a diary (Holly, 1984; Tripp, 1987; McLaren, 1980) as a way of accumulating an account that could be revisited and shared. Having to write required that we be clear about certain things that we regarded as the elements of the situation – the 'who', 'what', 'when' and 'where'. We believed that organizing and creating a narrative of our experiences was a crucial part of being able to find and speak our own voices. We found that sometimes these descriptions were very brief, while at other times they were more expansive, even going beyond mere description into being speculative. Here are three examples of teachers' journal entries from the project, along with some interpretation:

Year 7 Social Learning
Yesterday was Friday again! Friday bloody Friday. It's the third Friday that I've *had* those year 7's – emphasis on the *had*. . . . I am the principal of a

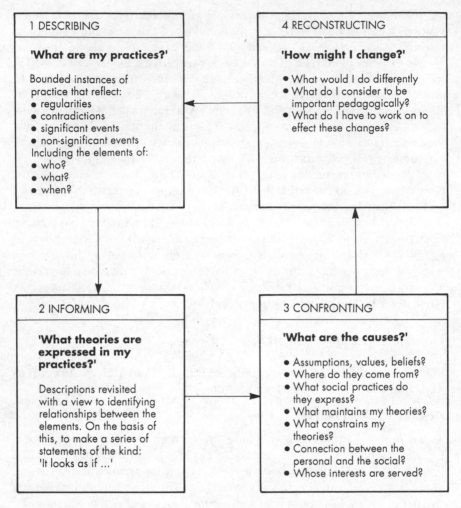

Figure 2   Critical pedagogy of classroom practice

primary school of 150 kids. I've just come from a smaller school of 50 kids; had been there for 5 years. Kids were beautiful . . . independent, reliable, self-directed, self-motivated. Great. Now, after 20 years of teaching I meet 21 year 7's, half of whom act like caged bastards. God I've been angry. . . . [T]ook them for a lesson intending to get to know them and do some social learning activities. I told them to work in small groups on a task – read a story and answer some questions. They did everything but. Roamed around, talked about everything else, annoyed the class next door, drew and colored-in. . . . I couldn't believe it. I'd been so used to asking year 7's in previous years to do so and so, and they would; but not this mob.

Using my theory of social learning and group development as a guide, I tried to explain [to them] my modus operandi and why I was doing it this way. Half of them wouldn't even listen. I asked them several times to sit down. Because I didn't know them by name, I walked over to the offenders and said: 'Excuse me, but I would like you to sit down so I can tell you what I would like you to do'. Some complied with my request. After almost pleading for co-operation, I did by block and yelled at them. That got their attention, but it is not the way I tend to operate.

Year 10 Mathematics

I was teaching a year 10 maths class in which we were doing Pythagoras' geometrical application. I decided to feign forgetfulness and hand over responsibility for the conduct of the lesson to the students so they could help one another. They found the notion of the teacher sitting down among them as a student disarming. A suggestion from a student that drawing on the blackboard was necessary was taken up, so Darren was asked whether he would take up the chalk. While the intention had been to get a volunteer, the direct cue to Darren, on reflection, was loaded with covert teacher power. It seemed to Darren to be a directive, and while he did proceed to the blackboard, his initial drawings were an inadequate representation, but eventually he came up with one without assistance from me. . . . When he was asked to explain, Darren faltered, about half-way through. . . . The students were surprised when no real help was forthcoming from me as the teacher.

Year 11 Modern History

Today in my Modern History class I was struck with the ongoing problem of making material as relevant as I can to the experiences of students. We had been looking at primary source material on the preparation for the war on the Western Front in World War One. The material included extracts from the training manuals and a letter from Field Marshal Kitchener about the way the troops should behave in the field. I struggled to make this material relevant to the students and engage them with the material.

In each instance, the journal description has been of an incident that is significant to the teacher; in the case of the Year 7 Social Learning experience, an intense frustration by the teacher was manifested in an inability to adjust to a new group; with the Year 10 Mathematics group, an unexpected reaction by students to a different teaching strategy; and, with the Year 11 History class, a desire to want to provide material that was more relevant to the experiences of the students.

It became clear when we started with descriptions of our practice, and used these as a basis for discussion and further elaboration, that it was possible to avoid the circumstances in which outsiders colonized our world and provided answers to issues that were non-questions for us. We needed not only to discover those things we 'thought [we] knew, but [which we] now realize [we] need to know' (Harris, 1979: 175). We were 'naming' our world (Freire, 1974) in the sense of concretely describing those elements of it that alienate and confuse us, so as to begin to reconstrue actions in ways that amount to changing them. The intent, then, was to see the social settings of our classrooms not as given, immutable and unchangeable, but as 'limit-situations that can be transcended' (Fay, 1977 220).

As we began to describe the situatedness of the concrete instances of our teaching, we also started to challenge the view that there is a set of universal laws of what constitutes 'good teaching'. We could see in a practical way what Shor and Freire (1987) meant when they spoke about conventional forms of research on teaching amputating teachers from the realities within which they work. Although it was not entirely clear to us at the time, what we had begun to do here was to strike out at the teacher education enterprise that has succeeded in promulgating a view that the act of teaching can somehow exist separately and apart from the lives, cultures, aspirations and problems of teachers and students. It was the practices, and the social processes they encapsulated, that we had started to describe and analyse.

Informing: 'What is the meaning behind my teaching?'

Having started to capture limited descriptions of those aspects of our practice that perplexed us (although we were not entirely clear about the reasons for our unease), we were able to revisit the descriptions and start doing what Young (1981) called 'untying the text' for what it might reveal. Obviously, it was not enough simply to have described something – it may have been the beginning of understanding, but on its own it was not informative as to the principles that lay behind the action. To that extent, action still remained in the realm of the mystical, caused as it were by vague magical forces that we did not really understand or control. Put another way, what we were really doing here was theorizing about our teaching in the sense of unpicking the broader pedagogical processes that lie behind specific actions. What we came up with were 'local theories' (Tripp, 1987; Geertz, 1983; Schibeci and Grundy, 1987) that were not universal but which nevertheless seemed to us to be embedded in the particular incidents we chose to describe. These theories may not have been generalizable but, more importantly to us, we saw them as highly significant in explaining the nature of our work contexts.

The previous examples from the journals were theorized as follows:

Year 7 Social Learning. The teacher on this occasion found that he was trying to put into effect a theory that says: learning cannot occur unless students are paying attention so they can hear directions. As he began to reflect on it, he found that he appeared to be prepared to pursue that theory to the point of verbal violence, if necessary. The students, on the other hand, seemed to have a different and competing set of values and beliefs (a theory) about learning that said they had the right to communicate with one another and to determine what went on in class, a circumstance the teacher was powerless to abrogate.

What they were expressing was a form of opposition to what they saw as the teacher's exercise of hierarchical control, despite his claim to be doing otherwise.

Year 10 Mathematics. When he stood back from his described incident, and sought to make sense of what was occurring, the teacher here was able to see that he held a theory about peer learning that failed to acknowledge that students come to class with a long history of expectations about what they see as likely to happen. They hold certain views about who has a right and a duty to impart knowledge. What the teacher had overlooked here was that students cannot always cope with quick, unexpected and dramatic shifts in power, especially if they have been socialized in particular ways.

Year 11 History. As he reflected on the incident he had described, this teacher concluded that the instigating event (his perceived need to inject relevance into his teaching) had caused him to ask questions about the relationships between his students and the wider authority structures within which they lived. As he put it: 'Today I was able to lock onto the idea of society and authority. I asked [them] the question, "Would you go to war out of patriotism?" We discussed the ways in which today we have less respect for authority. We are much more sceptical of "motives" and we tend to question and doubt those in authority, such as parents, schools, governments, etc. This seemed to form at least a partial bridge between the material and the experiences of the students.'

In each of the above examples, what we see is evidence of teachers beginning to 'inform' their classroom practices in the sense of theorizing or looking for broad explanatory principles that lie behind their actions. In the normal course of our daily teaching, we tend not to look for or talk about universal laws of teaching, nor for the existence of what the 'experts' claim to be true about teaching. Rather, what tends to preoccupy us, if anything does, are the 'local theories' (Tripp, 1987) that help us to make sense of particular situations and moments we encounter. While putting this kind of complexion on the notion of theory is certainly not new, as Schwab (1969) has shown, actually being able to see the embeddness of local theories in the normal act of teaching is something we may experience difficulty with because of the mythology surrounding the enforced separation of theory from practice. In practical terms, when we are able to get behind the habitualness and taken-for-grantedness of what we do, we gain a measure of control and ownership over what counts as knowledge. Carr (1982: 26) makes the point more generally when he says that the prevailing view is that educational theory is something developed independently of teachers and which has to be exported to classrooms:

> What this image conceals, of course, is not only that these consumers have themselves produced and already possess a map of their situation, and rules and guiding principles about what they are trying to achieve; it also

disguises the fact that since these theoretical products are the outcome of non-educational activities, they will always reflect the use of non-educational concepts and categorizations and so re-draw the map of the 'real world of education' in non-educational ways.

What is at issue, then, is the political question of who defines, articulates and legitimates knowledge about teaching. As McDonald (1986) points out, as teachers we have historically been led to believe that we should have only a benign part in this. Our acquiescence is not altogether surprising either, given the ideology behind hierarchical regimes of teacher evaluation and supervision, an argument that is well put by Carr (1982: 26):

> Once it is conceded that to undertake a practical activity like education, involves engaging in some recognizable set of practices, and once it is acknowledged that these practices are not . . . free from theoretical preconceptions, then it becomes apparent that 'educational theory' is not something that is created in isolation from practice and then has to be 'applied', 'implemented' or 'adopted' through a 'sustained effort' on the part of the two reluctant parties. 'Education' is not some kind of inert phenomenon that can be observed, isolated, explained and theorized about. There are no 'educational phenomena' apart from the practices of those engaged in educational activities, no 'educational problems' apart from those arising from these practices and no 'educational theories' apart from those that structure and guide these practices. The only task which 'educational theory' can legitimately pursue, then, is to develop theories of educational practice that are intrinsically related to practitioners' own accounts of what they are doing, that will improve the quality of their involvement in these practices and thereby allow them to practice better.

If the point being made by Carr (1980) were not true, that teachers have ways of making sensible and intelligible quite complex aspects of their teaching, then teaching would

> have to be some kind of mechanical behavior performed by robot-like characters in a completely unthinking way. But teaching is not like that. . . . [Teachers do have a] 'way of thinking' that provides the theoretical background against which teachers explain and justify their actions, make decisions and resolve real problems. Anybody engaged in teaching, then, must already possess some 'theory' which guides their practices and makes them intelligible (Carr, 1980: 7).

An inescapable part of theorizing is, therefore, its transformative potential or its capacity to stimulate the kind of critical questioning that challenges taken-for-granted assumptions and practices and brings about changes in the way practice itself is experienced and understood (Carr, 1980).

The associated issue has to do with how we came to hold these theories about teaching in the first place, because they were not a natural occurrence.

Confronting: 'How did I come to be this way?'

Describing and informing teaching is one thing, but actually positioning ourselves so as to question the world as we know and experience it is a much more difficult task. Seeking to locate or situate teaching in a broader cultural, social and political context amounts to engaging in critical reflection about the assumptions that underlie methods and classroom practices.

While there were a variety of ways in which people chose to engage in this confrontation of their teaching, we were especially mindful in our project of the problem disclosed by Fuller and Manning (1973), that when teachers confront themselves (at least on videotape) the result is apprehension, guilt and the search for individualistic solutions. The kind of paralysis that emerges out of individualistic self-attribution and victim blaming, was something we all wanted to avoid. Starting out by focusing on questions of the kind alluded to on p. 116, generated issues for exploration and provided a structure with which to begin the daunting task – they also provided a springboard for developing and pursuing other questions.

Commencing with historically located sociological questions not only gave us a direction with which to start, but it also enabled us to bring into question many ignored contextual factors that surround teaching. This was not easy, but as Berlak (1987: 7) said:

> it would be hard to over-estimate the difficulty of the challenge, the complexity, and the enveloping nature this net of taken-for-granted ideas presents for those who want to encourage independent thought in classrooms – and outside of classrooms as well.

Tripp (1984: 28) provides an example that illustrates nicely the difficulty we collectively faced in trying to develop a sociological and political analysis of our teaching. He cites the case of a teacher who noted the following in her journal: 'John didn't finish his work again today. I must see that he learns to complete what he has begun.' As a *description* this may not appear to be a particularly startling, problematic or even significant entry. It was only when the teacher 'massaged' this description a little that she began to see that the issues went much deeper than simply a problem to be solved. When she sought to ask what was the pedagogical theory that seemed to be *informing* her teaching on this occasion, she was able to see that what lay behind her journal entry was a belief about teaching that had to do with a sequential mode of learning – this task must be finished first because it is a prerequisite to the one that is to follow. Sharing her journal item with a group of colleagues enabled her to *confront* the fact that there was more to it than just a problem to be solved; in fact, there was a series of other questions:

- Why doesn't John finish his work?
- Why should he finish his work?
- How does John see the tasks demanded of him?
- Are the tasks of the right kind, quality and quantity? (Tripp, 1984: 28).

Starting out with the question 'How can I get John to finish his work?', Tripp noted how the question became transformed through dialogue into the more important question of 'Why must John finish his work before going onto the next task?' In a sense, it was her own unquestioned professional history as a successful teacher that prevented her from asking the 'why' questions – she had become fixated at the 'how' level. Asking the question 'Why am I doing this'?, can produce some quite startling answers. In the case of John's unfinished work, Tripp (1984: 28) argues that:

> In everyday life outside the classroom we continually leave unfinished what we have begun, so how is it that we are in a position of having to enforce upon these students the rule that they must finish one thing before they can go onto the next? Where did that rule come from, and when is it necessary?

The issue here, therefore, is one that transcends the domain of the individual teacher and has a lot to do with the hidden curriculum of social control in schooling. As Tripp argues, for reasons of orderliness and the general smooth and efficient running of the school, it is desirable that teachers have students complete tasks in a linear fashion. There may be little or no educational rationale for this requirement.

Let us return to the earlier examples from our project. Notwithstanding that some teachers found it difficult (if not impossible) to confront the theories of teaching that had emerged through description, they were able at least to begin to put a different complexion on matters.

Year 10 Mathematics. The teacher in this scenario could see more clearly the nature of the power relationships involved in his own teaching, and the fact that what he was doing was going against an established norm. Even as he tried to move beyond this to reconstruct the way in which he worked with groups of students, he was sensitive to the feelings of uncertainty as students tried to adjust to the new kind of risk-taking and exposure that was involved.

Year 7 Social Learning. On other occasions, some of us struggled hard to try and see the nature of our own implication in processes in which we were 'caught up'. In this particular instance, the teacher found it difficult to envisage how his own actions might be inextricably bound up in perpetuating a particular power relationship with his students, despite the fact that he thought he was actually divesting power to students. He found it difficult to accept the possibility that student opposition could be an expression of their unwillingness to submit to what they saw as a thinly veiled authoritarian form of control, albeit dressed up as democratic intent. While this teacher was able to see the more general point about the historical domination of students by teachers, he still found it very difficult to see the possible contradiction in his own practice. As he put it:

It seems to me that it's always been the practice for teachers to 'bark' orders at students, just as if they were in the army. . . . It's the way teachers have spoken to students ever since schools began; it's never been questioned. . . . I believe that asking students for co-operation . . . goes hand in hand with an explanation of why the request is being made. This gives children more information to go on when they make their choices about co-operating or not . . .

[And later] . . . it seems I am the person with the power in that I have decided what the class is going to do, but I am willing to 'give the power away' to the students by negotiating what I intend to do. What I am saying is that I hold the power, because I am making decisions about how I want the students to behave while I tell them my intentions for the lesson. But *then*, they have the power to re-negotiate the activities.

None of this *in any way* reflects personal adequacies on the part of the teachers concerned. In large part, the difficulty facing all of us in situations like this is our form of cultural upbringing that involves us in believing that schools (and what transpires within them) is construed as objectivist, neutral and apolitical. This can be a difficult view to dislodge, especially in a context where it is being reinforced continually and massaged by what Giroux (1985) calls a management pedagogy and a 'scientific' view of schooling. Because the notion of social critique is so foreign to us we either end up acting in self-denigrating ways that generate enormous guilt feelings about the way we do things, or we seek to rationalize and justify our practices on the basis of what we consider to be the perceived needs of children or the communities which schools exist to serve. In both cases, the end result is much the same: an unwillingness to confront the systematic way in which our teaching is being progressively dictated to us by forces outside of schools.

What the evidence from our descriptions of practice seemed to be saying is that there is a kind of conformity and failure to struggle with, to understand and, ultimately, to challenge our history as teachers. In the case of the Year 7 class, while there was a certain reluctance in accepting the apparently irrational behaviour of the class as they responded to what they saw as a form of social engineering (albeit in the guise of democratic relations), the teacher felt trapped within an overlapping set of relationships. To be fair to the teacher, there was also a rationality in his behaviour. He was caught in the difficulty of trying to sort out the interrelated complexities of school norms, what Willis (1977) described as the 'official' (what the institution says are its statements of purposes), the 'pragmatic' (how teachers deal with day-to-day problems relating to social control) and the 'cultural' (how they speak about both of the others in the staffroom and with colleagues). The interpenetration of these presented this teacher, as with many of us, with what Anderson (1987: 11–12) calls an 'inchoate social reality from which he or she must extract a rationale for his or her actions. The practitioner, then, cannot be blamed for possessing contradictory goals and rationales which he or she uses in different contexts.'

Sorting out such confusing and perplexing situations requires that as teachers we engage in dialogue with one another about the social, cultural and political structures around us that have caused us to regard as natural and unquestioned the ideas we have about teaching. In large part, this means seeing teaching practices as social constructions of reality, and even misrepresented ones at that. We found ourselves in agreement with commentators like Jackson (1968), Lortie (1975) and Sarason (1982) on the way the structures of schooling work against teachers. Mohr and MacLean's (1987: 1) point captured in nicely:

> In both elementary schools and high schools, teachers are isolated from one another, and the regimented quality of the school day perpetuates that isolation. In one day of teaching it is possible to have many intense emotional and intellectual exchanges with students, to experience in less than an hour a wide range of thought and emotion that people outside the profession can imagine, and yet at the end of the day to feel as if you have ben separated from the world, solitary and lonely. . . . As a result, teachers may shun further human interaction in their professional lives. The isolation, the exhaustion, and the need to pull away conflict directly with a teacher's corresponding need for more contact with colleagues, both for friendly support and for professional discourse.

The difficulty we had in this project developing and sustaining a critical dialogue was as much epistemological as it was a resistance based upon exhaustion and a lack of time – but at least we had identified that much. It was partly an artefact of our preparedness to see that there was far more involved in what we were attempting than simply discarding a few false beliefs. By the end of the project, we could see that what we had commenced was Fay's (1977: 214) process of confronting a 'set of interrelated illusions about human needs . . . about what is good and of value, and about how one should act in one's relations with others to achieve these things'. We were able to empathize with Fay (1977: 214) when he said that the systematic, shared and deeply rooted nature of these illusions means that dislodging them is extremely difficult: 'This is because giving up such illusions requires abandoning one's self-conceptions and the social practices that they engender and support, things people cling to because they provide direction and meaning in their lives.' Sometimes we were able to see these contradictions in varying degrees, and sometimes we were able to talk about our own confusion in trying to come to some kind of reconciliation so as to live with the incoherence. One of the group spoke about this in terms of his endeavours to negotiate the content of the curriculum with his students, while feeling trapped within a dilemma. He put it in these terms: 'I am negotiating from the position of wanting the other party to see reason. . . . [Yet at the same time, I am saying] . . . be reasonable, see my way!' Part of this was a feeling of powerlessness about the way in which he felt trapped by social forces he neither controlled nor understood:

I don't have any desire to exert control over others, but it is an inherent part of my practice (as I've seen from this project). [But] more and more I am feeling the influence of the accountant mentality of 'politicians'. More and more decisions are being made about schooling by people who are not part of the schooling scene.

For this teacher, and countless others like him, the kind of social relationships he was forced to endure in the workplace, and the way these are unwittingly reproduced in his pedagogy and in the relationships he develops with his students, produces an apparently inescapable contradiction:

As the teacher I see myself as a creator of the appropriate learning environments *which will encourage kids to construct the knowledge the teacher has planned.* . . . I still tend to be the teacher and the giver of information [my emphasis].

The further we went the more it became clear to us that as an occupational group we had become 'proletarianized', as Poulantzas (1973) and Derber (1982) put it, in the sense of losing control over our teaching. One of our group was able to see this graphically through locating himself historically in relation to his opposition to the Vietnam War and his subsequent support for traditionally oppressed social groups during the 1960s. Yet, at the same time, he could also see the contradiction in this of how individual competitiveness and upward social mobility had thwarted his ideals and caused them to become twisted and tarnished in the intervening period:

All of these social phenomena seemed to me to indicate that something was wrong with the traditional authority structures. This, combined with my school experience (rigid, hierarchical, privileged, private school . . . [caused me to leave] the place angry and rebellious), and made me an enthusiastic radical. [But now] I am part of the structure that I once daubed with slogans; survival has become a priority. . . .

Symptomatic of his feelings of entrapment, this teacher expressed difficulty in achieving 'the level of political analysis called for [in this project]' and of having 'struggled without much success to identify the nature of the ideological domination at work in the school'. Clearly, he had travelled much further than he was able to give himself credit for.

There can be little doubt that the notions of professionalism we carry with us as teachers actually get in the way of the process of confrontation. Grace (1978), for example, found that teachers held a view of themselves and their work as lying largely outside of social and political structures and to that extent they were relatively immune from analysing them. The teachers in Grace's (1978: 216–17) research:

were able to maintain this position with conviction because *control* of their activities and, consequently, *notions of a 'dominant order' or of a 'controlling apparatus' and of the necessity for struggle against it were*

insubstantial in their consciousness, whereas notions of autonomy were
real and actual [emphasis in original].

Grace's argument is essentially that in teaching there is a considerable
inertia that prevents us from challenging the network of invisible controls
(examination boards, curriculum guidelines, community pressures on
teachers to achieve results, etc.) that have come to envelop teaching. At least
when controls over teaching were more visible and obvious, it was much
easier to challenge such practices as inspection. Lawn and Ozga (1986) have
cogently argued that current relationships between teachers and the state has
meant a very unequal and uneasy partnership. The game seems to have
changed quite dramatically with controls over the work of teachers becoming
much less obtrusive but no less potent. The problem with the apparently
benign and unobtrusive nature of these controls is that teachers *can* be
deluded into developing a mistaken belief as to the true limits of their own
autonomy. As one American teacher quoted by Bullough *et al.* (1984: 349) said
of her freedom: 'If I'd rather use a different worksheet or create a worksheet of
my own, as long as it meets the [mandated] objectives, I feel free to do that';
while another said, 'The objectives are spelled out, but they are left open-
ended enough so that you can approach them from any angle you want.'
Bullough *et al.* (1984) argue that such a constrained view of what it means to be
free is symptomatic of the very nature and power of technocratic values in
shaping the consciousness of teachers. The ideology is one that 'takes the form
of a hierarchy controlled by seemingly benign, value-neutral, progressively
wiser experts who will settle all our moral, political, social, and educational
problems by applying some variation of the production model of efficiency'
(ibid.: 349).

As part of the workforce, teachers have come rather too readily to accept the
ideology of professionalism as a 'first line of defence against pedagogic and
cultural imposition' (Grace, 1985). This 'ethic of professionalism' (Grace,
1985) or 'licensed autonomy' (Lawn and Ozga, 1981) has been accompanied by
a belief among teachers that the political has no place in classrooms or schools.
In practice, this has meant an unreal detachment by teachers from the political
and economic agendas of the state and an 'avoidance of the controversial [in
the] naive belief that "being political" is "being socialist"' (Grace, 1978: 249).
With the shift of control over teaching from a 'visible, prescriptive and
centralized system to an essentially invisible and diffuse mode' (Grace,
1985: 11), and the disappearance of the 'malevolent invader' from their
classrooms, teachers have not always been quick to grasp the significance of
the shift in the locus of control:

This invisible control is constituted, among other things, by the activities
of examination boards and their definitions of valid knowledge; by the
constraints of the work situation; and, crucially, by what 'being a good
teacher' and 'being a professional' are taken to imply. These controls are
invisible to the majority of teachers in so far as they form part of the taken-

for-granted and unchallenged social world within which they operate (Grace, 1978: 217–18).

Reconstructing: 'How might I do things differently?'

The earlier claim about the need for teachers to start with the concrete lived reality is not based on convenience; rather, by starting with reality, we are able to work on it, see its limits, and hence begin to overcome it (Shor and Freire, 1987: 107). Because of the way our culture accommodates us to working in unthinking and unquestioning ways, and because we have come to accept as natural the ways we teach and the social relationships we develop with our students, we tend to accept as bearable forces around us which ought to be quite intolerable. This happens because of the way in which teaching is construed as being a technical process that only requires fine-tuning in order to achieve predetermined educational objectives.

To give some substance to this, one of the group described how he began to problematize his teaching by speculating about the courses of action he needed to adopt to make some incursions into the wider structures that surrounded him. He related an incident in which he called the class to attention, gave them permission to proceed with a 'set' assignment, and what happened when a student came to him with a 'puzzled look' on his face:

S: Mr . . . What's the answer to number five?
T: [referring to the question] What is meant by the texture of the soil?
S: I don't know, that's why I'm asking you.
T: Well, . . . you should be able to find the answer to this question. Have you read the information sheets I gave you when the assignment was handed out?
S: No.
T: What about searching through your notes on soil texture? Have you done that?
S: No.
T: Well you should refer to your notes first, read them through and then if you don't understand something come and see me.
[student left still looking puzzled].

An analysis of his own aspirations and the way in which he was implicated in this little incident led the teacher to ask:

Why do I maintain a situation where student participation, negotiation and construction of learning is minimized? Why do I continue with non-negotiable forms of teaching and learning processes? If I expect my students to assume increasing levels of responsibility for their own learning, then surely I must begin to allow them to participate in deciding how they are expected to learn.

The kind of questions he was raising here caused him to think about his teaching in an entirely different way. While time ran out for him in this project, he was adamant about the nature of the action he needed to take. Being able to see that shortcomings in teaching do not necessarily equate with personal inadequacies actually provided him with some avenues for action. As he put it:

> the school's current practice of rank ordering students through competitive assessment means that some students are locked out of future life options. Those who succeed are being rewarded for their compliance in following the rules which have been laid down by the community and endorsed by the school. My school demands that the quality of a student's work be judged. Why then do I allow such a requirement to pervade classroom life in such a manner that it discourages learning for some of the students I teach?
>
> [M]y practices are constrained within the philosophical constraints laid down by the . . . values of the school. One of the goals of the school is to provide an ordered, structured environment so that learning and willingness to apply effort to worthwhile tasks is facilitated. I may ask myself, who decided which tasks are worthwhile? Why do I expect the full attention of students when addressing them? Why do I demonstrate to the students my ultimate power over the classroom? The answer is becoming more and more apparent. The accepted political order within the school makes it that way.
>
> The established political order of the school dictates the curriculum. It decides what is taught and where resources are allocated, even down to the timetable allocations. The same political order restricts students from being involved in any meaningful decision-making within the school.
>
> Why are the students excluded from decision-making?
> What kinds of decisions should they be involved in?
> Why do I expect my students to gracefully accept decisions being handed down to them?
> Why are students precluded from possessing effective power within this school?

Reconstructing their practice was not something that was feasible or possible for everyone in the project in the short time that was available. On some occasions it was regarded by participants as sufficient to have engaged in the analysis and to have reached the informed decision not to act. To have done that knowingly was an important advance for some people. On other occasions, it became clear that people had experienced a form of rejuvenation that would last well after the project had terminated. In each case, participation in the project at least provided the opportunity for each individual to work with others in shifting from 'how to' questions to 'what and why' questions about their teaching.

Final reflections

What I have sought to do in this chapter is to show how it might be possible for teachers to use their own capacities to formulate and implement agendas for change. In doing that, however, I have attempted to show how we first need to uncover the relationships between the ideas we hold and act upon. Teachers working with other teachers to create a critical pedagogy of classroom practice through processes like clinical supervision can reveal the existence of a number of major impediments, quite apart from the general issue of 'why would I want to do that, it sounds uncomfortable?' The major shortfalls in this strategy are inextricably bound up with our political, historical and theoretical practices as teachers and our capacities to grapple successfully with them.

One thing we found out in this project was that our own inertia and unwillingness to question where particular teaching practices came from resulted in us accepting teaching actions as 'natural' or 'common sense', and to that extent exempt from questioning. For example, that there may have been a marked shift over time from overt to covert forms of teacher surveillance through the 'rational' and 'scientific' nature of knowledge itself, and that this may have had an effect on self-discipline and social regulation generally, was not something that we were especially sensitive to. Failure to understand the nature and course of our own professional history makes it difficult to see the changing nature of power relationships. As Walkerdine (1986: 55) put it, denial of this kind holds important pedagogical implications:

> The transformation of governmental forms, and therefore of the notion of power, is located . . . [in] the shift from an overt sovereign power to a 'suspicious' and invisible power located within those aspects of the sciences . . . which came to be used as the basis . . . [of] technologies and apparatuses of social regulation. . . . Basically, Foucault argues that the form of government depends not on authoritarianism but on normalization, the concept of a calculated, known population. In that sense a variety of governing practices . . . began to be based on a concept of a norm, a normal individual.

Understanding that normalization and naturalism have important histories that need to be unpicked, and that they are themselves potent forms of social control, are factors that should not go unheeded in the analysis of pedagogy and schooling. Using Walkerdine's (1986: 56) words again:

> the advent of naturalism, that is, the ensuring of a correct passage from animal infant to civilized adult, became understood both as 'progressive' (according to scientific principles) and effective. It would prevent the threatened rebellion *precisely because* children who were not coerced would not need to rebel – the lessons would be learned and this time properly.

The point to all of this is that a fixation with the here-and-now, and a denial of where we have come from in our personal and professional biographies, actually prevents the broader picture from being brought into focus.

Inextricably related to the apolitical and the ahistorical way in which teaching is construed, is the prevailing view that the creation of pedagogical knowledge is and should remain the purview of people other than teachers. Perhaps it is the enforced immediacy of the classroom, with its constant demands for matters to be attended to here-and-now, that bolsters our view of ourselves as hard-nosed pragmatists concerned only with issues of instrumental practicality. Certainly, gender issues are not unimportant in this. Historically, the largely female nature of the teaching workforce provides a partial explanation. Walkerdine (1986) has alluded to the move by women into teaching in the nineteenth century and of the way in which this has served to continue to bolster a view (albeit extremely insulting) that teachers are incapable of bringing a reflective stance to their work. As Walkerdine (1986: 59) says:

> The emerging human sciences, building upon previous philosophical tenets, had deemed women's bodies as unfit for reason, for intellectual reason. The possession of a womb was thought to render a woman unfit for deep thought, which might tax her reproductive powers or make her less amenable to rearing children. Given the state of Empire, the concern with the race as with the species, it was considered potentially injurious to allow bourgeois women to reason.

Given the enormous resilience of sexist views like this it is not difficult to see how hierarchical forms of teacher surveillance can continue to have popularity while masquerading under the guise of supervisory effectiveness and accountability. Even with the more recent influx of males into teaching, and the accompanying macho image portrayed by Goodman (1986), the official emphasis continues to remain largely upon the technical as distinct from the intellectual nature of the pedagogical enterprise. Teachers, by and large, are encouraged by those at managerial levels to shy away from construing their work in abstract, philosophical or theoretical terms.

All of this has had quite profound effects in terms of attempts to develop a critical pedagogy of classroom practice. In this chapter, therefore, I have sought to do two things. First, by showing that it is possible to contest the apparently common-sense bureaucratic way of construing schools and to posit in its place more democratic and informed ways of thinking and working. When discussion about the work of teachers is constrained and limited to the purely technical domain, it is not altogether surprising that the focus is restricted to the means of teaching, leaving the ethical and philosophical ends of teaching to be treated non-problematically at the whim of those outside of classrooms and schools. Secondly, through exploring the notions of critical pedagogy I have sought to provide a rationale and some general principles by which teachers *themselves* might begin to move beyond questions of technical competence and thereby challenge the rules, roles and structures within which teaching occurs. Throughout, I have sought to argue and demonstrate that when teaching is situated in the cultural politics of schooling, that teachers are better able to see more clearly how they and their students might better resist incursions by the state and its influence in shaping and structuring what counts as knowledge and pedagogy in schooling.

Notes

1 An expanded version of this chapter was presented to the Ninth Curriculum Theorizing and Classroom Practices Conference, Dayton, Ohio, November 1987. I want to express my gratitude to those teachers in the 'Teachers' Theories of Action' Group (1987) who, in all respects, were co-authors with me in this paper. To Alistair, Linda, Brian, Leo, Malcolm, Phil and Quentin, I am especially grateful for the gracious way in which they allowed me privileged access to their work and for their permission to incorporate it here. To my teaching colleagues Judy Mousley, Liz Murphy, Annette Street and Rob Walker who had the forbearance to stick with me, I am indebted to them for their enthusiasm and insights throughout. I am grateful too to David Tripp for his assistance and insights in the formative stages of developing a perspective on what might it mean for teachers to theorize their practice. 'Teachers' Theories of Action' is part of the graduate programme in the School of Education at Deakin University, Australia. I wish to thank the anonymous reviewers for the thoughtful provocation that challenged me to rewrite a draft of this chapter in its previously published form, and I am grateful also to Noel Gough for his patience and insightful comments in the re-drafting stage. Some of the examples used here appeared in a different form in Gitlin and Smyth (1989).

One of the teachers involved in this project published her experiences. It deserves to be read for the substantiation it provides for the processes spoken about here (see Garbutcheon-Singh, 1987).

2 For a more exhaustive treatment of my reflections on my own pedagogy on the issue of 'Teachers' Theories of Action', see Smyth (1989b).

References

Alfonso, R. (1977) Will peer supervision work? *Educational Leadership* 34(8): 594–601.

Alfonso, R. and Goldsberry, L. (1982) Colleagueship in supervision. In T. Sergiovanni (ed.), *Supervision of Teaching*, pp. 90–107. Alexandria, Va.: Association for Supervision and Curriculum Development.

Anderson, G. (1987) Towards a critical ethnography of educational administration. Paper presented at the annual meeting of the American Educational Research Association, Washington, D.C., April.

Anderson, R. and Snyder, K. (1982) Why such an interest in clinical supervision. *Wingspan, The Pedamorphasis Communique* 1(1): 3.

Apple, M. (1975) Scientific interests and the nature of educational institutions. In W. Pinar (ed.), *Curriculum Theorizing*, pp. 120–30. Berkeley, Calif.: McCutchan.

Apple, M. (1981) The process and ideology of valuing in educational settings. In R. Bates (ed.), *Organizational Evaluation in Schools*, pp. 79–102. Geelong: Deakin University Press.

Apple, M. (1983) Controlling the work of teachers, *Delta* 32: 3–15.

Apple, M. (1985) Teaching and 'women's work': A comparative historical and ideological analysis. *Teachers College Record* 86(3): 455–73.

Apple, M. (1986) *Teachers and Texts: A Political Economy of Class and Gender Relations in Education*. Boston, Mass.: Routledge and Kegan Paul.

Apple, M. and Teitelbaum, K. (1985) Are teachers losing control of their jobs? *Social Education* 49(5): 372–5.

Argyris, C. and Schön, D. (1974) *Theory in Practice: Increasing Professional Effectiveness*. London: Jossey-Bass.

Ashenden, D. (1987) Information and inequality: A systematic approach to increasing educational equity. Paper prepared for the State Board of Education, Victoria.

Austin, A. (1961) *Australian Education, 1788–1900*. Melbourne: Pitman.

Ayres, W. (1988) Teaching and being: Connecting teachers' accounts of their lives with classroom practice. Paper presented at the annual meeting of the American Educational research Association, New Orleans, April.

Bagenstos, N. (1975) The teacher as an inquirer. *The Educational Forum* 39: 231–7.

Bagley, W. C. (1907) *Classroom Management: Its Principles and Techniques*. New York: Macmillan.

Baker, R. (1977) *Whither Bureaucracy*. Occasional paper series, University of New South Wales.

Barrow, R. (1987) Skill talk. *Journal of Philosophy of Education* 21(2): 195.

Bastian, A., Fruchter, N., Gittell, M., Greer, C. and Haskin, K. (1985) Choosing equality: The case for democratic schooling. *Social Policy* pp. 34–51.

Bates, R. (1980) The framework of control: Bureaucracy, psychology and ideology. In W. J. Smyth (ed.), *Educational Leadership in Schools*, pp. 47–58. Study Guide 1, Open Campus Program. Geelong: Deakin University.

Beasley, B. (1981) The reflexive spectator in classroom research. *Inset* 1(2): 8–10.

Beasley, B. and Riordan, L. (1981) The classroom teacher as researcher. *English in Australia* 55: 36–41.

Bents, R. and Howey, K. (1980) Staff development: Change in the individual. In B. Dillon-Peterson (ed.), *Staff Development/Organizational Development*, pp. 11–36. Alexandria, Va.: Association for Supervision and Curriculum Development.

Berger, P. and Luckman, T. (1966) *The Social Construction of Reality: A Treatise in the Sociology of Knowledge*. Harmondsworth: Penguin.

Berlak, A. (1985) Back to the basics: Liberating pedagogy and the liberal arts. Paper presented to the annual meeting of the American Educational Research Association, Chicago, March–April.

Berlak, A. (1987) Teaching for liberation and empowerment in the liberal arts: Towards the development of a pedagogy that overcomes resistance. Paper presented at the annual meeting of the American Educational Research Association, Washington, D.C., April.

Berlak, A. and Berlak, H. (1981) *Dilemmas of Schooling: Teaching and Social Change*. London: Methuen.

Berliner, D. (1984) The halffull glass: A review of research on teaching. In P. Hosford (ed.), *Using What We Know About Teaching*, pp. 51–77. Alexandria, Va.: Association for Supervision and Curriculum Development.

Bernstein, R. (1976) *The Restructuring of Social and Political Theory*. London: Methuen.

Beyer, L. (1986) Critical theory and the art of teaching. *Journal of Curriculum and Supervision* 1(3): 221–32.

Beyer, L. (1989) *Critical Reflection and the Culture of Schooling: Empowering Teachers*. Geelong: Deakin University Press.

Beyer, L. and Apple M. (1988) *Curriculum: Problems, Politics and Possibilities*. Albany, N.Y.: State University of New York.

Bloom, A. (1987) *The Closing of the American Mind: How Higher Education has Failed Democracy and Impoverished the Souls of Today's Students*. New York: Simon and Schuster.

Blumberg, A. (1980) *Supervisors and Teachers: A Private Cold War*. Berkeley, Calif.: McCutchan.

Blumberg, A. (1984) Where we come from: Notes on supervision in the 1840s. Paper presented to the annual meeting of the American Educational Research Association, New Orleans, April, pp. 3–5.

Bolster, A. (1983) Toward a more effective model of research on teaching. *Harvard Educational Review* 53(3): 294–308.

Bobbitt, F. (1924) *How to Make a Curriculum*. Boston, Mass.: Houghton Mifflin.

Bodine, R. (1973) Teachers' self-assessment. In E. House (ed.), *School Evaluation: The Process and the Politics*, pp. 169–73. Berkeley, Calif.: McCutchan.

Bonser, S. and Grundy, S. (1988) Reflective deliberation in the formulation of a school curriculum policy. *Journal of Curriculum Studies* 20(1): 35–45.

Boomer, G. (1985) A celebration of teaching. *The Australian Teacher* 11: 13–20.

Borthwick, A. (1982) A collaborative approach to school focused in-service for teacher development and curriculum improvement. Paper presented to the annual meeting of the Australian Association for Research in Education, Brisbane, November.

Braverman, H. (1975) *Labor and Monopoly Capital*. New York: Monthly Review Press.

Breinin, C. (1987) A complaint and a prediction. *Phi Delta Kappa* September, pp. 15–16.

Buchmann, M. (1984) The use of research knowledge in teacher education and teaching. *American Journal of Education* 92(4): 421–39.

Bullough, R. and Gitlin, A. (1985) Schooling and change: A view from the lower rungs. *Teachers College Record* 87(2): 219–37.

Bullough, R. V., Jr, Gitlin, A. and Goldstein, S. L. (1984) Ideology, teacher role and resistance. *Teachers College Record* 86: 339–58.

Burlingame, M. (1979) Some neglected dimensions in the sudy of educational administration. *Educational Administration Quarterly* 15(1): 1–18.

Bussis, A., Chittenden, E. and Amarel, M. (1976) *Beyond the Surface Curriculum: An Interview Study of Teachers' Understanding*. Boulder, Col.: Westview Press.

Carnine, D. (1981) Barriers to increasing student achievement: What they are, where they come from, and some thoughts on how they can be overcome. Unpublished manuscript, University of Oregon.

Carr, W. (1980) The gap between theory and practice. *Journal of Further and Higher Education* 4(1): 60–69.

Carr, W. (1982) Treating the symptoms, neglecting the cause: Diagnosing the problem of theory and practice. *Journal of Further and Higher Education* 6: 19–29.

Carr, W. (1984) Adopting an educational practice. *Cambridge Journal of Education* 14(4): 1–4.

Carr, W. and Kemmis, S. (1983) *Becoming Critical: Knowing Through Action Research*. Open Campus Program. Geelong: Deakin University Press.

Ceroni, K. (1987) The Madeline Hunter phenomenon: Questions bothering a trainer. Paper presented to the annual meeting of the American Educational Research Association, Washington, D.C., April, pp. 20–24.

Cogan, M. (1973) *Clinical Supervision*. Boston, Mass.: Houghton Mifflin.

Collingwood, R. (1956) *The Idea of History*. New York: Oxford University Press.

Comstock, D. (1982) A method for critical research. In E. Bredo and W. Feinberg (eds), *Knowledge and Values in Social and Educational Research*, pp. 370–90. Philadelphia, Penn.: Temple University Press.

Connelly, M. and Clandinin, J. (1988) Narrative, experience and the study of curriculum. Paper presented to the American Educational Research Association, New Orleans, April.

Cooper, T. and Meyenn, R. (1984) A school-based project and educational change. Paper presented to the annual conference of the Australian Association for Research in Education, Perth, December.

Costa, A. (1984) A reaction to Hunter's knowing, teaching and supervising. In P. Hosford (ed.), *Using What We Know About Teaching*, pp. 196–203. Alexandria, Va.: Association for Supervision and Curriculum Development.

Crane, A. (1975) *Supervision*. Transcript of a television broadcast. Armidale: University of New England.

Cross, K. (1984) The rising tide of school reform reports. *Phi Delta Kappa* 66(3): 167–72.

Cruiskshank, D. (1985) Uses and benefits of reflective teaching. *Phi Delta Kappa* 66: 704–6.

Cruiskshank, D. and Applegate, J. (1981) Reflective teaching as a strategy for teacher growth. *Educational Leadership* 38(7): 553–4.

Cubberley, E. (1922) *Public School Administration*. New York: Houghton Mifflin.

Curtis, D. (1975) Supervision of teachers: The Cogan cycle and its applicability to the Australian scene. In W. Mulford *et al.* (eds), *Papers on ACT Education*, pp. 53–7. Canberra: Canberra College of Advance Education.

D'Alcan, F., Alexander, M., Machej, K. and McCafferty, J. (1986) Those having matches . . . an alternative approach to teacher appraisal. *Cambridge Journal of Education* 16(2): 154–6.

Davis, A. and Odden, H. (1986) How state instructional improvement programs affect teachers and principals. *Phi Delta Kappa* 67(8).

Day, C. (1985) Professional learning and research intervention: An action research perspective. *British Educational Research Journal* 11(2): 133–51.

Derber, C. (1982) *Professionals as Workers: Mental Labor in Advanced Capitalism*. Boston, Mass.: C. K. Hall.

Devaney, K. (1977) Warmth, concreteness, time and thought in teachers' learning. In K. Devaney (ed.), *Essays on Teachers' Centers*, pp. 13–27. San Francisco, Calif.: Teachers' Center Exchange, Far West Laboratory for Educational Research and Development.

Dewey, J. (1933) *How We Think: A Restatement of the Relation of Reflective Thinking to the Educative Process*. Chicago, Ill.: Henry Regnevy.

Dewey, J. (1965) Theory and practice in education. In M. Borrowmann (ed.), *Teacher Education in America: A Documentary History*. New York: Teachers College Press.

Diamond, P. (1988) Benchmarks for progress, or teacher education on the rails. *Australian Educational Researcher* 15(4): 1–7.

Dippo, D. (1988) Making ethnographic research count: Review of becoming clerical workers by Linda Valli. *Curriculum Inquiry* 18(4): 481–8.

Dockrell, B., Nisbet, J., Nutall, D., Stones, E. and Wilcox, B. (1986) *Appraising Appraisal: A Critical Examination of Proposals for the Appraisal of Teachers in England and Wales*. Birmingham: British Educational Research Association.

Doyle, W. (1978) Paradigms for research on teacher effectiveness. In L. Shulman (ed.), *Review of Research in Education* 5: 163–98.

Duckworth, E. (1986) Teaching as research. *Harvard Educational Review* 56: 481–95.

Dunn, W. (1982) A theory of exceptional clinicians. Paper presented to a conference on the Production of Useful Knowledge for Organization, Graduate School of Business, University of Pittsburgh, October.

Eggleston, J. (1979) Evaluating teachers or teaching? *Forum* 21(2): 40–42.

Eisner, E. W. (1978) The impoverished mind. *Educational Leadership* 35: 615–23.

Eisner, E. (1982) An artistic approach to supervision. In T. Sergiovanni (ed.), *Supervision of Teaching*, pp. 53–66. Alexandria, Va.: Association for Supervision and Curriculum Development.

Elbaz, F. (1988) Critical reflection on teaching: Insights from Freire. *Journal of Education for Teaching* 14(2): 171–81.

Elliott, J. (1976a) Preparing teachers for classroom accountability. *Education for Teaching* 100: 49–71.

Elliott, J. (1976b) Development of hypotheses about classrooms from teachers' practical constructs: An account of the work of the Ford teaching project. *Interchange* 7(2): 2–27.

Elliott, J. (1979) Self-accounting schools: Are they possible? *Educational Analysis* 1(1): 67–71.

Elliott, J. (1987) Educational theory, practical philosophy and action research. *British Journal of Educational Studies* 35: 149–69.

Elliott, J. (1989) The emergence of teacher appraisal in the UK. Paper presented to the annual meeting of the American Educational Research Association, San Francisco, April.

Erickson, E. (1969) Verstehen and the method of 'disciplined subjectivity': The nature of clinical evidence. In L. Krimerman, (ed.), *The Nature and Scope of Social Science: A Critical Anthology*, pp. 721–35. New York: Appleton-Century-Crofts.

Erickson, G. and Grimmett, P. (1988) *Reflection in Teacher Education*. New York: Teachers College Press.

Evans, A. and Tomlinson, J. (1989) *Teacher Appraisal: A Nationwide Approach*. London: Jessica Kingsley.

Everhart, R. (1979) Ethnography and educational policy: Love and marriage or strange bedfellows. In R. Barnhardt *et al.* (eds), *Anthropology and Educational Administration*, pp. 409–28. Tucson, Ariz.: Impresora.

Fay, B. (1977) How people change themselves: The relationship between critical theory and its audience. In T. Ball (ed.), *Political Theory and Praxis*, pp. 200–33. Minneapolis, Minn.: University of Minnesota Press.

Fay, B. (1987) *Critical Social Science: Liberation and its Limits*. Oxford: Polity Press.

Fenstermacher, G. (1983) How should implications of research on teaching be used? *The Elementary School Journal* 83(4): 469–99.

Fine, M. (1987) Silencing in public schools. *Language Arts* 64: 157–74.

Flinders, D. (1988) Teacher isolation and the new reform. *Journal of Curriculum and Supervision* 4(1): 17–29.

Floden, R. and Feiman, S. (1980) Should teachers be taught to be rational? Paper presented to the annual meeting of the American Educational Research Association, Boston, April.

Florida Coalition for the Development of Performance Measurement Systems (1983) *Domains: Knowledge Base of the Florida Performance Measurement System*. Talahassee, Fl.: Office of Teacher Education and In-Service Staff Development.

Forester, J. (1980) Critical theory and planning practice. *American Planning Association Journal* 46: 275–86.

Foucault, M. (1980) *Power/Knowledge: Selected Interviews and Other Writings* (translated and edited by C. Gordon). New York: Pantheon.

Freedman, P. (1986) Don't talk to me about lexical meta-analysis of criterion-referenced clustering and lap-dissolve spatial transformations: A consideration of the role of practising teachers in educational research. *British Educational Research Journal* 12(2): 197–206.

Freedman, S., Jackson, J. and Boles, K. (1983a) The other end of the corridor: The effect of teaching on teachers. *The Radical Teacher* 23(3): 2–23.

Freedman, S., Jackson, J. and Boles, K. (1983b) Teaching: An imperilled 'profession'. In L. Shulman and G. Sykes (eds), *Handbook of Teaching and Policy*, pp. 261–99. New York: Longman.

Freedman, S., Jackson, J. and Boles, K. (1986) *The Effect of Teaching on Teachers*. Grand Forks, N. Dak.: North Dakota Study Group on Evaluation, Centre for Teaching and Learning, University of North Dakota.

Freire, P. (1972) *Pedagogy of the Oppressed*. Harmondsworth, Penguin.

Freire, P. (1974) *Education for Critical Consciousness*. London: Sheed and Ward.

Fried, R. (1980a) *Empowerment vs. Delivery of Services*. Concord, N. H.: New Hampshire State Department of Education, Office of Community Education.

Fried, R. (1980b) *Learning in Community: An Empowerment Approach*. Concord, N. H.: New Hampshire State Department of Education, Office of Community Education.

Fuller, F. and Manning, B. (1973) Self-confrontation review: A conceptualization for video playback in teacher education. *Review of Education Research* 43: 469–525.

Gadamer, H. (1975) *Truth and Method* (translated and edited by G. Barden and J. Cummings). New York: Seabury Press.

Galloway, C. and Mulhern, E. (1973) Professional development and self-renewal. In J. Frymier (ed.), *A School for Tomorrow*. Berkeley, Calif.: McCutchan.

Garbutcheon-Singh, L. (1987) A teacher's theories of action: An approach to theorising teaching practice. *The Journal of Teaching Practice* 7(2): 21–31.

Garman, N. (1982) The clinical approach to supervision. In J. Sergiovanni (ed.), *Supervision of Teaching*, pp. 35–52. Alexandria, Va.: Association for Supervision and Curriculum Development.

Garman, N. (1984) *Reflection, the Heart of Clinical Supervision: A Modern Rationale for Professional Practice*. Open Campus Program. Geelong: Deakin University Press.

Garman, N. (1986a) Reflection, the heart of clinical supervision: A modern rationale for professional practice. *Journal of Curriculum and Supervision* 2(1): 1–24.

Garman, N. (1986b) Clinical supervision: Quackery or remedy for professional development. *Journal of Curriculum and Supervision* 1: 148–57.

Garman, N. (1987) A study of the Madeline Hunter/clinical supervision movement in Pennsylvania. *Research Report*, University of Pittsburgh.

Garman, N. (1990) Theories embedded in the events of clinical supervision: A hermeneutic approach. *Journal of Curriculum and Supervision* 5(3): 201–13.

Garman, N. and Hazi, H. (1988) Teachers ask: Is there life after Madeline Hunter? *Phi Delta Kappa* 69: 669–72.

Garrison, J. and MacMillan, C. J. B. (1984) A philosophical critique of process-product research. *Educational Theory* 34: 255–74.

Geertz, C. (1973) *The Interpretation of Cultures*. New York: Basic Books.

Geertz, C. (1983) *Local Knowledge*. New York: Basic Books.

Gibboney, R. (1987) A critique of Madeline Hunter's teaching model from Dewey's perspective. *Educational Leadership* 44(5): 46–50.

Gibboney, R. (in press) The killing field of reform. *Phi Delta Kappa*.

Giddens, A. (1976) *New Rules of Sociological Method*. New York: Basic Books.

Giddens, A. (1979) *Central Problems in Social Theory*. Berkeley, Calif.: University of California Press.

Gilligan, C. (1982) *In a Different Voice*. Cambridge, Mass.: Harvard University Press.

Giroux, H. (1982) Critical theory and schooling: Implications for the development of a radical pedagogy. Paper presented to the annual meeting of the American Educational Research Association, New York, April.

Giroux, H. (1983) *Theory and Resistance in Education: A Pedagogy for the Opposition.* Amherst, Mass.: Bergin and Garvey.

Giroux, H. (1985) Teachers as transformative intellectuals. *Social Education* 49: 376–9.

Giroux, H. (1986) Curriculum, teaching, and the resisting intellectual. *Curriculum and Teaching* 1(1–2): 33–42.

Giroux, H. (1987) Educational reform and the politics of teacher empowerment. *New Education* 9(1–2): 33–42.

Giroux, H. and Freire, P. (1987) 'Series Introduction'. In D. Livingstone *et al.* (eds), *Critical Pedagogy and Cultural Power*, pp. xi–xvi. Minneapolis, Minn.: University of Minnesota Press.

Gitlin, A. and Goldstein, S. (n.d.) A dialogical approach to understanding horizontal evaluation. Unpublished manuscript.

Gitlin, A. and Smyth, J. (1989) *Teacher Evaluation: Educative Alternatives.* Philadelphia, Penn.: Falmer Press.

Glaser, B. and Strauss, A. (1967) *The Discovery of Grounded Theory: Strategies for Qualitative Research.* New York: Aldine.

Goldhammer, R. (1969) *Clinical Supervision: Special Methods for the Supervision of Teachers.* New York: Holt, Rinehart and Winston.

Goldhammer, R., Anderson, R. and Krajewski, R. (1980) *Clinical Supervision: Special Methods for the Supervision of Teachers*, 2nd edn. New York: Holt, Rinehart and Winston.

Goldsberry, L. (1980) Colleague consultation: Supervision augmented. In L. Rubin (ed.), *Critical Issues in Educational Policy: An Administrator's Overview*, pp. 335–44. Boston, Mass.: Allyn and Bacon.

Gondak, D. (1986) Madeline Hunter/clinical supervision sweeps the state. *The Mideasterner* 8(1).

Goodlad, J. (1978) Educational leadership: Toward the third era. *Educational Leadership* 35(4): 322–31.

Goodman, J. (1986) Masculinity, feminism, and the male elementary school teacher. *Journal of Curriculum Theorizing* 7(2): 30–60.

Gordon, D. (1988) Education as text: The varieties of educational hiddenness. *Curriculum Inquiry* 18(4): 425–49.

Gore, J. (1987) Reflecting on reflective teaching. *Journal of Teacher Education* 38(2): 33–9.

Goswami, D. and Stillman, P. (eds) (1987) *Reclaiming the Classroom: Teacher Research an Agency for Change.* Upper Montclair, N.J.: Boynton Cook.

Grace, G. (1978) *Teachers, Ideology and Control: A Study in Urban Education.* Henley: Routledge and Kegan Paul.

Grace, G. (1985) Judging teachers: The social and political context of teacher evaluation. *British Journal of Sociology of Education* 6(1): 3–16.

Greene, M. (1986a) Reflection and passion in teaching. *Journal of Curriculum and Supervision* 2(1): 68–81.

Greene, M. (1986b) In search of a critical pedagogy. *Harvard Education Review* 56(4): 427–41.

Grumet, M. (1979) Supervision and situation: A methodology of self report for teacher education. *Journal of Curriculum Theorizing* 1(1): 191–257.

Grundy, S. (1987) *Curriculum: Product or Praxis?* Philadelphia, Penn.: Falmer Press.

Guditus, C. (1982) The pre-observation conference: Is it worth the effort? *Wingspan: Pedamorphosis Communique* 1(1): 7–8.

Habermas, J. (1973) *Theory and Practice.* Boston, Mass.: Beacon Press.

Habermas, J. (1978) *Knowledge and Human Interest.* London: Heinemann.

Habermas, J. (1979) *Communication and the Evolution of Society.* Boston, Mass.: Beacon Press.

Halberstam, D. (1986) *The Reckoning.* New York: Avon.

Hargreaves, A. (1982) The rhetoric of school-centered innovation. *Journal of Curriculum Studies* 14: 251–66.

Hargreaves, A. (1988) Teacher quality: A sociological analysis. *Journal of Curriculum Studies* 20: 211–31.

Harris, B. (1976) Limits and supplements to formal clinical procedures. *Journal of Research and Development in Education* 9(2): 85–9.

Harris, I. (1986) Communicating the character of 'deliberation'. *Journal of Curriculum Studies* 18(2): 115–32.

Harris, K. (1979) *Education and Knowledge: The Structured Misrepresentation of Knowledge.* London: Routledge and Kegan Paul.

Hartley, L. and Broadfoot, P. (1986) Assessing teacher performance. *Journal of Educational Policy* 3(1): 39–50.

Hartnett, A. and Naish, M. (1980) Technicians or social bandits: Some moral and political issues in the education of teachers. In P. Woods (ed.), *Teacher Strategies: Explorations in the Sociology of the School*, pp. 254–74. London: Croom Helm.

Hawkins, D. (1973) What it means to teach. *Teachers College Record* 75(1): 7–16.

Hazi, H. (1987a) Teacher evaluation incognito: The Madeline Hunter movement and school reform. Paper presented to the Annual Meeting of the American Educational Research Association, Washington, D.C., April.

Hazi, H. (1987b) *The Madeline Hunter Movement and School Reform in Pennsylvania.* Morgantown, W. Vir.: West Virginia University.

Held, D. (1980) *Introduction to Critical Theory: Horkheimer to Habermas.* London: Hutchinson.

Hextall, I. (1984) Rendering accounts: A critical analysis of the assessment performance unit. In P. Broadfoot (ed.), *Selection Certification and Control: Social Issues in Educational Assessment*, pp. 245–62. Philadelphia, Penn.: Falmer Press.

Hirsch, E. D., Jr (1987) *Cultural Literacy: What Every American Needs to Know.* New York: Houghton Mifflin.

Hirst, P. (1983) Educational theory. In P. Hirst (ed.), *Educational Theory and Its Foundation Disciplines*, pp. 3–29. London: Routledge and Kegan Paul.

Hogben, D. (1980) Research on teaching, and teacher training. *Australian Journal of Education* 24(1): 56–66.

Holly, M. (1982) Teacher reflections on classroom life: Collaboration and professional development. Paper presented to the annual meeting of the American Educational Research Association, New York, March.

Holly, M. (1984) *Keeping a Personal-Professional Journal.* Geelong: Deakin University Press.

Holly, M., and Smyth, J. (1989) The journal as a way of theorizing teaching. *The Australian Administrator* 10(3–4): 1–8.

Hosford, P. (1984) *Using What We Know About Teaching.* Alexandria, Va.: Association for Supervision and Curriculum Development.

House, E. (1972) The conscience of educational evaluation. *Teachers College Record* 73: 405–14.

Hult, R. (1979) On pedagogical caring. *Educational Theory* 29: 237–43.

Hunt, D. (1975) Person–environment interaction: A challenge found wanting before it was tried. *Review of Educational Research* 45: 209–30.

Hunt, D. (1978) In-service training as persons-in relation. *Theory into Practice* 17: 239–44.

Hunter, M. (1980) Six types of supervisory conferences. *Educational Leadership* 37(5): 408–12.

Hunter, M. (1984) Knowing, teaching and supervising. In P. Hosford (ed.), *Using What We Know About Teaching*. 1984 Yearbook, pp. 169–92. Alexandria, Va.: Association for Supervision and Curriculum Development.

Hunter M. (1985) What's wrong with Madeline Hunter? *Educational Leadership* 42(5): 57–60.

Hustler, D., Cassidy, T. and Cuff, T. (1986) *Action Research in Classrooms and Schools*. London: Allen and Unwin.

Hymes, D. (1979) Ethnographic monitoring. In E. Briere (ed.), *Language Development in a Bilingual Society*. Pomona, Los Angeles, Calif.: National Multilingual Multicultural Materials Development Centre, California State Polytechnic University.

Jackson, P. (1968) *Life in Classrooms*. New York: Holt, Rinehart and Winston.

Johnson, B. (1982) Teaching ignorance: L'ecole des Femmes. *Yale French Studies* 63: 165–82.

Jonathan, R. (1983) The manpower service model of education. *Cambridge Journal of Education* 13(2): 3–10.

Joyce, B. and Showers, B. (1980) Improving in service training. The messages of research. *Educational Leadership* 37(5): 379–85.

Kanpol, B. (1988) Teacher resistance and accommodation to structural factors of schooling: Possibilities and limitations. Paper presented to the annual meeting of the American Educational Research Association, New Orleans, April.

Karier, C. (1982) Supervision in historic perspective. In T. Sergiovanni (ed.), *Supervision of Teaching*. 1982 Yearbook, pp. 2–15. Alexandria, Va.: Association for Supervision and Curriculum Development.

Karier, C., Violas, P. and Spring, J. (1973) *Roots of Crisis: American Education in the Twentieth Century*. Chicago, Ill.: Rand McNally.

Kemmis, S. (1985) Action research and the politics of reflection. In D. Boud, D. Keogh and D. Walker (eds), *Reflection: Turning Experience into Learning*, pp. 139–64. London: Kogan Page.

Kemmis, S. and Smyth, J. (1989) Management of the performance of academic staff. Unpublished manuscript, Deakin University.

Kilbourn, B. (1980) Ethnographic research and the improvement of teaching. In H. Munby, G. Opwood and T. Russell (eds), *Seeing Curriculum in a New Light: Essays from Science Education*, p. 174. Toronto: OISE Press.

Kilbourn, B. (1982) Linda: A case study of clinical supervision. *The Canadian Journal of Education* 7(3): 162–81.

Kohl, H. (1983) Examining closely what we do. *Learning* 12(1): 28–30.

Knowles, M. (1978) *The Adult Learner: A Neglected Species*. Houston, Texas: Gulf Publishing.

Krajewski, R. (1976) Preface to thematic issue on clinical supervision. *Journal of Research and Development in Education* 9(2): 1–3.

Kretovics, J. (1985) Critical literacy: Challenging the assumptions of mainstream educational theory. *Journal of Education* 67(2): 50–61.

Lather, P. (1984) Critical theory, curricular-transformation, and feminist mainstreaming. *Journal of Education* 166: 49–62.

Lather, P. (1986) The absent presence: Patriarchy, capitalism, and the nature of teacher work. Paper presented to the Bergamo Curriculum Theorizing Conference, Dayton, Ohio, October.

Lawn, M. (1987) *Servants of the State: The Contested Control of Teaching 1900–30*. Lewes: Falmer Press.

Lawn, M. and Ozga, J. (1981) The educational worker? A reassessment of teachers. In L. Barton and S. Walker (eds), *Schools, Teachers and Teaching*, pp. 45–64. Lewes: Falmer Press.

Lawn, M. and Ozga, J. (1986) Unequal partners: Teachers under indirect rules. *British Journal of Sociology of Education* 7(2): 225–38.

Levy, T. (1985) A hired hand responds. *Social Education*, May 366–7.

Lieberman, A. (1982) Practice makes policy: The tensions of school improvement. In A. Lieberman and W. McLaughlin (eds), *Policy Making in Education*, pp. 249–69. 81st Yearbook of the National Society for the Study of Education. Chicago, Ill.: University of Chicago Press.

Lieberman, A. and Miller, L. (1979) The social realities of teaching. In A. Lieberman and L. Miller (eds), *Staff Development: New Demands. New Realities, New Perspectives*, pp. 54–68. New York: Teachers College Press.

Lightfoot, S. (1973) Politics and reasoning: Through the eyes of teachers and children. *Harvard Educational Review* 43(2): 197–244.

Liston, D. and Zeichner, K. (1987) Reflective teacher education and moral deliberation. *Journal of Teacher Education* 38(6): 2–8.

Little, D. (1989) Criteria for assessing critical adult education research. Paper presented to the American Association for Adult and Continuing Education, Atlantic City, N.J., October.

Little, J. (1982) Norms of collegiality and experimentation: Workplace conditions of school success. *American Educational Research Journal* 19(3): 325–40.

Lokan, J. and McKenzie, P. (eds) (1989) *Teacher Appraisal: Issues and Approaches*. Melbourne: Australian Council for Educational Research.

Lortie, D. (1975) *School Teacher: A Sociological Study*. Chicago, Ill.: University of Chicago Press.

MacDonald, J. (1988) Curriculum, consciousness and social change. In W. Pinar (ed.), *Contemporary Curriculum Discourses*, pp. 156–200. Scottsdale, Ariz.: Gorsuch Scarisbrick.

MacKay, D. and Marland, P. (1978) Thought processes of teachers. Paper presented to the annual meeting of the American Educational Research Association, Toronto, April.

Mackie, R. (1980) *Literacy and Revolution: The Pedagogy of Paulo Freire*. New York: Continuum.

Marks, J., Stoops, E. and King-Stoops, J. (1978) *Handbook of Educational Supervision: A Guide for the Practitioner*, 2nd edn. Boston, Mass.: Allyn and Bacon.

McCoombe, M. (1984) Clinical supervision from the inside. In J. Smyth (ed.), *Case Studies in Clinical Supervision*, pp. 43–56. Geelong: Deakin University Press.

McDonald, J. (1986) Raising the teacher's voice and the ironic role of theory. *Harvard Educational Review* 56: 355–78.

McFaul, S. A. and Cooper, J. M. (1984) Peer clinical supervision: Theory *vs* reality. *Educational Leadership* 41: 4–9.

McLaren, P. (1980) *Cries from the Corridor*. Toronto: Methuen.

McLaren, P. (1987) Critical pedagogy and the dream of emancipation. *Social Education* 5(2): 146–50.

McLaren, P. (1988a) Foreword in H. Giroux, *Teachers as Intellectuals: Towards a Pedagogy of Practical Learning*, South Hadley, Mass.: Bergin and Garvey.

McLaren, P. (1988b) Language, social structure and the production of subjectivity. *Critical Pedagogy Networker* 1(2–3): 1–10.

McLaren, P. (1989) *Life in Schools: An Introduction to Critical Pedagogy in the Foundations of Education*. New York: Longman.

McLaughlin, M. and Pfeifer, R. (1988) *Teacher Evaluation*. New York: Teachers College Press.

McNeil, J. (1982) A scientific approach to supervision. In T. Sergiovanni (ed.), *Supervision of Teaching*, pp. 18–34. Alexandria, Va.: Association for Supervision and Curriculum Development.

McNergney, R. and Carrier, C. (1981) *Teacher Development*. New York: Macmillan.

McTaggart, R. and Kemmis, S. (1988) *The Action Research Reader*, 3rd revised edn. Geelong: Deakin University Press.

Mezirow, J. (1977) Perspective transformation. *Studies in Adult Education* 9(2): 153–64.

Mezirow, J. (1981) A critical theory of adult learning and education. *Adult Education* 32(1): 3–24.

Millman, J. and Darling-Hammond, L. (1990) *The New Handbook of Teacher Evaluation: Assessing Elementary and Secondary School Teachers*. Newbury Park, Calif.: Sage.

Mills, C. (1959) *The Sociological Imagination*. Harmondsworth: Penguin.

Mishler, E. (1986) Meaning in context and the empowerment of respondents. In E. Mishler (ed.), *Research Interviewing: Context and Narrative*, pp. 117–35. Cambridge, Mass.: Harvard University Press.

Mohlman, G., Kierstead, J. and Gundlach, M. (1982) A research-based in-service model for secondary teachers. *Educational Leadership* 40(1): 16–20.

Mohr, M. and MacLean, M. (1987) *Working Together: A Guide for Teacher-researchers*. Urbana, Ill.: National Council of Teacher of English.

Moore, B. and Reid, A. (1990) Appraisal: Teachers or teaching. *Curriculum Perspectives* 10(4): 56–83.

Mosher, R. and Purpel, D. (1972) *Supervision: The Reluctant Profession*. Boston, Mass.: Houghton Mifflin.

Murray, M. (1975) *Modern Critical Theory: A Phenomenological Introduction*. The Hague: Martinus-Nijhoff.

National Commission on Excellence in Education (1983) *A Nation at Risk: The Imperative for Educational Reform*. Washington, D.C.: Government Printing Office.

National Governors' Association (1986) *The Report of the National Governors' Association Committee*.

New Jersey State Department of Education (1986) *New Jersey's Plan for the Supervision of Instruction*. N.J.

Nixon, J. (ed.) (1981) *A Teacher's Guide to Action Research: Evaluation, Inquiry, and Development in the Classroom*. London: Grant McIntyre.

Noddings, N. (1986) Fidelity in teaching, teacher education, and research for teaching. *Harvard Educational Review* 56: 496–510.

Parekh, B. (1970) Scholarship and ideology. *Cross Currents* pp. 455–75.

Pavan, B. (1980) Clinical supervision: Some signs of progress. *Texas Technical Journal of Education* 7(3): 241–51.

Perrone, V. (1988) Teachers and schools. Paper presented to the Summer Institute, Teachers College, Columbia University, July.

Piccone, P. (1973) Phenomenological Marxism. In B. Grahl and P. Piccone (eds), *Towards New Marxism*. St. Louis, Mo.: Telos Press.

Pollard, A. (1987) Reflective teaching – the sociological contribution. In P. Woods and A. Pollard (eds), *Sociology and Teaching: A New Challenge for the Sociology of Education*, pp. 53–73. London: Croom Helm.

Poulantzas, N. (1973) *Political Power and Social Classes*. London: New Left Books.

Preston, B. (1990) Teacher appraisal: Inherently contestable. *Curriculum Perspectives* 10(4): 49–50.

Proppe, O. (1982) Educational evaluation as a dialectical process. *Discourse* 2(2): 11–20.

Raphael, R. (1985) *The Teacher's Voice*. Portsmouth, N.H.: Heinemann Educational.

Retallick, J. (1983) Supervision and teacher development: A critical perspective. *The Australian Administrator* 4(5): 1–4.

Robinson, J. (1984) A second pair of eyes: Clinical supervision – a case study of a supervisor's view. In J. Smyth (ed.), *Case Studies in Clinical Supervision*, pp. 5–42. Geelong: Deakin University Press.

Romberg, T. (1979) Systematic monitoring of planned school change. Unpublished paper, University of Tasmania. Cited in *Educational Leadership in Schools*, Study Guide 2, pp. 5–22, J. Smyth (ed.). Geelong: Deakin University Press.

Ross, E. and Hannay, L. (1986) Toward a critical theory of reflective inquiry. *Journal of Teacher Education* 37(4): 9–15.

Rudduck, J. (1984) Teaching as an art, teacher research and research-based teacher education. Second annual Lawrence Stenhouse Memorial Lecture, University of East Anglia, July.

Rudduck, J. (1985) Teacher research and research-based teacher education. *Journal of Education for Teaching* 11(3): 281–9.

Ryan, B. (1982) Accountability in Australian education. *Discourse* 2(2): 21–40.

Ryan, W. (1971) *Blaming the Victim*. New York: Pantheon.

Sarason, S. (1982) *The Culture of the School and the Problem of Change*. Boston, Mass.: Allyn and Bacon.

Sawada, D. and Calley, M. (1985) Dissipative structures: New metaphors for becoming in education. *Educational Researcher* 14(3): 14–15.

Schibeci, R. and Grundy, S. (1987) Local theories. *Journal of Education* 81(2): 91–6.

Schön, D. (1979) Generative metaphor: A perspective on problem-setting in social policy. In A. Ortony (ed.), *Metaphor and Thought*. Cambridge: Cambridge University Press.

Schön, D. (1983) *The Reflective Practitioner: How Professionals Think in Action*. New York: Basic Books.

Schön, D. (1984) Leadership as reflection-in-action. In T. Sergiovanni and J. Corbally (eds), *Leadership and Organizational Culture: New Perspectives on Administrative Theory and Practice*, pp. 36–63. Urbana, Ill.: University of Illinois Press.

Schön, D. (1987) *Educating the Reflective Practitioner*. San Francisco, Calif.: Jossey-Bass.

Schwab, J. (1969) The practical: a language for curriculum. *School Review* 78(1): 1–24.

Sergiovanni, T. (1976) Towards a theory of clinical supervision. *Journal of Research and Development in Education* 9: 21–2.

Sergiovanni, T. (1982a) Toward a theory of supervisory practice: Integrating scientific clinical and artistic views. In T. Sergiovanni (ed.), *Supervision of Teaching*, pp. 67–80. Alexandria, Va.: Association for Supervision and Curriculum Development.

Sergiovanni, T. (1982b) Supervision and the improvement of instruction. In T. Sergiovanni (ed.), *Supervision of Teaching*, pp. vi–viii. Alexandria, Va.: Association for Supervision and Curriculum Development.

Sergiovanni, T. (1984a) Landscapes, mindscapes and reflective practice in supervision. Paper presented to the annual meeting of the American Educational Research Association, New Orleans, April.

Sergiovanni, T. (1984b) Liberating supervision in search of meaning. *Impact on Instructional Improvement* 19(1): 54–5.

Sergiovanni, T. (1984c) Expanding conceptions of inquiry and practice in supervision and evaluation. *Educational Evaluation and Policy Analysis* 6(4): 355–65.

Sergiovanni, T. and Starratt, J. (1979) *Supervision: Human Perspectives*, 2nd edn. New York: McGraw-Hill.

Shapiro, S. (1984) Choosing our educational legacy: Disempowerment or emancipation. *Issues in Education* 2: 11–22.

Shor, I. (1980) *Critical Teaching: And Everyday Life*. Boston, Mass.: South End Press.

Shor, I. (1987) *Freire for the Classroom*. Portsmouth, N.H.: Boynton Cook.

Shor, I. and Freire, P. (1987) *A Pedagogy for Liberation: Dialogues on Transforming Education*. South Hadley, Mass.: Bergin and Garvey.

Simons, H. and Elliott, J. (1989) *Re-thinking Appraisal and Assessment*. Milton Keynes: Open University Press.

Simon, J. (1979) Who and what is the APU? *Forum* 22(1): 7–11.

Simon, R. (1985) Critical pedagogy. In T. Husen and T. Postlethwaite (eds), *International Encyclopedia of Education Research and Studies*, pp. 118–20. London: Pergamon Press.

Simon, R. (1987) Empowerment as a pedagogy of possibility. *Language Arts* 64(4): 370–82.

Simon, R. (1988) For a pedagogy of possibility. *Critical Pedagogy Networker* 1(1): 1–4.

Slavin, R. (1987) The Hunterization of America's schools. *Instructor* 96(8): 56–60.

Small, R. (1978) Educational praxis. *Educational Theory* 28(3): 214–22.

Smart, D. (1977) The status of the teacher in the penal and early colonial New South Wales society, 1788–1848. In A. Spaul (ed.), *Australian Teachers from Colonial Schoolmasters to Militant Professionals*, pp. 2–15. Melbourne: Macmillan.

Smith, F. (1986) *Insult to Intelligence: The Bureaucratic Invasion of our Classrooms*. New York: Arbor House.

Smyth, J. (1982) Teaching as learning: Some lessons for staff development from clinical supervision. Paper presented to the annual meeting of the Australian Association for Research in Education, Brisbane, November.

Smyth, J. (1983a) Theory, research and practice in clinical supervision: A view from 'down under'. Paper presented to the annual meeting of the Association for Supervision and Curriculum Development, Houston, Texas, March.

Smyth, J. (1983b) Teaching as learning: Some lessons for staff development from clinical supervision. *The Developer, National Staff Development Council*, pp. 2–7.

Smyth, J. (1983c) There's got to be a better way: A follow-through approach to introducing clinical supervision into schools. *The Canadian School Executive* 3(2): 2–5.

Smyth, J. (1984a) *Clinical Supervision – Collaborative Learning About Teaching: A Handbook*. Geelong: Deakin University Press.

Smyth, J. (1984b) Toward a 'critical consciousness' in the instructional supervision of experienced teachers. *Curriculum Inquiry* 14: 425–36.

Smyth, J. (1984c) Using research on teaching for on-going teacher development. *Unicorn* 10(1): 68–71.

Smyth, J. (1984d) Teachers as collaborative learners in clinical supervision: A state-of-the-art review. *Journal of Education for Teaching* 10(1): 24–38.

Smyth, J. (1984e) Teachers as collaborators in clinical supervision: Co-operative learning about teaching. *Teacher Education* 24: 60–68.

Smyth, J. (1985a) Developing a critical practice of clinical supervision. *Journal of Curriculum Studies* 17:1–15.

Smyth, J. (1985b) Educational administration: A critique of the tradition. In L. Rattray-Wood (ed.), *Tradition and Turmoil in Educational Administration*, pp. 2–12. Geelong: Deakin University Press.

Smyth, J. (1985c) An educative and empowering notion of leadership. *Educational Administration Review* 3(2): 3–12.

Smyth, J. (1986a) An alternative and critical perspective for clinical supervision in schools. In K. Sirotnik and J. Oakes (eds), *Critical Perspective on the Organization and Improvement of Schooling*, pp. 131–61. Hingham, Mass.: Kluwer-Nijhoff.

Smyth, J. (1986b) *Reflection-in-action*. Geelong: Deakin University Press.

Smyth, J. (ed.) (1986c) *Learning About Teaching Through Clinical Supervision*. London: Croom Helm.

Smyth, J. (1987a) Cinderella syndrome: A philosophical view of supervision as a field of study. *Teachers College Record* 88(4): 567–88.

Smyth, J. (1987b) Leadership, enabling teachers to become 'transformative intellectuals'. *The Australian Administrator* 8(3): 1–4.

Smyth, J. (1987c) Teachers-as-intellectuals in a critical pedagogy of schooling. *Education and Society* 5(1–2): 11–28.

Smyth, J. (ed.) (1987d) *Educating Teachers: Changing the Nature of Pedagogical Knowledge*. Lewes: Falmer Press.

Smyth, J. (1987e) A critical pedagogy of classroom practice. Paper presented to the Ninth Curriculum Theorizing and Classroom Practice Conference, Dayton, Ohio, October.

Smyth, J. (1988a) A 'critical' perspective for clinical supervision. *Journal of Curriculum and Supervision* 3: 136–56.

Smyth, J. (1988b) *A 'Critical' Pedagogy of Teacher Evaluation*. Geelong: Deakin University Press.

Smyth, J. (1988c) Teachers theorizing their practice as a form of empowerment. *The Educational Administrator* 30: 27–37.

Smyth, J. (1989a) Collegiality as a counter discourse to the intrusion of corporate management into higher education. *Journal of Tertiary Educational Administration* 11(2): 143–55.

Smyth, J. (1989b) When teachers theorize their practice: A reflexive approach to a distance education course. In D. Nation and T. Evans (eds), *Critical Practices in Distance Education*, pp. 197–233. Lewes: Falmer Press.

Smyth, J. (ed.) (1989c) *Critical Perspectives on Educational Leadership*. Lewes: Falmer Press.

Smyth, J. (1990) Teacher evaluation as the technology of increased centralism in education. In C. Bell (ed.) *Assessment and Evaluation: World Yearbook of Education*, pp. 237–57. London: Kogan Page.

Smyth, J. and Henry, C. (1983) A case study experience of a collaborative and responsive form of professional development for teachers. Paper presented to the annual meeting of the Australian Association for Research in Education, Canberra, November.

Smyth, J., Henry, C., Marcus, A., Logan, T. and Meadows, M. (1982a) Follow-through case study of clinical supervision. *Deakin University Report to the Educational Research and Development Committee*, Canberra, Australia.

Smyth, J., Martin, J. and Henry, C. (1982b) Clinical supervision: Evidence of a viable strategy for teacher development. *The Australian Administrator* 3(5): 1–4.

Snyder, K. (1981) Clinical supervision in the 1980's. *Educational Leadership* 38(7): 521–4.

Spring, J. (1977) *A Primer for Libertarian Education.* New York: Free Life Editions.

Sprinthall, N. and Sprinthall, L. (1980) Adult development and leadership training for mainstream education. In D. Corrigan and K. Howey (eds), *Special Education in Transition: Concepts to Guide the Education of Experienced Teachers*, pp. 35–51. Reston, Va.: The Council for Exceptional Children.

St Maurice, H. (1987) Clinical supervision and power: Regimes of instructional management. In T. Popkewitz (ed.), *Critical Studies in Teacher Education: Its Folklore, Theory and Practices*, pp. 242–64. Lewes: Falmer Press.

Stenhouse, L. (1978) Using research means doing research. Unpublished paper, University of East Anglia.

Stenhouse, L. (1983) The relevance of practice to theory. *Theory Into Practice* 22(3): 211–15.

Stephens, M. (1983) Captivated by our own words. *Education News* 40(6): 3–4.

Stevens, P. (1987) Political education and political teachers. *Journal of Philosophy of Education* 21(1): 75–83.

Streeter, S. (1967) Phenomenology and the human science. In J. Kocklemans (ed.), *Phenomenology.* New York: Doubleday.

Strieb, L. (1985) *A (Philadelphia) Teacher's Journal.* Grand Forks, N. Dak.: North Dakota Study Group Evaluation.

Suffolk Department of Education (1985) *Those Having Torches . . . Teacher Appraisal: A Study.* Suffolk: Department of Education and Science.

Taylor, C. (1971) Interpretation and the science of man. *The Review of Metaphysics* 25(1).

Taylor, F. (1911) *The Principles of Scientific Management.* New York: Holt, Rinehart and Winston.

Thornburgh, R. and Smith, M. A. (1983) *Turning the Tide: An Agenda for Excellence in Pennsylvania's Public Schools.* Harrisburg, Penn.: Department of Education.

Tom, A. (1985) Inquiring into inquiry-oriented teacher education. *Journal of Teacher Education* 36(5): 35–44.

Toulmin, S. (1972) *Human Understanding: The Collective Use and Evolution of Concepts.* Princeton, N.J.: Princeton University Press.

Traver, R. (1987) Autobiography, feminism, and the study of teaching. *Teachers College Record* 88(3): 443–52.

Trethowan, D. (1987) *Appraisal and Target Setting.* London: Harper and Row.

Tripp, D. (1984) From autopilot to critical consciousness: Problematising successful teaching. Paper presented to the Sixth Curriculum Theory and Practice Conference, Bergamo, Ohio, October.

Tripp, D. (1987) *Theorizing Practice: The Teacher's Professional Journal.* Geelong: Deakin University Press.

Tronc, K. and Harris, H. (1985) Victims of history: The establishment and growth of the Australian inspectorate. *Practicing Administrator* 7(1): 43–8.

Turner, G. and Clift, D. (1988) *Studies in Teacher Appraisal.* Lewes: Falmer Press.

van Manen, M. (1977) Linking ways of knowing with ways of being practical. *Curriculum Inquiry* 6(3): 205–28.

Walker, S. and Barton, L. (eds) (1987) *Changing Policies, Changing Teachers: New Directions for Schooling.* Milton Keynes: Open University Press.

Walkerdine, V. (1986) Progressive pedagogy and radical struggle. *Screen* 27: 54–60.

Walsh, K. (1987) The politics of teacher appraisal. In M. Lawn and G. Grace (eds), *Teachers: The Culture and Politics of Work,* pp. 147–66. Lewes: Falmer Press.

Wehlage, G. (1981) Can teachers be more reflective about their work? A commentary on some research about teachers. In R. B. Tabachnick, T. S. Popkewitz and B. B. Szekely (eds), *Studying Teaching and Learning: Trends in Soviet and American Research,* pp. 101–13. New York: Praeger.

Weller, R. (1969) An observational system for analyzing clinical supervision of teachers. Unpublished doctoral dissertation, Harvard University, Cambridge, Mass.

Welton, M. (in press) *Critical Perspectives on Adult Learning.* Lewes: Falmer Press.

White, J. and White, P. (1986) Teachers as political activists. In A. Hartnett and M. Naish (eds), *Education and Society Today,* pp. 171–82. Lewes: Falmer Press.

Wiles, J. and Bondi, J. (1980) *Supervision: A Guide to Practice.* Columbus, Ohio: Charles E. Merrill.

Williamson, J. (1981–82) How does girl No. 20 understand ideology. *Screen Education* 40: 80–87.

Willie, R. and Howey, K. (1981) *Reflections on Adult Development: Implications for In-service Teacher Education.* Minneapolis, Minn.: University of Minnesota.

Willis, P. (1977) *Learning to Labour: How Working Class Kids Get Working Class Jobs.* London: Gower.

Winter, R. (1989) Teacher appraisal and the development of professional knowledge. In W. Carr (ed.), *Quality in Teaching,* pp. 183–99. Lewes: Falmer Press.

Wise, A. (1977) Why educational policies often fail: The hypernationalization hypothesis. *Journal of Curriculum Studies* 9(1): 43–57.

Wise, A., Darling-Hammond, L., McLaughlin, M. and Bernstein, H. (1984) *Teacher Evaluation: A Study of Effective Practices.* Santa Monica, Calif.: Rand Corporation.

Withall, J. and Wood, F. (1979) Taking the threat out of classroom observation and feedback. *Journal of Teacher Education* 30(1): 55–8.

Wright, O. (1980) Class and occupation. *Theory and Society* 9: 177–214.

Yonemura, M. (1982) Teacher conversations: A potential source of their own professional growth. *Curriculum Inquiry* 12: 239–56.

Young, R. (ed.) (1981) *Untying the Text.* Boston, Mass.: Routledge and Kegan Paul.

Zeichner, K. and Teitelbaum, K. (1982) Personalized and inquiry-oriented teacher education: An analysis of two approaches to the development of curriculum for field-based experiences. *Journal of Education for Teaching* 8: 95–117.

Index